SAILING
7 CONTINENTS
SOLO

SAILING 7 CONTINENTS SOLO

HARRY R. ANDERSON, Ph.D. P.E.
Bainbridge Island, WA USA

Sailing 7 Continents Solo

Copyright © 2025 by Harry R. Anderson

All rights reserved. No part of this publication may be reproduced, distributed, or transmitted in any form or by any means, including photocopying, recording, or other electronic or mechanical methods, without the prior written permission of the publisher, except in the case of brief quotations embodied in critical reviews and certain other noncommercial uses permitted by copyright law. For permission requests, write to the publisher, addressed "Attention: Permissions Coordinator," at the address below.

Phywave, Inc.
250 Eagle Place NE
Bainbridge Island, WA 98110
www.phywave.com
Email: *publishing@phywave.com*
Printed in the United States of America

First Edition

ISBN 978-0-9967450-5-5

Cover photo by Harry R. Anderson

Contents

Introduction		1
Chapter 1	Planning the Route	9
Chapter 2	Buying the Boat	15
Chapter 3	Outfitting Phywave	25
Chapter 4	Eastward to the Azores	36
Chapter 5	Landing in Portugal	50
Chapter 6	Across to Morocco	58
Chapter 7	The Canary Islands	64
Chapter 8	Onward to Brazil	70
Chapter 9	Mar del Plata	80
Chapter 10	To Tierra del Fuego	88
Chapter 11	Puerto Williams	98
Chapter 12	Antarctica	106
Chapter 13	Puerto Montt	124
Chapter 14	Patagonia to the Marquesas	135
Chapter 15	French Polynesia	150
Chapter 16	Vava'u, Tonga	159
Chapter 17	Across to Australia	168
Chapter 18	The Great Barrier Reef to Darwin	176
Chapter 19	Darwin to Lombok	186
Chapter 20	Cocos (Keeling) Islands	199
Chapter 21	Réunion Island	207
Chapter 22	Crossing to Richards Bay	218
Chapter 23	South Africa	229
Chapter 24	Namibia	243
Chapter 25	Across the Atlantic Again	252
Chapter 26	The Caribbean	263
Chapter 27	Florida—Voyage Completed!	273
Epilogue		281
Glossary		287

Appendices

Appendix A – Route Details	293
Appendix B – Boat Gear	296
Appendix C – Tools	299
Appendix D – Spares	302
Appendix E – Electronics	304
Appendix F – Medical Supplies	307
Appendix G – Charts, Books, and Flags	309
Appendix H – Antarctica Documents	311

Introduction

I was trying to get some sleep in the shallow Antarctic night when there are only a few hours of solid darkness between long half-light dusks and dawns, a sunlight limbo, that reinforced my feeling of being stuck in between. I was sailing back from Antarctica across the renowned and feared Drake Passage, about halfway toward my destination of Puerto Williams, a small town in Tierra del Fuego. I had heaved-to and essentially let the boat drift for 48 hours to wait out a violent storm north of me that refused to abate. I finally gave up waiting and started sailing north again in spite of 6-meter waves and gale-force winds. My tentative sleep was disturbed by a new motion of the boat that seemed much faster and more heeled over than when I had turned in. Getting out of my bunk, pulling on my boots and jacket, and going out on deck, I saw the genoa headsail was fully unfurled instead of having three reefs where I had left it. It made no sense. Then I looked at the genoa furling line on the port side deck that's used to wind the sail up around the forestay. It was lying slack on the deck, having snapped at some point while I slept, letting the headsail fully deploy. The boat was ripping along in 40-knot winds and violent waves driven by a large sail I could no longer control.

That was one of several crisis moments on the voyage I had undertaken, a voyage that began with an airplane or, more specifically, while writing a book about flying an airplane to seven continents. Between 2011 and 2014 I had flown solo in my single-engine airplane N788W, a Lancair Columbia 300, to all seven continents. In 2015 I published a book about those flights, *Flying 7 Continents Solo*.

As I was finishing the book it occurred to me that if I were to sail solo to seven continents, I'd become the first person to do both. I know the other solo pilots who have landed on all the continents—there's only a few—and none of them are offshore sailors. Becoming the first person to both fly and sail solo to all the continents became the primary objective that drove the voyage described in this book.

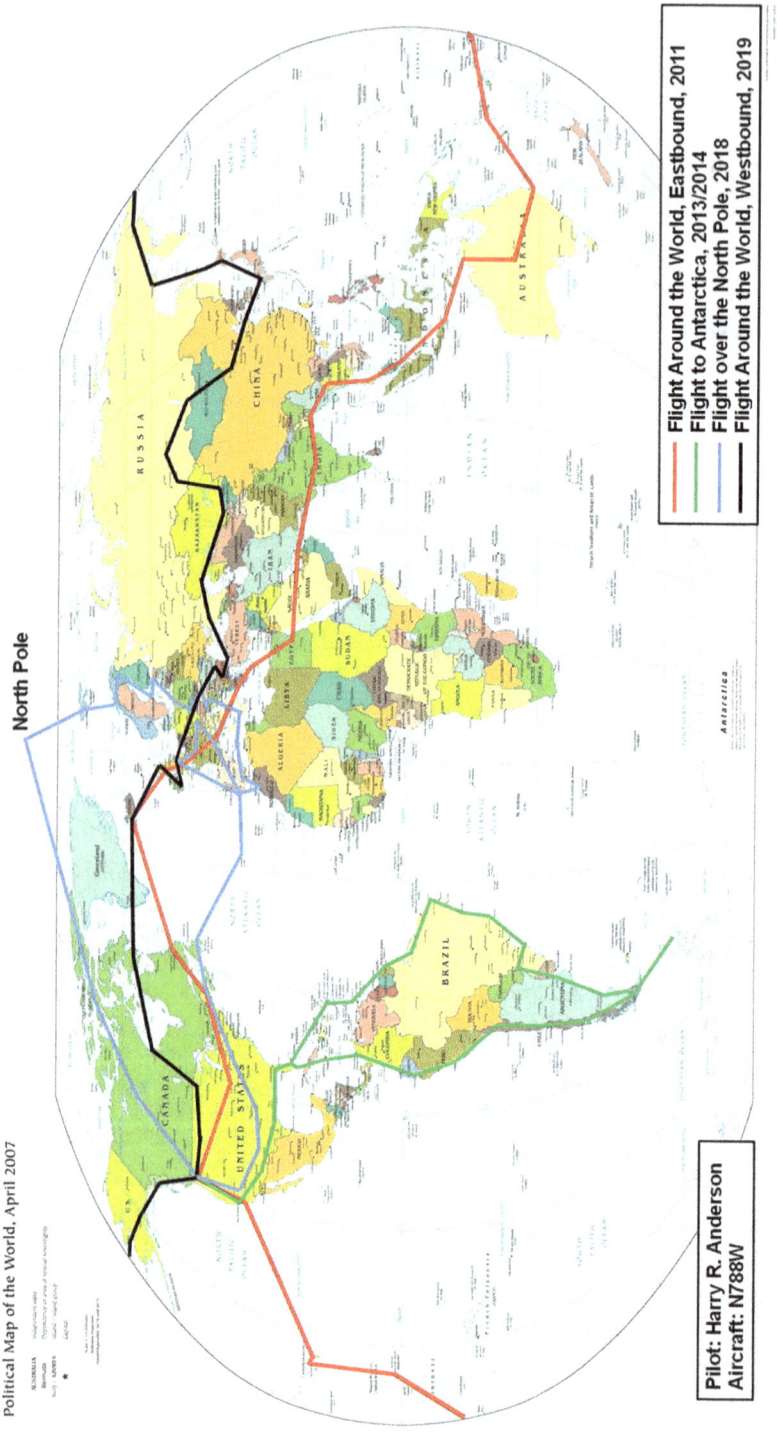

In boating terms, being alone on a boat is referred to as being "single-handed," meaning only one "hand" (crew member) is on board. It doesn't mean, as some might guess, that I would be sailing with one hand tied behind my back. To avoid confusion, and to employ the same terminology used in flying, I will use the term "solo" throughout this book in place of "single-handed."

I had sailed for many years, first as a teenager in my dad's boat off the coast of Southern California and later in a small Capri 22 sailboat on Fern Ridge Reservoir near Eugene, Oregon, where I lived for many years. After I sold my wireless engineering software business, EDX Engineering, Inc., at the peak of the tech boom in 2000, I moved to Bainbridge Island, Washington, sold the Capri 22, and eventually bought a Bavaria 37 sloop in 2006. I named it *Raytrace* after an engineering technique called ray-tracing for predicting wireless signal propagation that I commercially pioneered in 1994. Over 12 years I sailed *Raytrace* around the Pacific Northwest and along the Inside Passage toward Alaska, learning a lot about the various systems on cruising boats and about boat maintenance. I never took it offshore through the Strait of Juan de Fuca. In 2018 I sold *Raytrace* to my neighbors across the street. I wasn't sure I would ever own another sailboat—it seemed like sailing was a chapter of my life that had come to an end.

My plane, N788W, in Antarctica. I used it for all my international flights

While the idea of sailing solo to seven continents was compelling, I had many reservations about it. With my previous sailing experience, I knew that sailing could be a lot of work and physically demanding. It was also really slow compared to flying my plane. Ocean crossings that took hours in the plane would take weeks in a sailboat. Being on the ocean for such extended periods also meant I would be much more exposed to bad weather. With the plane I could easily outrun bad weather or fly around it, something I'd done many times. If the weather was really bad, I could always stay on the ground and wait for a better day. I couldn't do any of those things while sailing. Once I was offshore, I would have to deal with whatever weather came along. With sufficient warning I could run for shelter, but shelter could be days away. Considering all of this, while writing the flying book in 2015, I dismissed the idea of sailing solo to seven continents. "Nope, not for me," I thought.

Fast forward five years to 2020 when I changed my mind about it for two reasons. First, in the intervening years I had completed two more solo international flights I really wanted to do. In 2018 I flew my plane over the geographic North Pole from Resolute in northern Canada to Longyearbyen in the Svalbard Islands, a part of Norway. Though not the longest flight I've made, it was by far the most isolated; I was out of radio contact for almost the entire 1,630–nautical mile (nm), 10.5-hour flight. The second flight was a westbound solo circumnavigation that took me through Alaska, Russia, Japan, China, Kazakhstan and across Europe. With those two flights completed, in addition to my original flights to seven continents, I felt satisfied with what I'd accomplished in solo international flying. I didn't feel a need to do more flying; I wanted to turn my attention to something that offered a new challenge.

The second reason I changed my mind was the global COVID pandemic. Like most people in 2020, I was sitting around my house, not able to travel anywhere, and frustrated by an inability to do something truly engaging. To deal with that, I decided to resurrect the idea of sailing solo to seven continents. If nothing else, thinking about it and planning it would give me something interesting to do.

I began my research into such a voyage by reading the many online blogs written by people who have been cruising the world's oceans in sailboats, sometimes for years. I was surprised at the size of the cruising community, especially compared to the community of small-plane pilots flying internationally. There are thousands of cruising boats out there, both sailboats and powerboats, located all over the world. Many have turned cruising into a lifestyle; the boat is their home and their transportation. They don't have a house on land. For some older couples, it's a way to downsize, maybe reduce living expenses, while providing an opportunity to see the world.

I also started buying books, mostly cruising books but also books about equipping and provisioning a sailboat for long ocean passages. Books written and published by Jimmy Cornell, in particular *World Cruising Routes* and *Cornells' Ocean Atlas*, have become fundamental sources of information for anyone undertaking their own voyage across an ocean. There are many other books I consulted listed in appendix G.

This research led to planning a route that would let me efficiently sail to and land on seven continents while taking best advantage of the ocean winds and currents, and avoiding tropical storm seasons. Some places, particularly Antarctica, are only accessible for a few months a year in the austral summer (the summer months in the Southern Hemisphere), when the ice pack is at a minimum. Chapter 1 discusses my process for choosing a route in some detail.

No less important than having the right route is having the right sailboat. As a successful high-tech entrepreneur, the cost of the boat was never an issue for me. I was encouraged by the many blogs I'd read of people in old boats, in small boats, in poorly equipped boats, successfully sailing across the ocean. Some misgivings I had about undertaking this voyage were mitigated when I knew I could afford a great boat with no compromises regarding how it would be equipped. The process of choosing and buying a boat and outfitting it are discussed in chapters 2 and 3.

With the route planned and the boat purchased and equipped, the seven-continents project was done except for the sailing! Chapter 4 and the chapters that follow it describe my amazing sailing adventures to these continents and many points in between. It turned out to be a much different experience than I anticipated, requiring me to adjust my schedule, my route and my equipment as I was incrementally educated from being a novice offshore sailor to someone who could confidently cross any of the world's oceans.

I have included a spreadsheet showing the details of my sailing route, distances and dates in appendix A. Other appendices list various equipment, tools, spares and other supplies I took on my voyage, primarily the things I started with but which were added to and subtracted from as the voyage progressed. Appendix H includes copies of the complete documents I submitted to the Environmental Protection Agency (EPA) and the National Science Foundation (NSF) to get permission to sail solo to Antarctica.

Finally, there are many sailboat and nautical terms used throughout this book. To make the book more accessible to non-sailors, I have included a glossary following the appendices where explanations of these terms, as well as abbreviations, can be found.

As I mentioned in my flying book, I'm not a pilot's pilot. You will never hear me say I "love" flying, as many other pilots might say. The plane is a vehicle that opened the door to some unique and challenging adventures, like flying over the North Pole, that I couldn't have had any other way. Becoming skilled at flying through difficult circumstances gave me a satisfying sense of accomplishment.

I feel the same way about the boat and sailing. I'm not a sailor's sailor, definitely not an "old salt" with decades of engaging nautical stories to tell in a pub over a beer. The boat is a vehicle that, like the plane, opened the door to the rare and amazing adventures described in this book, adventures I couldn't have experienced any other way.

One of the positive surprises I've had from these flying and sailing adventures was meeting great people along the way, especially while sailing. Because fuel and other logistics often had to be arranged ahead of time, flying internationally was a fairly scheduled activity. I was rarely in any place longer than about three days unless some maintenance was being done on the plane. Even so, I made lasting friendships within the international pilot community.

Because it's much slower, sailing was very different in that regard. I would typically spend a week in any place I stopped, often longer. Other cruisers (people who sail the world on their own boats) I met would stay in places much longer. That provided an opportunity to meet people and get to know them, joining them for dinner or drinks on each other's boats or ashore. What set me apart in most cases was the fact that I was on a mission; I had the particular sailing objective of efficiently landing on all the continents while most everyone else was truly "cruising," enjoying just hanging out in the places they stopped. Some were intent on completing a circumnavigation but taking a leisurely approach with maybe a five or ten year plan to complete it. In crossing the oceans to get where we were, we all shared common experiences and difficulties—one of the quickest ways to form friendships with other people, whether short-term or enduring.

After studying electrical engineering in college, during which I lived in a van for my junior and senior years, and getting my bachelor's degree in 1972, I took a job with a small consulting firm in the San Francisco Bay Area. After three years of the daily grind, it became clear to me I would never get to do the things I really wanted to do with annual two-week vacations. I was 25 years old. I asked for and got a one-year leave of absence from my job. During that year I hitchhiked from Nairobi to Cape Town and back, climbed Mt. Kilimanjaro, lived in the South of France for several months and rode trains all over Europe. That year changed my life. I returned to the same job for a few years but eventually went into business for myself. The sense of independence and self-reliance I experienced during my year off gave me a new perspective on what I was capable of doing on my own. In many ways my career as a high-tech entrepreneur, my solo flights all over the world, and my solo voyage to seven continents are ongoing extensions of that year of independence. It's a perspective that will continue to drive my life.

1

Planning the Route

The world's oceans cover about three-quarters of the surface area of the earth so there are many possibilities for where a boat can go. However, for a sailboat, the oceans can have many "one-way streets," defined by prevailing winds and currents, where it's more difficult to sail a boat in the wrong direction, against the winds and currents. The sailors in the early 16th century who first crossed the oceans soon realized that the quickest way to get between two places was rarely achieved by sailing along a route with the shortest great circle distance. Without any weather-forecasting tools, they discovered by trial and error that sailing with the prevailing winds and currents, though not the shortest route, was faster. This quickly became apparent for ships sailing around Cape Horn at the southern tip of South America with the intention of crossing the Pacific to Asia for trading. Instead of taking a direct route, it was faster to sail north to the vicinity of the equator where (now) aptly named "trade winds" could be found that would push them westward with relative ease. Similar trade winds are found in the Atlantic Ocean around the equator, making sailing from West Africa to the Caribbean and the east coast of North America an easy downwind voyage, at least for much of the year.

Over the decades—in fact, centuries—mariners crossing the oceans have logged the winds and currents they've experienced on their voyages at different times of the year. This information has been collected and compiled in ocean "pilot charts." Pilot charts are maps of the oceans with "wind roses" set in 2.5, 5, or 10 degree latitude and longitude boxes forming a grid of information that illustrates the winds that have been experienced in each box. The wind roses themselves have wind arrows showing the percentage of time the wind arrives from compass directions spaced every 45 degrees. The wind roses also show the relative strength of the wind every 45 degrees at the wind rose location. The pilot charts are prepared for each ocean/sea and for each month of the year, allowing a mariner who is contemplating an ocean crossing to choose the best time to make that crossing. Using the pilot charts as a guide, it's possible to plan a voyage anywhere in the world that takes best advantage of the prevailing wind conditions.

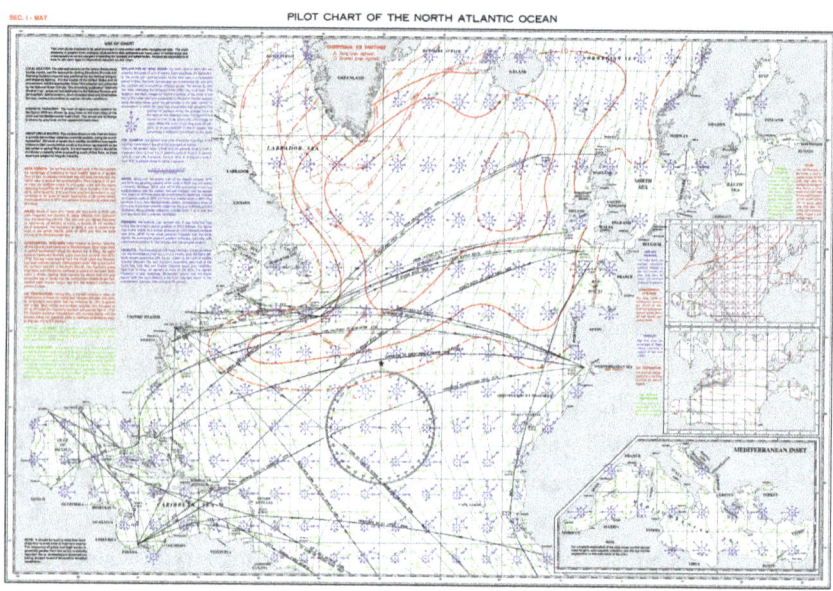

Sample pilot chart for the North Atlantic in the month of May

Pilot charts can be found online and downloaded for free. They have also been compiled into a convenient large-format book, along with interpretive information, named *Cornells' Ocean Atlas*, published by Jimmy Cornell (see appendix G).

In the sample pilot chart shown here for the North Atlantic in the month of May, the wind roses along a line eastward from Chesapeake Bay to the Azores generally show the longest wind arrows (prevailing wind) from the southwest and west. This would be a good time to sail east because the wind would be generally behind the boat, resulting in efficient and comfortable downwind sailing. Once past the Azores, the longest wind arrows are generally from the northwest and north along a route approaching the coast of Portugal. These are still favorable wind conditions, with the boat sailing on a port beam reach.

There are other significant weather phenomena that are important to consider when planning a voyage to all seven continents or around the world. Chief among them are hurricanes in the Atlantic Ocean and tropical cyclones (typhoons) in the Pacific and Indian Oceans. These occur during reasonably well-understood seasons. The Atlantic hurricane season has traditionally been considered to occur from June 1 to November 30 each year. Similarly, the Pacific tropical cyclone season lasts from November 1 to April 30. The Indian Ocean also has a tropical cyclone season in the austral summer months that's further affected by the northeast and southwest monsoon seasons.

However, climate change has begun to break down the long-held understanding about when these potentially violent storms will occur. Increasingly, storms are forming outside of these well-known storm seasons and following unexpected paths across the oceans. For a small sailboat, encountering such a big storm at sea can be catastrophic and life threatening. Even when a boat is at anchor in a sheltered harbor, or in a marina, it can be seriously damaged if hit by a tropical storm. An initial plan to sail around the world must avoid, to the extent possible, being at sea in the affected ocean during these tropical storm seasons, with the realization that violent storms may occur in months outside of what has been traditionally defined as the storm season.

As I discuss in the next chapter, I wasn't able to start this voyage on the date I wanted primarily due to the delay in delivering the boat. I had hoped to make my first ocean crossing eastward from North America to Europe early in the year, ideally in April or May, well ahead of when the Atlantic hurricane season would usually start. As a result of the delay, I didn't actually leave Norfolk, Virginia, in Chesapeake Bay, sailing eastward until August 2, 2022, well into the hurricane season. Fortunately, no hurricanes or tropical depressions crossed my route to Europe, but that was a matter of luck, not good planning. The point is, even a good plan that considers weather conditions can be upset by other factors such as boat preparation, maintenance, repairs and other voyage logistics like country arrival formalities.

12 | SAILING 7 CONTINENTS SOLO

Original planned sailing route

For the first part of my seven-continents voyage, the main imperative driving the schedule was crossing the Drake Passage to Antarctica in a suitable month. Because of ice conditions and extreme cold, the months when it's possible and advisable for small boats to sail in Antarctic waters is typically limited to December, January, February and part of March—the austral summer months. Even large cruise ships usually limit their season in Antarctica to these months, as do some Antarctic research stations that remove or reduce their research teams at the end of February. Wherever and whenever I started my voyage, I had to get to Antarctica during one of these months or I would have to wait a year for another opportunity. I definitely did not want to do that.

Considering all the ocean weather factors and timing to make the crossing to Antarctica, I came up with the route and schedule shown on the world map as the original planned route. I've shown only a few planned departure/arrival months from my original route map, a schedule that was immediately thrown off by the late delivery of my boat. As the voyage progressed, I changed my mind about where I wanted to go, in part due to information I gathered along the way that made one destination more desirable than another. For example, I had originally planned to visit the Cape Verde Islands on my way to Brazil, but once underway from Lanzarote in the Canary Islands I decided this stop was superfluous. I was already behind schedule getting to Tierra del Fuego and Antarctica, so I was looking for ways to eliminate unnecessary stops and resulting delay.

Such on-the-go adjustments to the original plan were not that unusual for me. On my first flight around the world in 2011 I made several changes to the places I would land primarily due to changing logistics—i.e., changes in the places where high-octane aviation gas was available and where I could get permits to land. Jet fuel, which is basically kerosene, is available pretty much everywhere because it's essential for commercial jet and turboprop planes. Small planes like mine have piston engines with big cylinders that need high-octane gasoline. Standard-octane gasoline for automobiles is generally not good enough. Small private planes are a relative rarity in many parts of the world, so naturally the availability of the fuel needed to support them can be correspondingly limited.

After reviewing my planned route, it occurred to me that I could accomplish my goal of sailing to all the continents by turning north after landing in Australia, landing somewhere in Malaysia or Thailand for my landing in Asia, then continuing north and ultimately east to return to North America for my seventh continent landing. That plan would also put me back in my home cruising grounds, and at my home, in the Pacific Northwest. However, taking that route wouldn't result in completing a circumnavigation—sailing around the world. Although a circumnavigation was not my primary goal, I thought it would be shortsighted to sail most of the world's oceans and not complete a solo circumnavigation. I therefore rejected that plan and stayed with the original route, which would take me across the Indian Ocean to a landing in India and Asia. From there I would sail around the southern tip of Africa and across the Atlantic for the third time for my return to North America at Florida. By adding a solo circumnavigation, I now had two goals.

Beyond those two goals I could imagine many secondary goals—mainly stopping in places that might be interesting or unique where I hadn't been before. Having routinely traveled internationally during almost 50 years, and having visited more than 100 countries, I'd had the opportunity to visit most of the places that someone might put on a travel bucket list. I had already been to many islands that commonly draw cruisers, like Easter Island (Rapa Nui), the Galapagos Islands, Fiji and Tahiti, whether via commercial flights or in my own plane. Even Tierra del Fuego at the southern tip of South America was not a stranger to me, as I had flown my plane there twice and landed in places like Puerto Williams, Punta Arenas and Puerto Montt. Of course, visiting places I'd been before but doing it in my own boat would make the experience new. Would it be different enough to justify detours off my primary route, and schedule delays, to go there? I decided that would be an ongoing, case-by-case judgment call, not part of my original plan.

2

Buying the Boat

With my decision in the summer of 2020 to attempt a solo voyage to seven continents, I began the process of choosing and buying the right boat for what I now saw as a mission, a process that can be very arduous and time-consuming. The variety and types of sailboats available for the voyage I had planned is really enormous. People can spend months, even years, searching for the right boat for their own ocean cruising dreams that will fit their budget. They'll hire consultants, presumably experts in oceangoing boats, to help them find just the right boat. The boat they seek could be nearby or almost anywhere in the world.

After they've found a candidate boat, a serious evaluation of its status is needed. Hiring a boat surveyor to evaluate the boat comes next. The surveyor will conduct an on-site inspection of the boat and all its systems and prepare a detailed report. Analyzing the engine oil alone, and cutting open the oil filter to examine it for metal particles, can reveal serious internal problems with the engine. Boats have many systems—plumbing, electrical, navigation electronics, autopilots, solar panels, wind generators, pumps, etc.—that must all be assessed when deciding if the boat is worth buying and, more importantly, how much work and expense there'll be to fix it up so it's sound enough to take across the ocean.

For a sailboat, an experienced rigger is also needed to inspect the rigging, including going up to the top of the mast(s). An older boat may have a lot of wear and tear not only on the standing rigging but on the sails and the running rigging—lines, blocks, clutches, and winches. A boat that's been sitting in or around saltwater for years will naturally show the effects of that environment with rusty metal components and corrosion.

Depending on the boat, taking it out on the water for sea trials to assess its performance may also be warranted, or necessary if the boat is sitting on land in a boatyard and can't be tested for leaks until it's put in the water.

I've touched on a few of the general points to consider when buying a boat for offshore sailing. This list is by no means comprehensive. There are entire books devoted to the subject of evaluating and buying a boat for this purpose, or for other sailing purposes, and as I mentioned, many consultants are available to assist with the process.

Fortunately, I already had enough sailing experience with a cruising boat to quickly narrow down the possibilities for what I wanted for my sailing mission to seven continents. As I mentioned in the introduction, I had previously owned a 37-foot Bavaria sloop, *Raytrace*, that I sailed mostly solo for 12 years in the Pacific Northwest. I wanted something of a similar size that felt comfortable for me to handle alone. That size would also be large enough to easily handle offshore sailing; in fact, people have crossed the oceans in far smaller boats. From owning the Bavaria, I also had a great deal of experience with operating and maintaining the many systems on a cruising boat. I knew several attributes I wanted when buying another boat, like large fuel and fresh water tanks, two things the Bavaria lacked.

The destination on my planned route that really narrowed down and simplified the boat selection process was Antarctica. Even though many have sailed to Antarctica, and along the Antarctic Peninsula, in fiberglass hull boats without a problem, I was convinced I wanted a boat with an aluminum hull. If a serious encounter with floating ice occurred, an aluminum hull will deform and dent but still stay watertight. Under similar circumstances, a fiberglass hull could potentially crack, compromising its watertight integrity and perhaps requiring some temporary level of repair just to make the return voyage to Tierra del Fuego, or farther north, for more permanent repairs. From my research, the yacht repair facilities in Tierra del Fuego, at either Puerto Williams or Ushuaia, are not capable of handling major repairs. A sailor would have to go farther north to Puerto Montt in Chile or even Uruguay to accomplish the repairs.

While at the time there were a few used aluminum hull boats meeting my criteria on the market, I would still be left with the challenging task of evaluating their seaworthiness, especially since some of them were far away in Europe where it was impossible to travel in 2020. If I bought a used boat, I would also be paying for equipment upgrades, especially electronic upgrades, to make it the boat I really wanted. Also, even the best boat surveyor's evaluation can still fail to find some hidden problems. Like buying a used car, there's always the risk of buying someone else's problems.

Fortunately, I was in a position to greatly simplify the process. As a successful high-tech entrepreneur, I had made a lot of money when I sold my software businesses. I wasn't restricted to a budget as many cruisers are; I could afford to buy exactly the boat I wanted. I therefore decided to order a new boat directly from the factory, thus eliminating any hidden, unknown problems I might encounter buying a used boat. I would get a new engine with zero hours on it and be able to specify exactly the optional equipment I wanted on board.

With that decision made, the choices were reduced to three French yacht manufacturers that specialize in building standard-model aluminum hull sailboats that can be customized with a wide variety of options. These manufacturers are Allures, Ovni and Boréal, all located on the west coast of France. All of their boats have retractable aluminum centerboards. When the centerboard is in the up position, these boats have a draw (their depth in the water) of about 1 meter, unlike fixed keel boats which draw much more. The shallow draft makes it possible to navigate some very shallow water and even beach the boat on its forefoot with the boat remaining upright. It's not possible to do that with a fixed keel boat. I didn't have any plans to beach the boat, but having a shallow draft could be important in some places I planned to visit, like coral atolls in the South Seas.

Of the candidate boat manufacturers, the smallest Boréal 44.2 was larger than I wanted, so that eliminated them. Ovni had just come out with the Ovni 400, which was the right size and had some other characteristics I liked such as large fuel and water tanks, but in sailing videos I'd seen putting the Ovni head-to-head against the Allures 40.9 (a boat of a similar size), the Allures definitely looked like the better boat sailing upwind.

There was also the question of delivery time. Even though it was 2020 and in the middle of the COVID pandemic, I knew it would take at least a year to build the boat after ordering it. I anticipated taking delivery when the pandemic was hopefully winding down. As a practical matter, I had been reading blogs written by other sailors who reported being pinned down all over the world, wherever they happened to be, when the pandemic hit. They could not travel home; in some cases, they could not even leave their boats to go ashore. Provisions had to be brought out to them where they anchored. The borders of many countries were completely closed to foreigners, including those on visiting yachts. I didn't want to launch a voyage, and probably couldn't launch a voyage, under such circumstances.

The hull of my boat under construction

The final factor that ultimately made my decision was the representation for Allures and Ovni in the US. I called the Ovni brokers in Florida and spoke to a woman who told me she really didn't handle Ovni sales and that I should call back the next day when her husband returned from sailing. He could help me. It was not the full-service involvement I wanted when buying a new boat that would eventually cost more than US$500,000.

Allures is represented in the US by Swiftsure Yachts, conveniently based on Lake Union in Seattle, a short ferry ride across Puget Sound from my home on Bainbridge Island. Ryan Helling of Swiftsure responded to my inquiry right away, sending me detailed information on the Allures 40.9, available options and initial pricing. He also said they had an American project manager by the name of Kevin Bray on-site in Cherbourg, France, where Allures yachts are built. Both Ryan and Kevin are expert sailors with considerably more sailing experience than I had at the time. Given that, and a promised delivery time from Allures of about a year, and my view that the Allures 40.9 was probably the better sailboat compared to the Ovni 400, I decided to order the Allures 40.9. That began a process that would occupy a lot of my time for the next several months.

The list of options available for the Allures 40.9 was several pages long. The first step was deciding on a model with two sleeping cabins or three. I chose the two-cabin version because it offered a larger head (bathroom) with the third cabin space turned into a "technical room" with drawers for tools and storage space for other equipment like spare lines, spare parts, and so forth. When setting off on a voyage that would take me around the world, having a full set of tools and spares to fix the boat myself was important.

The deck of my boat before attaching to the hull

Beyond that, there were a myriad of other available options. I chose from among those additional options with expert advice from Ryan and Kevin, who understood my sailing objective and had that in mind when making their recommendations. One thing I opted for were electric winches for the halyards and genoa sheets. By pressing a button instead of cranking a winch handle, I could quickly raise and lower the mainsail, and trim the mainsail and genoa sheets, with very little effort. As my voyage progressed and I experienced the physical demands of solo sailing and learned how quickly I wanted to adjust the sails when suddenly hit by a violent rain squall, selecting electric winches proved to have been a great decision.

For redundancy, I also opted for dual autopilot (AP) computers and drive units. Sailing solo, I would be relying on the autopilot extensively as a second "crew member" to steer the boat not only while I was sleeping but essentially all the time. That approach would free me to trim sails, prepare meals, take care of other chores around the boat, or simply relax. In those situations where I was navigating a narrow passage or coming into a marina or anchorage, I would be manually steering the boat instead of using the autopilot. I also ordered wireless remote controls for the autopilot so I could make course adjustments from any place on the boat.

I chose to have two 9-inch chartplotters, with one at the starboard helm position and one at the navigation (nav) station inside the cabin. This also proved to be a good move because I could steer the boat and control all its functions from inside the cabin instead of outside in the weather. Typically, the only time I would go on deck would be to adjust the sails or to sit and watch the hypnotic motion of ocean waves and the many brilliant sunsets and sunrises.

At the starboard helm (where the engine throttle is located), I had the boat equipped with a remote control for the anchor windlass, a control which included a chain counter showing me how much anchor chain I had deployed when dropping the anchor. This was far more convenient than the arrangement I had on the Bavaria 37 which required me to go to the bow to raise and lower the anchor. Without a chain counter, I had to use small fluorescent cable ties evenly spaced every 30 feet on the chain links to determine how much anchor chain I had lowered. Knowing how much chain has been released is a critical matter when anchoring a boat. The typical objective is to have the length of chain deployed be five times the depth of the water where the anchor is dropped. This number is called the anchor scope. Generally, the higher the scope, the more secure the anchor will be and the less likely it will be to drag across the bottom. When expecting high winds or seas, a considerably larger scope than five may be advisable. If the water is deep at an anchorage, a scope of five may not be possible with the available chain length. I had 80 meters of chain on my Allures 40.9. At St. Helena Island in the Atlantic, the water depth in the anchorage was 17 meters. Even using all the chain, the best scope I could achieve was 4.7.

All the boat electronics including chartplotters, supplemental sailing displays, radios, AIS (automatic identification system), radar and autopilots were the latest available gear from B&G, renown as one of the premier man-ufacturers of electronics for sailboats.

In terms of rigging, I chose to include a staysail on a furler. A staysail is a second smaller headsail on a mast stay (or guy wire) attached to the deck behind the genoa, which is the primary headsail and is on a furler mounted on the forestay. The staysail is useful in high winds where it's better to have less sail set and better to have the center of force from the sails closer to the center of the boat. I specified that both headsails supplied by Allures be made of Hydra Net sailcloth, the most durable sailcloth available at the time.

The biggest change I made with the rigging was to order the boat without a mainsail boom. I had been thinking about the effort involved in reefing the mainsail when the winds pick up. If the winds increase rapidly, like when encountering a squall, it's best to reduce the amount of sail quickly. In reefing with conventional booms, so-called slab reefing, the mainsail is pulled down with reefing lines and secured to the boom with ties. Instead of this approach, an increasing number of sailboats are equipped with in-mast furling where the sail is reduced by winding it up on a roller inside the mast. My Bavaria 37 had such in-mast furling. In the early days, these systems were problematic, but evolving technology has made them a reliable choice. The drawback is that you can't include battens in the sail because they won't roll up, meaning the sail shape itself can't include a roach and is less efficient for that reason.

The other approach to reducing the mainsail is to wind it up, or furl it, inside the boom. This allows the mainsail to have battens and better sail shape because the battens, which run parallel to the deck, can be rolled up with the sail inside the boom. There are a handful of boom furling systems available; the best of them is made by Schaefer Marine. That is the system I chose to have on my boat. Unfortunately, Allures would not (or could not) install a Schaefer boom on my new boat. Consequently, I ordered the boat without the boom or mainsail with the plan to have the Schaefer boom installed once the boat was delivered to the US, as described in the next chapter. With the Schaefer boom, the mainsail needed was a custom design to fit the boat and the boom. I ordered that mainsail from Neil Pryde Sails, who have made many sails for Schaefer booms in the past

Phywave **being launched in Cherbourg**

and had a close working relationship with them. Like the two headsails supplied by Allures, I had Neil Pryde use Hydra Net material for the mainsail.

Throughout the process of specifying the details for the boat, I traded literally hundreds of emails, and a few video calls, with Kevin and Ryan to get the boat built the way I wanted. It was not a simple process. Kevin compiled and sent me hundreds of photos he had taken showing the state of the construction at various times. These photos proved invaluable later when I was trying to investigate installation details and troubleshoot various things on the boat.

One of the final steps was deciding on a name for my new boat. I wanted a name that was absolutely unique in the US Coast Guard vessel registry. As I prepared a short list of candidate names, I checked each one on the Coast Guard website to see if anyone else was using it, or had used it. I also didn't want a personal name like many sailors who name their boats so they can speak to them like a friend or partner. Mulling over names went on for months, it seemed, until the deadline approached for finally choosing a name and applying for Coast Guard registration and documentation. I chose "Phywave" more by default than any compelling reason—I simply couldn't get enthusiastic about any of the other names on my short list. Those names seemed too oblique, too contrived, somehow phony. "Phywave" is a name I came up with many years ago for an engineering consulting business I started after selling my software business in 2000. I already had a website: *www.phywave.com*. At some point I stopped doing engineering consulting work and Phywave, Inc. became the corporation that published my flying book. Phywave is still an active corporation but doesn't make much money. I decided to continue with "Phywave" as the name for the boat and convert the Phywave website into a personal website that could include information about many of my activities like flying, sailing and wireless engineering. I also considered how recognizable and easy to use it would be as a boat name when sailing around the world and visiting many foreign ports with different languages. I was surprised and amused when I later heard over the radio how "Phywave" was pronounced in Spanish and French.

The boat was ordered and the contract signed with Allures in September 2020. The contract called for the boat to be finished and ready for delivery in October 2021. As that date approached, it was clear that construction was well behind schedule. Allures kept pushing the completion date back into 2022. The boat was not actually put in the water for the first time until March 22, 2022. A small leak was found and required the boat to go back to the assembly building for a welding repair on the aluminum hull. The boat was launched again on April 12, when it was confirmed the leak was fixed. The final delivery documents were signed on April 22, 2022, and *Phywave* was officially mine and free to leave the Cherbourg boatyard for delivery to the US.

Overall, the boat was delivered fully six months late. My contract with Allures called for a penalty to be paid to me for late delivery that would have amounted to several thousand euros. Allures refused to pay the late delivery penalty in spite of my arguing by letter that I was entitled to it. I think Swiftsure Yachts also agreed Allures should pay the penalty. I contacted a bilingual lawyer in Paris who reviewed the contract documents and agreed with me that Allures owed me the penalty amount. He was willing to take the case. After thinking about it for a week, I decided not to pursue legal action. It would only serve to further delay delivery of the boat and the beginning of my voyage to seven continents. While I like the boat they built, I now consider Allures to be an untrustworthy company for refusing to pay the penalty. Although the boat is great, I would hesitate to buy a boat from Allures because of the way they do business.

Now that I owned *Phywave*, I arranged for Kevin to sail it across the English Channel to Southampton in the UK, the port where a Sevenstar Yacht Transport ship would pick it up and carry it to Baltimore, Maryland, where it would be offloaded. Sevenstar ships are equipped with cradles on the deck that allow a fully rigged sailboat with the mast stepped (erected) to be transported across the ocean. Boats are lifted from the water onto the deck

Phywave **being offloaded from transport ship in Baltimore**

with a shipboard crane, tied down and then dropped into the water again by crane at the delivery destination. To prepare *Phywave* for transport, Kevin had to remove the headsails, stow them below and take down the backstays so the slings could be fitted under the hull with the boat alongside the ship. The boat was then picked up out of the water and placed in its cradle on the ship's deck. Once it was in the cradle, the slings were removed and the backstays reconnected to make sure the mast was properly supported during the ship's passage. With that done, Kevin could leave the *Phywave* keys with the ship's captain and return to Cherbourg by ferry.

The boat was first scheduled to be picked up by Sevenstar in April. But with the leak repair, that pickup date was missed. Kevin was finally able to get *Phywave* to Southampton on April 26. The next Sevenstar pickup date in Southampton was May 21, so *Phywave* sat in the Town Quay Marina there for nearly a month. On May 21 *Phywave* was finally loaded on the ship, which then sailed for the US that day. After dropping off some other yachts in Newport, Rhode Island, the ship would make it to Baltimore harbor and be in position to offload *Phywave* on June 1.

I would have to be in Baltimore when the ship arrived to climb on board as *Phywave* was lowered over the side, ready to drive it away when it hit the water and the lifting straps were removed. Ryan from Swiftsure joined me for this offload process since he had been through it many times before. From there, the closest place to have extensive boat rigging and other work done was in Annapolis, Maryland, where there are several boatyards, chief among them the Bert Jabin Yacht Yard. As my first experience with *Phywave*, I drove it from the offload point in Baltimore to Bert Jabin where Ryan and I put it in a slip I had already reserved. From there the additional *Phywave* outfitting would start.

Getting my hands on *Phywave,* I felt like the adventure I had been thinking about and planning since the summer of 2020 was finally underway. The long preamble to my voyage had become a real boat that floated and sailed and would carry me across the sea. It was a time for an incremental mini-celebration, so Ryan and I went to a restaurant for Maryland-famous crab cakes and margaritas.

There was relief that all the work I had done specifying the boat, and the large amount of money I had paid to buy it, had turned into something tangible. That relief was tempered by knowing I was just approaching the starting line, not yet in the race, and that there was still an enormous amount of effort ahead of me to achieve my sailing goals.

3

Outfitting *Phywave*

With the available Allures options decided for *Phywave*, and the boat under construction, I created a list of additional equipment I wanted that Allures couldn't or wouldn't install, or where the option they offered was inferior to the equipment I really wanted. As the date for *Phywave*'s arrival in Annapolis approached, I started lining up contractors to install this additional equipment. Fortunately, Annapolis has a huge sailing community that supports a wide range of contractors who can furnish all manner of boating supplies and equipment as well as provide installation services.

Schaefer Furling Boom

Since I ordered *Phywave* without a boom or mainsail, these were the first essential items I needed to add. I wanted to install a Schaefer furling boom, which the Allures boatyard wouldn't do. In October 2022, during the annual Annapolis Boat Show, I hired The Rigging Company, located at the Bert Jabin boatyard, to buy and install the Schaefer boom. They had worked with Schaefer before so they were a logical choice for this work.

My Schaefer Gamma boom was delivered to the boatyard the day after I arrived in Annapolis with *Phywave*, having already been cut to the right length at Schaefer. All the gear Schaefer sells is known for being very heavy-duty, including this boom and the pivoting gooseneck that connects it to the mast. Once I saw it all installed, I was impressed with how much more substantial it looked compared to conventional booms and goosenecks on other sailboats of similar size. It looked like it was ready for rough ocean travel.

The new Hydra Net mainsail from Neil Pryde was delivered a few weeks later. A single continuous roll of fiberglass batten material was also delivered. The batten material had to be cut to exactly fit the batten sleeves in the sail. I enlisted the help of a local sail loft that could lay out the sail on a huge table, measure the sleeves, and cut the battens to the correct length. With that done, they delivered the sail to *Phywave* and fitted the foot tape into the slot on the boom. Next, we fitted the sail luff tape into the Schaefer hinged mast track and raised the sail, inserting the newly cut battens as we did that. For the first time I saw *Phywave* with its fully hoisted mainsail, a moment worth a few photos.

Phywave at the Bert Jabin Yacht Yard

Forespar Whisker Pole

A whisker pole is attached to the mast on one end and the clew of the headsail on the other end. It's used to pole out the headsail so it catches more wind when sailing downwind. Allures wouldn't install the track-mounted telescoping whisker pole I wanted, instead offering to install their standard spinnaker pole as an option. I declined that and had The Rigging Company furnish and install the track and Forespar whisker pole I wanted.

Watermaker

Though watermakers are often reported to be troublesome by other cruisers, I decided I wanted one on *Phywave*. Watermakers turn seawater into fresh water using a high-pressure pump that pushes the seawater through a very fine membrane that filters out the salt and discards the brine overboard. They're essentially desalinators. There are many companies that manufacture watermakers for yachts. I chose model 260-DML-1 from ECHOTec, which has separate components connected with hoses so there is more flexibility in how it can be installed in the boat. Sailing solo, my fresh water usage would be less than a sailing couple or a family. Even so, the watermaker would eliminate any concern about running out of fresh water. Allures did offer a watermaker preinstall option that provided the thru-hull fitting for the seawater supply already welded into the hull. This watermaker can nominally provide about 15 gallons per hour (gph) of fresh water, more than enough to easily refill *Phywave*'s water tank in a reasonable amount of time. The high-pressure pump in the watermaker requires a fair amount of 12-volt power, so it's best to run it only when either the engine or generator is also running to keep the batteries charged. The watermaker was installed by J. Gordon & Co. in Annapolis.

Diesel Generator

Electrical power on a sailboat is a critical resource that's used to run a number of essential devices including chartplotters, radios, the autopilot, lights and the refrigerator. The power on *Phywave* is 12 volts DC that comes from a 440-amp-hour bank of batteries, known as house or service batteries. That distinguishes them from a second, independent battery that is reserved for starting the engine, the start battery. As standard options from Allures, *Phywave* came equipped with a 520-watt solar panel array and a Silentwind wind generator to charge these batteries. The batteries are also charged by a 120-amp alternator when the engine is running. If the sky is cloudy or there is little wind, the solar panels and wind generator won't be much help in keeping the batteries charged. In that case, boats without an auxiliary generator have no choice but to run the engine to recharge the batteries. This is not a fuel-efficient thing to do, and diesel engines generally don't like to be run with such light loads. For these reasons, I decided to install a Northern Lights 6-kW generator in a place behind the main engine that was available for that purpose. Allures did offer an option to have a generator installed, but the make and model of generator they offered had a very bad reputation, so I rejected that option and chose to have the generator installed when the boat reached the US. As for the watermaker, Allures did offer a generator preinstall option that provided the thru-hull fittings already welded into the hull which are needed to supply cooling seawater to the generator and take exhaust seawater and fumes overboard. Northern Lights generators are the first choice for commercial fishing boats operating in the Pacific Northwest and Alaska. I took that as a solid recommendation on their quality and reliability.

With some research I decided the best place to get the generator installed was at the Haven Harbour Marina boatyard in Rock Hall, Maryland. Rock Hall is on the eastern side of Chesapeake Bay, opposite from Annapolis on the west side, so I would have to move *Phywave* over there when all the other outfitting was done in Annapolis. Among the Northern Lights dealers I talked to, the generator delivery times varied considerably. I finally ordered the generator from North Harbor Diesel and Yacht Service in Anacortes, Washington, and had it shipped to Haven Harbour for installation.

The generator installation alone took nearly a month, partly due to the boatyard being busy with other projects but also because it's a difficult installation. The generator weighs nearly 400 pounds and has to be lowered by a crane down *Phywave*'s companionway where, with a lot of muscle, it was maneuvered aft to its mounting location behind the engine. It then had to be connected to the thru-hull fittings for cooling seawater. A separate start battery and switch were installed, and a fuel hose was attached to the main diesel tank. The final step was to wire the generator output to a switch that would select between shore power and generator power. The output of that switch supplies power to the battery charger and to the few US-style 120-volt AC outlets installed on the boat. Having those outlets installed instead of French-style outlets was another custom option I specified when ordering the boat.

SSB (Ham) Shortwave Radio

Over short distances, boats communicate via VHF radio using frequencies in the 156 to 174 MHz range. Communication is more or less limited to boats or shore stations that are within line of sight of each other. For communication over longer distances, SSB radios operating on shortwave frequencies in the 3 to 30 MHz range have traditionally been used. They rely on the shortwave signal bouncing between the ionosphere and Earth, sometimes multiple times (called "skip") to get the signal from the boat to a shore station or another boat that can be thousands of miles away over the horizon. While once essential, over the past 10–15 years the use of SSB by boats has diminished significantly, having been replaced by satellite-based communications that can handle voice calls as well as email and text. Even so, being a ham radio operator

SSB radio installed at the nav station

since I was a kid, with a current call sign of KB6AF, I decided I wanted an SSB radio on my boat. I bought an Icom IC-7300 and modified it so it would transmit on all frequencies between 3 and 30 MHz, including the marine radio frequencies. The IC-7300 was connected to an Icom AT-140 antenna tuner that, in turn, was connected to an antenna wire that was attached to one of the backstays on *Phywave*. Allures had installed the backstay with two insulators, one near the top of the mast and the other near the deck. That provided a long wire electrically isolated from the rest of the boat that would serve as an antenna. Such a long-wire antenna, when used with the antenna tuner, could be tuned to work efficiently over a wide range of frequencies. For the antenna counterpoise, I connected the RF ground lug on the antenna tuner to a 12-foot wire in the bilge of the boat that inductively couples to the aluminum hull and the saltwater surrounding it. This turned out to be a very effective antenna arrangement. I was able to contact ham operators, and SSB cruiser nets, thousands of miles away with good signal reports.

Unlike the other equipment I was having installed on the boat in Annapolis, the SSB was something I could install myself as a wireless engineer. I mounted the IC-7300 radio at the nav station and supplied it with 12-VDC power through a 30-amp circuit breaker from the main power bus. I then mounted the antenna tuner in the technical room and connected it to the radio by running the RF coax cable and control wire through the bilge. I also had to drill a hole through the deck for the antenna wire, which required a watertight clamshell cable pass-through fitting. With the antenna wire connected to the insulated backstay, the installation was complete.

Satellite Communications

When I outfitted *Phywave* for my voyage, the Iridium GO! was the most economical satellite system available. It provides basic communication services such as email, voice calls and some data downloads. Most importantly, it can download weather forecast maps in the form of compressed binary GRIB files that can be displayed in various apps available for iPads and iPhones. I chose the PredictWind app for this purpose. I also bought the Iridium satellite airtime plan from PredictWind. The drawback of the Iridium GO! is that the data speed is extremely slow. As an older guy I remember using dial-up modems years ago to connect to remote computers, and the Iridium GO! speed is even slower than that connection. Even so, as I began my voyage in 2022 it was the best option and an obvious choice to have on board. One clear benefit of the Iridium GO! is that it would automatically transmit a GPS position report every hour via the Iridium satellite network. That position report could then be displayed on a web page map so anyone could see the position of *Phywave* at any time.

As with the SSB radio, I was able to do the Iridium GO! installation myself, including the outside antenna and a second watertight deck pass-through fitting for the cable connecting the antenna to the Iridium GO! unit mounted inside the technical room.

In the last few years, slow satellite systems like Iridium GO! on boats have been supplanted by Starlink flat-dish antennas that offer full high-speed internet access even far offshore. Later in my voyage I was able to install a Starlink system while *Phywave* was in Puerto Montt, Chile. I kept the Iridium GO! operational, but it became a backup system.

Dodger and Bimini

Although it interrupts the clean design lines of a boat, a dodger at the front of the cockpit area is essential for any ocean-going boat because waves are bound to come flying over the deck into the cockpit. The dodger is essential for protecting the crew from those waves. The bimini is situated across the aft part of the cockpit over both helms as a sunshade. A connecting panel is usually zipped in between the dodger and bimini to provide shade over the entire cockpit. I could have ordered the dodger and bimini from Allures but I was advised by Swiftsure that the canvas work available in Europe is inferior to what I could get in the US, so I delayed having the dodger and bimini designed and installed until the *Phywave* was in Annapolis. After interviewing a few yacht canvas companies, I decided to go with Cover Loft for the installation. The staff there came up with a custom design that responded to what I wanted. They were also able to fit the dodger with Makrolon polycarbonate windows, a material far superior to the polyvinyl windows traditionally used in dodgers, which can yellow and ultimately disintegrate with age and sun exposure. The dodger, bimini and connector panel were delivered while the boat was in Rock Hall.

Dinghy and Outboard Motor

I had an AB 9.5 Lammina UL RIB dinghy on the Bavaria 37 I owned. An RIB (rigid inflatable boat) dinghy has a solid hull, usually aluminum, attached to inflatable tubes. I used it frequently while sailing in the Pacific Northwest where even the better beaches can still have a lot of rocks. I liked its durability and straight tracking through the water, so I decided to get another AB dinghy for *Phywave*. While visiting the Annapolis Boat Show in October 2022, I put a deposit down on an AB 9.5 Lammina AL with a bow locker with Annapolis Inflatables. They seemed to be the premier inflatable boat company in Annapolis. They promised me my dinghy would be ready to pick up when I arrived the following spring to outfit *Phywave*. When I arrived my dinghy wasn't there, and they couldn't even give me a solid answer about when it would arrive. They talked about shipping containers arriving with new stock, but they weren't sure if my dinghy was in any of them. After a month of listening to their excuses and bait-and-switch tactics to sell me a different brand they had in stock, I canceled the order and got my deposit back. I found exactly the dinghy I wanted at Defender Marine in Connecticut. I drove up there in my 2011 Nissan Pathfinder, which I had driven east from home, rented a small flat trailer, picked up the dinghy (still in the box) and drove it back to Annapolis. I also bought a new 6-hp Yamaha outboard motor to drive it.

Boat Gear Brought from Home

Beginning a year before I expected to take delivery of *Phywave*, I started gathering the boat gear I wanted to place on board that wouldn't actually be installed there. This pile of stuff quickly occupied a significant area in my 20 x 20 foot shop at my home on Bainbridge Island. Some of the equipment was obvious, like all kitchen-related gear for the galley, an extensive collection of tools including cordless Milwaukee power tools, and clothes for all seasons. By reading the blogs of other cruisers who had been to the places I was going, and guidebooks for places like Tierra del Fuego, I assembled more esoteric equipment like shore lines on reels for tying the boat to shore in the narrow anchorages sometimes encountered where there isn't room for the boat to swing at anchor. There were also backup electronics like radios, an extensive medical kit derived from a variety of sources, and emergency gear like flares and an EPIRB emergency GPS satellite beacon that would eventually be mounted on *Phywave*. Spares were also a major part of the gear brought from home, including a spare anchor. I also included a telescoping ladder for accessing the elevated end of the Schaefer boom.

This pile continued to grow to the point that I had to address the question of how I would get all this stuff out of my shop and to a boat that would be arriving on the other side of the country. I investigated renting a van or truck, or a trailer, but finally decided on getting a U-Haul U-box that I could load myself and then have picked up and shipped to Annapolis for unloading there. Knowing I would be in Annapolis for a while, I also decided to drive my Pathfinder across the country so I would have transportation while there. I could take some gear in the car with me, like those items I considered most valuable or irreplaceable. I could keep them safe in my hotel rooms as I drove

Boat gear in my shop at home

across the country. Ultimately, I decided some of what I brought from home was superfluous and decided not to take it. Some I gave away to charities in Annapolis; the rest I put in a box and left in my Pathfinder. Appendices B through G have spreadsheets showing the equipment I had on board for most of my voyage, both items I brought from home and gear I added, or substituted, along the way.

I had arranged with my good friends Kathy Maher and Alec Vassiliades on Bainbridge Island to drive my Pathfinder back home from the East Coast. For generations Kathy's family has had a cabin on a lake near Camden, Maine. She routinely spends the summer there. For our arrangement, she would fly to Baltimore, pick up the Pathfinder from me and then drive it to Camden, where she would meet Alec. At the end of the summer, they would drive it back to Bainbridge Island and put it in my garage. It gave them transportation while in Camden for the summer and got my car back home. The plan worked great, a win-win for everyone.

Other Preparations

In addition to the boat, its equipment and the gear I placed on board, there were several other things I needed to do before a world voyage like this could begin.

Insurance

Finding boat insurance for a voyage across the ocean can be difficult and expensive. For someone intending to sail solo, it is almost impossible. I talked to a few US insurance companies who said "no way" as soon as I told them it was for a solo voyage. I finally got a lead on a company named Edward William based in Spain that would insure a solo offshore voyage. They had a poor reputation for paying claims but what I really needed from them was the policy paperwork I could show to gain entrance to harbors and marinas in some foreign countries along the way. Most of them require at least third-party liability insurance for foreign boats. The Edward William premium was very expensive, but I really had no choice after seeking policies from others. I started the voyage with full hull and liability insurance, but after I got to know the boat and could better understand the sailing risks involved, I eventually reduced that coverage to liability only, greatly reducing the premium cost.

Charts

While flying I had stopped using paper charts many years ago. I applied the same thinking to navigation charts for the boat. I used all-electronic Navionics charts in the chartplotters on the boat and on my iPads. Navionics charts did not cover Antarctica, but another charting app called iSailor did. I started using iSailor as an alternate to the Navionics (now Garmin) Boating app. As a backup, I did buy the British Admiralty paper charts for Antarctica. The iSailor's e-charts matched the Admiralty charts exactly for the places I was going in Antarctica.

Provisions

I spent a fair amount of time thinking about the food I'd bring, even buying various things at home to sample. I rarely eat anything out of a can, so I sampled a variety of canned fish and meat options. There are many (too many) books out there with recipes for cruising boats and recommendations for using more elaborate galley gear like pressure cookers. Recipes? I don't want to follow any recipes. Given the sometimes-difficult sea conditions encountered, the key to eating on a boat is simplicity. A can of tuna and a can of vegetables tossed into a saucepan and heated up became a very common dinner for me, along with a glass of red wine and a dark chocolate bar for dessert. Fresh food was OK for the first 10 days or so of the voyage, but having only a refrigerator and no freezer on *Phywave*, I knew I would end up eventually eating canned food on long passages.

Provisioning in the US was easy with the huge variety of food available in supermarkets. In other countries, depending on the size of the town and how remote it is, the choices could be very limited. Even so, there was always enough to get by. Later in the book there's more about the provisioning challenges I faced as my voyage progressed.

Country Entry Formalities

Every country has its own procedures for people entering on a private yacht. Some can be quite streamlined and sensible; others are arduous, bordering on ridiculous. A fairly up-to-date source of information on the current entry formalities for the many countries around the world is a website called Noonsite. By selecting the country name from a drop-down list, a concise summary of the essential information for visiting boats is presented. I consulted this website frequently during the voyage, beginning with my first stop in the Azores, a territory of Portugal.

Some places, like Réunion Island and Australia, require advanced notification from arriving yachts. The information on the Noonsite website explains this requirement to cruisers and provides them some basic instructions on how to proceed.

There were many other smaller issues to consider before setting off across the ocean, but at some point, I had to stop getting bogged down in those details and just go.

4

Eastward to the Azores

With the generator installation finally complete, I sailed south from Rock Hall down the Chesapeake Bay to Norfolk, Virginia, where I would top off the fuel tank and make that the departure point for my passage east to the Azores, about 2,500 nm away. I left Haven Harbour Marina on July 30 with two stops planned along the way, in Mill Creek, north of Solomon Island, and in Little Bay, south of Fleets Bay. This would give me an opportunity to anchor the boat at least twice. It seemed a little ridiculous to set off across the ocean in a boat I had never anchored.

During the first day of my southbound journey, I had reasonably good weather with sunshine, but immediately after leaving Rock Hall I discovered a serious problem with the autopilot. An alarm on the chartplotter reported a "no rudder position" error, so I had to hand steer all day to my first anchorage in Mill Creek. Investigating the problem the next morning, I discovered the small control arm that attaches to the rudder, and sends its position information to the autopilot, was disconnected. I'm pretty sure this happened during the generator installation, when disconnecting this control arm would have made it easier to connect the seawater discharge hose from the generator to the corresponding thru-hull. After I reconnected the control arm, the autopilot then worked properly. This was the first of many problems I would need to troubleshoot and fix myself during the course of my voyage.

The next day 20-to-25 knot winds and 2-meter waves were out of the south, impeding my progress and making for a long day getting to the next anchorage in Little Bay. While staying there overnight I moved the dinghy from the stern arch on *Phywave* to the foredeck where I strapped it down with stainless steel ratchet straps I brought from home. For an ocean passage, having the dinghy on the foredeck is usually the preferred location. With the dinghy hanging from the arch, it could swing around too much when at sea, especially in rough seas. With some clever use of straps, the swinging could be minimized—a project to consider in the future.

Hanging it from the arch certainly makes it easier to launch. With the dinghy on the foredeck, it's necessary to use the spinnaker halyard to pull the dinghy up and over the lifelines and then lower it into the water. From there, it has to be moved around to the stern where the outboard motor can be mounted and the fuel tank placed inside along with the oars and the seat. The whole process can take up to an hour. Putting the dinghy back on the foredeck is the reverse process. The work involved in launching and stowing the dinghy certainly dissuaded me from using it when I was only in an anchorage for a short time.

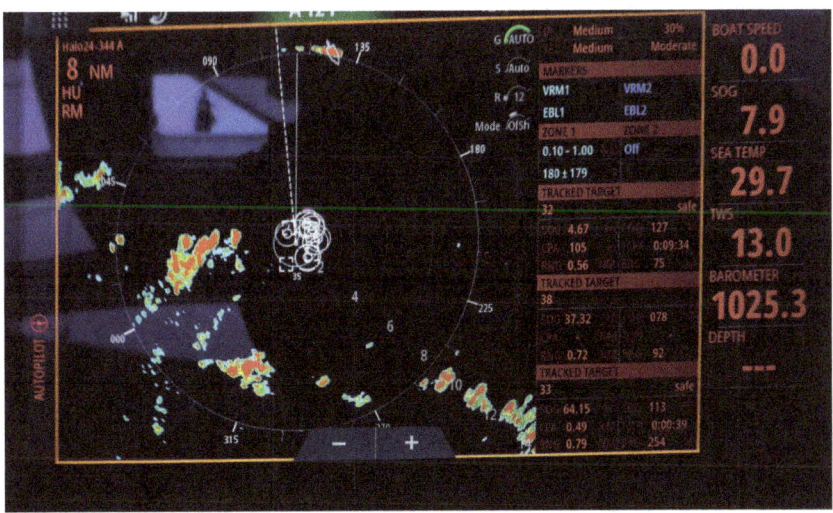

Rain squalls on the radar

From my Little Bay anchorage, I continued south to my final stop in the US at Cobb's Marina in Little Creek Harbor in Norfolk, Virginia, where there is an easily accessible fuel dock. I filled up my diesel tanks that afternoon and stayed tied there until the next morning when I would set off east across the Atlantic Ocean. Just before entering the Little Creek channel, I was hit with an intense rain squall, forcing me to turn my bow into the wind until it passed. Even a large navy ship attempting to maneuver into Little Creek was forced to break off its approach to the channel and head into the wind until the squall passed.

At Sea, at Night, Alone

On the morning of August 2 at 1200Z I set sail for Horta in the Azores. "Z" stands for Zulu time, which is the nomenclature we use as pilots. It's the same as Greenwich Mean Time (GMT) or Coordinated Universal Time (UTC). I expected the passage to Horta would take 18–20 days.

It was a big moment when I passed over the underwater road tunnel at the entrance to Chesapeake Bay and pointed *Phywave* east. I had never sailed offshore before, never sailed out of the sight of land, so it truly felt like the beginning of a new adventure. The weather was sublime, with filtered sunshine but without enough wind to sail, so I was motoring most of the day. I was primarily focused on intercepting the Gulf Stream current that would help propel me east. The location and strength of ocean currents can vary, so where exactly I would encounter it was a bit of a guess. There are some weather apps like Windy, one I use frequently in flying, that show the location of ocean currents over a few days. But Windy requires an internet connection that I would soon lose as I got farther away from land. As I finally began to lose that internet connection, I took a screenshot of the Windy current map with my iPad that would be approximately correct for a while.

I was thinking about getting into a daily routine, already rearranging the provisions and gear I had stowed and hoping to soon get some usable wind. I was also still learning the B&G chartplotter electronics and setting up the data displays the way I wanted. This turned out to be an ongoing process throughout my voyage. There are so many options it can be a small challenge to get the necessary information on the correct screens. I found the B&G SailSteer display on the chartplotter the most useful, rather than the chart display, because it graphically shows the relationship of the boat to apparent and true wind directions, essential for establishing an optimum sailing angle. Learning the electronics is something I probably should have done before I left, but once at sea there are long hours when there is nothing much to do so I had time for this ongoing education.

Many people have asked me how I sleep when sailing solo—who is running the boat and standing watch? It's a good question that solo sailors have answered for themselves in a variety of ways. Some will set fixed schedules, alternately sleeping for 45 minutes then standing watch for 45 minutes. For some sailors it's two hours instead of 45 minutes. For me, with my own personal sleep schedule, such a routine would have been impossible. At home I would normally fall asleep quickly but wake up after four hours. I'd be awake for an hour or more, then usually fall back asleep for three hours or so. Rarely, I would never fall back asleep and feel wiped out for the rest of the day. I decided not to impose a new, radical sleep schedule but simply do what I do at home. Being asleep for approximately four hours means the boat could move about 25 nm with an average speed of 6 knots. If I reviewed what was in front of me, and was satisfied there was nothing I could hit, I was comfortable with going to sleep for four hours.

Approaching rain squall

Of course, reviewing what was in front of me relied on using the electronics on the boat: specifically, the AIS and the radar. The acronym AIS stands for automatic identification system. It is legally required for large ships but optional on small private vessels like mine. The AIS on each ship broadcasts its GPS coordinates, its course and its speed. Using this data and corresponding data for your own vessel, the AIS receiver can calculate the potential for a collision and display that information. The AIS turned out to be the most critical system for avoiding other ships. Unfortunately, many small boats, especially small fishing boats, don't have expensive AIS systems, so there is substantial risk with them I'll discuss later in this book. Even some yachts cruising around the world don't have working transmit and receive AIS systems, which is totally crazy, in my opinion. Even if a sailor is on a limited budget, an AIS system is one of the first things they should invest in.

For detecting nearby boats that don't have AIS, the radar is the next system that can help. It's possible to set alarms that will sound if something comes close on radar. The radar is also useful for displaying the location and movement of nearby rain squalls or heavy rain. Small wooden fishing boats are not well-detected by the radar unless very close, so they can still represent dangerous obstacles at sea.

While I initially used the AIS and radar to review everything around me before going to sleep, I found using the radar far offshore was not efficient because it uses electrical power from the batteries. Any vessel far offshore will most likely have AIS running all the time, as I did. I therefore restricted my use of radar to those times when I was close to shore where small fishing boats could be encountered.

In effect, the electronics instead of a human crew member were standing watch while I slept. The first night at sea for me was a turning point. Letting the boat sail off into the darkness with nobody at the helm, nobody looking out for other boats or obstacles, nobody watching the chartplotter screens, was a necessary act of confidence if I were going to be a solo sailor and successfully complete my mission to sail alone to seven continents.

One happy realization came in those first days—I don't get seasick. Generally, I'm not prone to motion sickness and have never gotten sick in my plane, even in rough turbulence. A few times on other boats, like during a rough ferry crossing of the Strait of Gibraltar from Spain to Morocco many years ago, I've felt queasy but never actually gotten sick. I came prepared to deal with seasickness with various recommended drugs and wristbands that touch acupressure points. I had used the wristbands crossing the Drake Passage to Antarctica on a small 80-passenger cruise ship in 2011. They were effective then. I was delighted not to have to resort to the wristbands or drugs for seasickness. Interestingly, on my voyage I met many cruisers who do suffer from seasickness. Their first few days on passage were miserable until they got their sea legs. I think I'd be more reluctant to sail the oceans if every time I set off from shore or an anchorage I would have to suffer with seasickness.

It wasn't long before I had to deal with rain squalls in the middle of the night, rushing to get sails down with my headlamp on. Worse were patches of no wind where motoring was the only way to make progress. I hate to run the engine; it's noisy and hot. The voyage improved late the second day when I intercepted the Gulf Stream current. With a good wind sailing on a beam reach and a boost from the Gulf Stream flowing in my direction, I was getting 9–10 knots SOG (speed over ground), the best way to measure actual progress.

I saw dolphins playing around the boat three out of four mornings. A small fish of some sort jumped into the cockpit; I threw him back. Dead flying fish lying on the deck and in the cockpit became a common sight in the morning. I could see them flying across the water during the day and imagined they can avoid hitting the boat in daylight. At night it's a different story; they will fly up on the deck because they can't see the boat, get stuck there and die.

A dead flying fish on deck

One night on the passage a tanker came within a mile of me. Not a real hazard since I was tracking him on AIS and radar the entire time. It's rare for ships to pass so closely in the middle of the ocean.

Everything was generally running smoothly on board, but I discovered an issue with the new generator wiring. The generator only fed power to the US-style 120-volt AC outlets, not to the battery charger where I most needed it. I contacted the crew at Haven Harbour in Rock Hall by email. They acknowledged the mistake but there was nothing they could do about it with me already at sea. I added fixing the generator wiring to the list of projects I needed to complete when I arrived in Horta. In the meantime, the solar panels, the wind generator and very occasionally running the engine were needed to keep the batteries charged.

I managed to connect with a couple of cruiser nets on the SSB shortwave radio, checking in with my position report and to chat a bit. Small events like that helped to break up the daily routine. After four days, I'd put almost 600 nm under the keel, so on average I made pretty good time with the help of the Gulf Stream.

Making progress east largely became a hunt for following wind and the Gulf Stream, which meanders its way across the North Atlantic like a river. There are some charts showing its location but it's hard to keep its direction lined up with a sailing route and the restrictions wind direction present. During some of the first four days I got impressive speed gains from the current but then lost it, found it again for a while, but permanently lost it again west of 60 degrees west longitude.

The wind was generally at my stern, which can make for good sailing but can also be tricky, since it can throw the boom from one side of the boat to the other, sometimes with violent speed, as the variable wind shifts direction only 5 or 10 degrees. Fortunately, I equipped *Phywave* with a boom brake that lets me control the boom's motion and position regardless of the wind direction. Generally, it's better to sail just off the wind on a "broad reach" where the angle of the wind to the stern is about 30 to 40 degrees. Sailboats are usually fastest on a broad or beam reach, but this may mean you're not sailing on the most direct route to a destination. That was my situation for several days.

I arrived at the halfway point on this Norfolk–Horta passage on August 12, an important milestone, but from there the sailing got more difficult and much slower as a high-pressure system (essentially dead air with no wind in the center) built in across my route. I pivoted to the north with the intention of riding westerly winds on the north side of that high if it developed as forecast. It would take a few days to find out if this was a good strategy, very unlike flying, where I know within hours, sometimes minutes, whether I made a good or bad decision about the weather.

I was getting to know the boat better and how it likes to sail and monitoring consumptions of fuel, water and especially power. After running *Phywave* for several days, I calculated the average current needed from my 12-to-14 volt battery bank was about 12–13 amps with the navigation electronics, autopilot and refrigerator running. The refrigerator takes about 5 amps when the compressor is running, leaving about 8 amps of current demand from the navigation electronics, AIS and autopilot. Much of that is taken by autopilot to steer the boat, and it increases in rough seas when the autopilot has to work harder to steer. I have a 440-amp-hour battery bank on *Phywave*. With 8 amps of current drawn from the batteries, the stored battery power was being drawn down at a rate of about 2% an hour.

I was monitoring power consumption hoping I could rely on the solar panels and wind generator to fully recharge the batteries during the daytime after the overnight power drain. The solar panels in direct sun produce 10 times the power of the wind generator, sometimes 20–25 amps. It takes 20–30 knots of wind for the wind generator to produce 10 amps. If the solar panels could fully recharge the batteries, it would mean I wouldn't have to run the engine to do it, saving fuel. When it was cloudy for a significant part of the day, though, that was unlikely. If my generator had been wired the way I wanted, it would be available for charging the batteries too. Fixing the generator wiring became a priority task when I arrived in Horta. By email I lined up a contractor in Horta to correct it.

Trying to make the most of the wind, I was busy sailing with varying wind directions and speeds, requiring frequent adjustments to the sails. I sometimes would have to start the engine to keep moving when the wind was light or coming from a direction that was not useful for sailing along a course reasonably constructive toward reaching my destination. Many times, the wind would be just on the cusp of being useful for sailing. In such cases I would sometimes run the engine at the same time (motor-sailing), which would result in reasonably good progress.

For weather forecasting I employed the most commonly used and well-regarded weather models, primarily the European ECMWF model with 9-km resolution and the American GFS model with 22-km resolution. I downloaded forecast updates twice a day on the very-low-bandwidth Iridium GO! satellite link. Depending on how much data I requested and how large the

The Hemingway Sandwich

forecast area was, the download could take up to an hour. The most useful parts of the downloaded data were colored forecast maps sent as compressed data files (GRIB files) showing forecast wind speeds and directions for several days ahead. I was surprised by how far off the forecasts sometimes were, but I'd been through a fairly unsettled area of weather, so I would expect it to be more difficult to forecast. Fortunately, I hadn't been hit with any big storms, just a half dozen or so rain squalls where the wind speed could increase violently, the wind direction change significantly, accompanied by intense rainfall. Most squalls I encountered usually lasted only 20–30 minutes.

After crossing the halfway point, I was counting down the miles to Horta, trying to zero in on an estimated arrival date. The forecasts said I'd be crossing a high-pressure dead zone with no usable wind for 36 hours. More motoring. Considering the high-pressure system, I was projecting my arrival in Horta to be around August 22–23.

I finally got a little smarter dealing with the high-pressure systems that were following me. It became pointless to motor to make progress because that would just keep me inside the doldrums as it moved with me. The better strategy was to simply stop the boat and let it drift while the high-pressure system passed over me. I could then pick up the wind on the following side of the system and start sailing again. I did this for 24 hours and it worked out pretty well.

The Hemingway Sandwich

In Ernest Hemingway's book *Islands in the Stream*, he mentioned an unusual sandwich consisting of bread, peanut butter and a fat slice of raw onion. It's come to be known as the Hemingway Sandwich. Hemingway wrote, "One of the highest points in the sandwich-maker's art. We call it the Mount Everest Special. For Commanders only." Since I was now a commander of my vessel, I was entitled to eat one. Actually, it wasn't as bad as it may sound—the sweetness of the peanut butter offset the tang of the onion.

Arriving in Horta

As most sailors do, as I approached the Azores I first sighted the distinctive, sharp cone shape of Pico Island rising above the clouds just east of Faial Island, where Horta is located. After many days of looking at nothing but water around me, it was an odd sensation to see land. It served as a reminder of how significant an event this was for sailors centuries ago when navigation was less certain and actually finding your destination after weeks at sea was a big deal.

I arrived in Horta Harbor on the morning of August 23 after a 21-day passage from Norfolk, Virginia. It was a momentous occasion for me, my first offshore passage of any kind, and solo. Having been lucky to not get hit by any big storm probably made it easier for me than others sailing a similar route. Overall, the passage didn't stress me or make me question the ambitious project I had planned. If anything, that first long offshore passage encouraged me: What I had committed to do was feasible and within reach.

Passing the breakwater into Horta Harbor, I saw that things were busy but not as crowded as they might have been. The reception dock, which is

Pico Island

also where fueling is done in addition to clearing Immigration and Customs, was crowded with boats, so I had to drive around in circles for 45 minutes while refueling boats finished and moved on. Once on the dock, clearing in to Portugal went very efficiently with the first stop at the marina office followed by a stop at the Immigration office directly across the hall.

After being on a moving, rolling boat for 21 days, my first steps off the boat onto solid ground were wobbly; it felt like the ground was moving. It took several hours for this to start wearing off. Walking around didn't feel completely normal for a few days.

Fortunately, I arrived at a time when Horta Harbor was not as crowded as it can be in May through July. The marina had a roomy berth for *Phywave* at the south end on J dock, making it convenient to get to town from there. At busy times, many boats must anchor in the harbor and use their dinghies every time they want to go into town. Although I was unhappy about leaving late in August, the uncrowded conditions I encountered at Horta turned out to be a benefit of that late departure.

With *Phywave* securely tied up in its berth, I started exploring Horta. My lunch on the day I arrived was at the famous Peter's Café Sport, which I could see from my boat. Although famous for its past as a hangout for oceangoing sailors, it is now mostly a tourist place. It's open all day, every day unlike most restaurants here. I also paid a visit to the hipermercado (supermarket) where I would later buy provisions for my next passage to Lagos, Portugal.

Peter's Café Sport in Horta

While on passage I emailed a yacht services company (Mid Atlantic Yacht Services) in Horta that said they could install the necessary new switch and adjust the wiring for my generator. That process started the day after I arrived and was finished the next day. I also had them install a small stainless steel spigot over the galley sink for the watermaker sample water output, allowing me to easily test the salinity before diverting the water into the main water tank. It's something I should have had put in place when the watermaker was first installed, but having never used a watermaker before I didn't realize how big a convenience the sample spigot would be.

On the passage from Norfolk, I also had an issue with the mainsail battens working their way out of their pockets in the sail and, in a couple of cases, getting damaged. I found a sailmaker in Horta who came out the evening I arrived and replaced the damaged battens. For a more permanent solution to the battens moving, the original sailmaker Neil Pryde suggested a technique they have used. They told me to drill a hole through each batten and the sail and sew the battens in place. After finding large sewing needles and heavy sail thread at a local shop, I managed to do that a few days after the new battens were put in.

Volcano caldera on Faial Island

With the essential sailing problems dealt with, I had time to rent a car and explore Faial Island. There is a large caldera in the center of the island that is usually obscured by clouds, but I got a few decent photos. At the west end of the island there was a relatively recent (1958) volcanic eruption that resulted in a lighthouse being abandoned and a new small island being created. Faial Island is not very big; it's easy to drive the perimeter and across the interior in a day, seeing the highlights along the way. I stopped for a pleasant lunch at Aldina Restaurant and Bar in a village on the road along the north side of the island.

I originally planned to stay in Horta one week, which meant an August 30 departure. But there wasn't much wind to work with going east until Thursday, September 1, so I set that as my departure date. The night before my departure I had dinner at Pousada Forte da Horta, which had become one of my favorite restaurants in Horta.

I also completed the traditional ritual of painting the name of my boat and the year of my arrival on the jetty in Horta Harbor. It's supposed to be good luck. There are hundreds of these on the jetty, sidewalks and walls around the harbor making it a little difficult to find a spot for *Phywave*. In many places they have been worn away by weather and footsteps so only bare stone or concrete and remnants of paint remain. Compared to the truly artistic efforts of some, the painted sign for *Phywave* is very simple but leaves our mark here for as long as weather and time will allow it to stay.

Phywave's name on the jetty in Horta Harbor

I'm not generally inclined to join organizations, but for sailing there is one organization I did want to join. The Ocean Cruising Club (OCC) is a fairly exclusive club because becoming a full member requires a sailor to complete a nonstop ocean passage of at least 1,000 nm and have another OCC member sponsor them. My voyage from Norfolk to Horta was over 2,400 nm so I now qualified. I contacted Mike and Angie, cruisers with whom I had traded emails from when they were cruising around Tierra del Fuego on the sailboat *Madrone*. Mike was happy to serve as my sponsor so I became a member of OCC after arriving in Horta. The OCC has a network of port officers at various places around the world that assist cruisers who arrive in their ports with whatever they might need. It can be a real help, especially if a cruiser is looking for reliable contractors to make boat repairs. I made contact with several OCC port officers during my voyage.

5

Landing in Portugal

I left Horta the morning of September 1 bound for Lagos, Portugal, which would be my first landing on another continent. I stayed a total of nine days in Horta, two days longer than originally planned. Even with the extra days, and a day trip on the ferry to nearby Pico Island, I still felt like I'd hardly gotten to know the place. Horta is such a famous, iconic stop for sailors; I felt sentimental about leaving.

Unlike most other sailors, and many I met in the marina in Horta, I decided not to visit other islands in the Azores. It was the first time, among many to come, I was reminded that I was not a cruiser like the others but on a mission to sail to seven continents. I had to keep moving. Having sailed across oceans, cruisers want to explore the places they visit, learn something about the culture and people, and generally hang out with other cruisers and enjoy life on their boats and the freedom of being unburden by the speed and hustle of the modern world.

The solution of sewing the battens in place seemed to be working. They didn't start to slide out of the mainsail pockets during the passage to Portugal as they had before.

I had delayed my departure from Horta to take advantage of a favorable weather forecast, favorable weather that never materialized. The first few days moving east through the Azores, between Pico and São Jorge Islands, was difficult sailing into headwinds requiring motoring and upwind sailing. I saw large groups of dolphins in this channel, some coming just a few feet from the boat but difficult to photograph because just as quickly as they appeared, they disappeared beneath the waves. That evening, as the sun was setting off the eastern tip of Pico Island, I saw several whale spouts, the closest perhaps a half mile from the boat. Whale-watching is a popular tourist activity in the Azores, with many tour boats departing from Horta and other towns.

Moonlight on the water crossing to Portugal

After motoring into headwinds and contrary current past the north side of San Miguel Island, the last island I would pass in the Azores, the wind finally turned south in the middle of the night, onto my beam. I got out of bed, set the sails and shut down the engine.

With San Miguel Island behind me it was open ocean sailing, often with wind directly astern requiring me to jibe periodically across the wind to get a reasonable sailing angle. At least it was steadily pushing me east. I was also hit by much stronger-than-forecast winds that lasted several hours. When you're expecting 15 knots and you're hit with 30 knots, it's a scramble to reduce sail in a rolling boat in the middle of the night. The swells were around 3 meters, spinning out of a large low-pressure system to my north. Taking those swells on the beam of the boat made for a very rolly time below.

It was always necessary to hang on to something or brace myself against the roll.

The winds later rotated to the southwest and weakened below 20 knots so I had better, less turbulent sailing with a heading directly toward Lagos after veering north for a time to set up a better sailing angle. I expected, hoped, this condition would last for a couple of days.

I was planning to arrive in Lagos late Sunday, September 11, but thought I would eventually slow down when I got close so I would arrive at the Lagos Marina during daylight hours on September 12. Slowing down to arrive during daylight hours became a technique I employed in several other places on my voyage. Entering a new harbor, anchorage or marina at night can be tricky and dangerous, especially when the entrance channel is very narrow as it is in Lagos. Also, there usually aren't any personnel around to complete the clearing-in process. I'd have to wait for the next day in any event before I could complete formalities and leave the boat.

As it turned out, I was able to pick up some speed due to the current and arrive in Lagos around noon on September 11. I awoke the next morning to rain and cool temperatures. The last few days of the passage here were not satisfying, mostly with light and variable winds not suitable for sailing, so a lot of motoring was needed. Occasionally the wind would kick up to 9 or

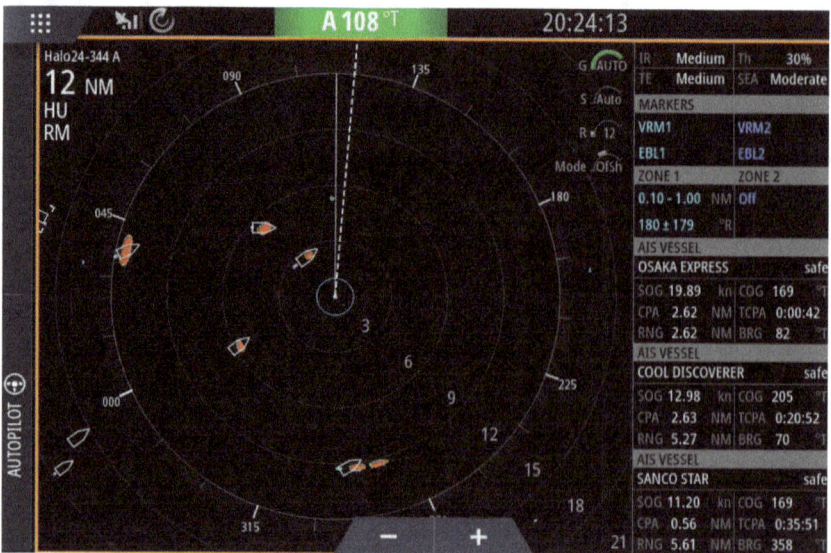

AIS and radar display of ships while crossing the shipping lanes along the coast of Portugal

10 knots, at a useful angle, so I'd set the sails and enjoy sailing for a while, but after a few hours the wind would die again. I'd take the sails down rather than have them flog around in the gentle, but not useful, breeze. This back and forth raising and lowering the sails became tiresome and annoying, and no doubt caused more wear on the sails.

Crossing the very busy shipping lanes that run north and south along the coast of Portugal in the middle of the night was a new experience. Amazingly, courses and positions were coordinated with very little ship-to-ship communication. I'm not sure what the big ships made of *Phywave*, but my AIS transmission would have given them all the details. As I mentioned before, the AIS system automatically uses the position, course and speed of other vessels and *Phywave* to determine whether there is a possibility of a collision, identifying each vessel as "safe" or not. Crossing a busy shipping lane is a place where this system is critically important. So that a boat's future position can be accurately estimated, it's important to maintain course and speed. If any vessel is making course adjustments to avoid me, those adjustments will be effective. That said, there were still what I considered tight spacings, like a 400-meter-long container ship that passed across my bow only 1,100 meters away at 1 a.m. It was amazing and ominous to see this black wall of a ship right in front of me.

Lifting fog approaching the coast of Portugal

Phywave **tied up at the dock at Lagos Marina**

Past the shipping lanes, I was faced with a fogbank just as dawn approached. I was particularly concerned about small fishing boats near the coast that wouldn't have AIS and would just be presented to me as intermittent blips on my radar, if that. The fog burned off and lifted just as I was rounding Ponta de Sagres for the turn to the east-northeast and Lagos. Though I was tired from being up all night while crossing the shipping lanes, the remaining 15 nm to Lagos was easy, with adrenaline keeping me energized as I drove toward my first continent landing.

After clearing through Portuguese Immigration and Customs, which were located in the Marina de Lagos office building, I was given a convenient berth in the large marina. Of course, the first night I went out for a steak dinner and Caesar salad—I definitely missed having fresh greens on board. Following dinner, I wandered into the narrow streets of the old section of Lagos, still lively and vibrant with the sidewalk restaurants full of people at 10 p.m. and street musicians in the little plazas. As I came around a corner a trio was playing John Denver's "Take Me Home, Country Roads" for a large crowd, some dancing, everyone singing along. It was good to get out, just walk around and see people enjoying life after being confined to my 43-foot boat for the last 10 days. In all, it was a great first night out for my arrival. I guess civilization does have some things to recommend it.

Benagil Cave, Algarve coast

One of the odd things about the marina at Lagos is a pedestrian bridge that separates the marina from the reception pontoon where boats first tie up to check into the marina and go through Immigration and Customs. The bridge is not high enough to accommodate a sailboat mast so it's necessary to call the bridge operator on the VHF radio and ask them to open the bridge. They won't open it immediately but will tell a boat when they can expect the next opening to occur, usually within 15–30 minutes. That way they can let pass a cluster of boats and reduce the times when the bridge is opened. Consequently, it may be necessary to hang out for a little while waiting for the next opening.

With my arrival in Europe, I could finally add a "one" to my tally of the seven continents where I'd sailed. It should have been a champagne moment of celebration, but what I mainly felt was relief that an important leg of the voyage was behind me without encountering any big storms or hurricanes while crossing the Atlantic during hurricane season. In planning the route, Europe always seemed out of the way to me, not where I would have gone if I were just trying to sail westward around the world following the trade winds. All the other continents, except Antarctica, were naturally along a world circumnavigation route. I had also been sailing east instead of west, so basically backtracking the generally westward circumnavigation I had planned. From here on I would be sailing south and west, consistently making progress toward my seven continents and circumnavigation goals.

Ponta de Sagres, Portugal

Exploring the Algarve Coast

I spent three largely inactive weeks in and around Lagos, relaxing, eating too much and listening to street music. The first week was mainly occupied with boat maintenance items. I arranged for an engine oil change to be done by Sopromar Centro Nautico, adjacent to the marina. I also bought a few items I needed, or thought I would need later, in their well-stocked chandlery.

I rented a car for a day and drove a loop through the Algarve. The first stop was Ponta de Sagres, sometimes called the "End of the World" because it's the most southwestern point in Europe. Nearby is Cabo de São Vicente, the first Portuguese land I saw as it emerged through the fog when I arrived from the Azores. From there it was north to Aljezur, then east on winding roads through the mountains toward Monchique and finally south to vineyard country around Estômbar. I stopped at Quinta dos Vales winery, one of the largest and best-known wineries in the Algarve to taste some of their red wines. The vines were incredibly dried out; I've never seen anything like it in the many vineyards I've visited over the years. The Quinta dos Vales winery is a curious place; the grounds are populated with a wide array of odd, mostly fat, statues of animals, and a few abstracts. From Estômbar I drove back west along highway N125 to Lagos.

If you're in Lagos it's pretty much essential to take a boat excursion by one of the tour companies operating out of Lagos Marina to see the many waterfront caves that are found along this part of the Algarve coast. There are hundreds of such caves, perhaps the most famous being Benagil Cave with its interior beach and a hole to the sky. Of course, everyone wants to see these caves so crowds of tourists in boats are inescapable.

Toward the end of my stay in Lagos I made a five-day side trip to Switzerland to visit pilot friends who have also flown small planes around the world, a group known as Earthrounders (*www.earthrounders.com*).

Street musicians in Lagos

My next stop would be Tangiers, Morocco, a landing in Africa, my second continent. The marina at Rabat in Morocco, in reality a more favorable stop in Africa, never responded to my emails inquiring about berth space. Tangiers is a short distance from Lagos across the Strait of Gibraltar. However, gale-force easterly winds routinely blow through the strait. It would take some weather planning finesse to get into Tangiers without driving straight into such wind.

6

Across to Morocco

The weather for a direct passage from Lagos to Tangiers was not favorable, with strong easterly winds that would be blowing almost directly on my bow. The distance was short but also not favorable, about 160 nm, more than a day's voyage. As I mentioned, I always plan the timing on passages to arrive at a new port, marina or anchorage during daylight hours. This always makes it easier to maneuver the boat but also, if it's a marina, helps me to arrive during office hours. A 160-nm passage is about 1.5 days, so there was no assurance I would get to the marina in Tangiers when they were open, although they claim access 24 hours a day, seven days a week.

For these reasons I decided to break up the trip into two legs: the first a short leg of about 40 nm east to an anchorage in a bay at the beginning of the boat channel leading to Faro, Portugal. It was a secure anchorage with good holding in heavy sand. I needed that holding. The next day the wind blew at 20–25 knots most of the day, the northern edge of the stronger wind flow to the south in the Strait of Gibraltar. Other boats were also taking shelter there for the same reason.

Fishermen in small boats working those waters. I'm always wary of where they drop their nets, concerned my boat might swing at anchor into one of them and get it caught in my propeller. However, they set the nets in the evening away from my boat, and picked them up in the morning before I got going so there were no issues. I'm sure they would not like to lose a net to my propeller, either.

Sunset at the Faro anchorage

I spent two nights in this anchorage until the easterlies in the strait abated, then set off in the morning for an overnight run that would get me to Tangiers during daylight hours. It was a long night with only occasional sleep as I avoided the heavy east–west shipping traffic in these waters.

One possible consequence of the wind dying down with a high-pressure system is fog, and that's what I got, very dense fog. I passed fishing boats that were marked as targets on the radar that were only a few hundred meters away, yet I never saw them. I could barely make out the yellow channel marker near the entrance to Tangiers harbor, the visibility reduced to only about 100 meters. The turning points around stone jetties leading to the marina entrance were equally obscured, but finally visibility improved a bit as I got to the marina entrance.

The Tanja marina reception pontoon where I needed to tie up the boat while I completed entry formalities for Morocco was already full of boats waiting for the fog to lift so they could leave. They didn't allow boats to raft together (to tie to one another) at the reception pontoon, so I had to anchor outside the marina entrance until they left late in the afternoon. These boats appeared to have radar, and I assumed modern chartplotters, so I was puzzled as to why they wouldn't venture out in the fog, the fog I had just navigated for several hours getting into Tangiers. Everyone has their own personal safety

In thick fog passing a buoy while entering Tangiers harbor

Phywave **in the Tanja marina**

criteria on the water, which is OK. As an instrument-rated pilot, I'm accustomed to flying through clouds where I can't see anything. That's a three-dimension navigation problem. A boat on the water driving through fog is a two-dimension navigation problem—inherently easier—so I guess it's understandable my criteria for safe navigation on water are different than what other sailors might have. Of course, when flying in the clouds a pilot has air traffic control watching and controlling various aircraft flight paths so collisions with other planes are avoided. No comparable service exists on the water; with a boat you're on your own avoiding collisions in fog.

Morocco does not permit camera drones in the country, so during the Customs inspection of my boat on arrival they confiscated one of my drones. They promised to return it when I left. I have two drones; the one I gave them was a cheap one, a sacrificial drone, I guess. I didn't tell them about the expensive DJI drone. It was "sacrificial" in the event they refused to return it when I left, but they did return it, so it wasn't a problem. Completing the paperwork for the seized drone and then having it released again introduced more bureaucracy and delay into the clearing-in, clearing-out process.

Like the clearing-in process, the clearing-out process was also a multi-hour ordeal, with a search of everyone's boat that was more thorough than the search on arrival. They even brought out a drug-sniffing dog that refused to get on my boat, even when they provided him with a ramp to walk up through the gate in the lifelines. The dog apparently spent five minutes inside the boat of another sailor I'd gotten to know while in the marina.

I only spent four nights in Tangiers and didn't take any side trips into the countryside. I've been to Morocco twice before. I first visited in 1976 when I was traveling all over Europe on Eurail Passes with my girlfriend Helen, whom I met in Montpellier, France. We spent a few days in Fez mostly getting hassled by street urchins who wanted to guide us through the markets and Kasbah. When we declined, they cursed us with obscenities in a variety of languages.

My second trip to Morocco was more enjoyable. After my solo flight over the North Pole in 2018 I spent several weeks touring Europe in my plane. One place I always wanted to visit was Casablanca. I spent a few nights in the city and discovered there was a Rick's Café, like in the movie *Casablanca*, not far from my hotel. Of course, I had to go there. It turned out to be much smaller than the one in the movie and not really a nightclub, but they tried to replicate the ambience and décor from the movie with archways, potted plants, a piano and even a roulette wheel. As they showed me to a table I thought, "This is great." A waiter came over and I ordered a gin and tonic. The waiter apologized. He said the ownership of the restaurant had changed six months before. The new owners were strict Muslims who didn't allow alcohol to be served. Are you kidding me? Of all the gin joints in all the towns in all the world, I walk into one with no gin. The food wasn't that great either. Of course, when I left Casablanca I wanted to fly the same escape route that was in the movie—I flew to Lisbon.

The terrace outside my hotel room in Tangiers

To get a break from the boat, and a long, hot shower, I did spend one night in a little hotel in the old city near the Kasbah. I had a great dinner with lamb couscous at a nearby restaurant. The hotel was a classic setup with a narrow staircase winding its way up around a small inside courtyard to a handful of distinctive guest rooms. My room, which had an outdoor terrace filled with plants, provided a great view overlooking the city and harbor. It was a nice break from sailing.

By landing in Morocco I could now increase my seven continents voyage total to two. It was not essential to stop here to claim a landing in Africa since rounding South Africa was part of my original route plan as described in chapter 1. However, I wanted to leave the option open to complete my seven continents voyage by returning to the US via the North Pacific after landing in Australia and Asia. As I mentioned before, with that option, I wouldn't complete a solo circumnavigation but I would end up on the west coast of North America with an easy return to my home near Seattle. Stopping in Tangiers after landing in Lagos was easy enough. It was worth the additional effort to leave options open to return via the North Pacific.

7

The Canary Islands

The Canary Islands are an archipelago controlled by Spain with seven main islands about 100 km off the west coast of Africa. They're a favorite stop for yachts planning to cross the Atlantic to the Caribbean. The ARC (Atlantic Rally for Cruisers) is a popular event where as many as 150 sailboats assemble at Las Palmas on Gran Canaria Island. On the appointed start day in November when the hurricane season has wound down, they sail west for Saint Lucia Island in the Caribbean. For cruisers who have never crossed the Atlantic Ocean, or any ocean, before, it's a good initiation with several seminars ahead of the departure to assist cruisers in preparing their boats and making their plans for the crossing. It's also sort of a race, with the boats that first arrive in Saint Lucia receiving prizes. I imagine it's reassuring to have several boats sailing along the same route in case something goes wrong and another boat may be nearby to lend assistance. I really don't have any interest in these group events. Besides, they don't accept solo sailors so I couldn't participate anyway.

However, these rallies are also a problem, something I came to realize later in my voyage. With a large group of boats arriving at small marinas at about the same time, they tend to consume all the resources at those marinas, like berth space, to the exclusion of other boats that are on their own, like mine. For example, the large group of boats that gather at Las Palmas for the ARC take up the available marina and anchorage space, so independent cruisers often have to go to a marina or anchorage at another island in the Canary Islands group until the ARC leaves.

Because the rally organizers make all the marina bookings and logistical arrangements for Immigration and Customs, land tours, weather forecasts, and departure "go–no go" decisions, I started to call them "nanny cruises. The boats that participate also pay a large amount of money to the organizers to be part of the rally. With all that assistance, the boats involved are not really

Choppy seas and strong wind leaving Tangiers

Glorious sunset on the way to the Canary Islands

getting the full experience of cruising the world's oceans. A lot of that experience is the feeling of freedom and independence that comes with preparing your own boat and making your own decisions. It can take a lot of research, and sometimes arrival formalities can be convoluted, but that leads to the satisfaction of doing it yourself instead of relying on someone else to do it for you.

After a three-hour process with Immigration and Customs to clear out of Tangiers, four sailboats all left within a few minutes of each other, all bound for the Canary Islands. It was nearly noon and the wind had kicked up to 20 knots at the marina entrance and 25–30 knots in the Strait of Gibraltar. Heading due north from the marina, *Phywave* was climbing and crashing down on the big waves the wind and tide had created. That lasted for a couple of miles, until we reached the point where all the boats could turn due west and the winds in the strait were on our sterns. At that point I started sailing with three reefs in the mainsail and no genoa set. That still pushed me along at 6–7 knots. After another seven nm we could all turn southwest and eventually out of the strong easterly winds coming through the strait.

After turning that corner, it was about 600 nm to the southern end of Lanzarote Island where I had booked a berth at Rubicon Marina. I soon lost sight of the other boats as each chose its own course and angle to the wind. This passage south lasted five days with variable winds on the stern. Sometimes they disappeared so I occasionally used the engine to keep making progress. There was a fair amount of north–south shipping traffic, and occasionally other yachts would pop up on the AIS. At one point I was intercepted by a small, fast fishing boat from the coast of Morocco that just came by to wave hello. I was wary of them having other intentions until they headed off toward their fishing grounds.

When I was finally within cellphone range of the Canary Islands, I was surprised to receive emails from friends telling me that the position tracking from the Iridium GO! was no longer working. I tried rebooting it several times by opening the case and pulling the battery out for 10 seconds and then replacing it—a very crude method. It didn't help, so I resigned myself to getting a replacement Iridium GO! at the Rubicon Marina.

The day and night before my arrival at Lanzarote the wind picked up considerably to the point where I had to slow down to time my arrival at Rubicon during daylight. I furled the mainsail and was only using a reefed genoa. That still was giving me 5–6 knots. The timing worked out fine, with the boat arriving at Rubicon late morning. Even in the relatively protected marina the wind was still 15–20 knots, making docking a little tricky. Help from the marina's dockhands (marineros) to handle the mooring lines was certainly needed.

Volcanic interior of Lanzarote Island

Rubicon is a great marina with wide berths and waterways (fairways) between pontoons. I expected that. What I didn't realize is that Rubicon Marina is in the middle of a large resort complex, generally known as Playa Blanca, with dozens of restaurants, many shops, luxury 5-star hotels and, of course, hordes of tourists drawn to all that. It was the beginning of the cold weather season when Europeans, especially the English, seek a sunny refuge from increasingly dreary weather at home. Among boat owners, I met a few who brought their boats to Rubicon for the entire winter season, six months or more, essentially floating waterfront condos for them.

I took advantage of the relaxing resort atmosphere and tried several of the restaurants that were within easy walking distance of the marina. The food choices were quite varied; I suppose this was to avert food boredom among resort guests. I was happy to be eating food I didn't prepare myself. They also had a selection of small grocery stores where I could stock up on basic provisions for the next leg of my voyage—eggs, UHT milk, fresh meat. UHT milk has been subjected to ultra-high temperatures to sterilize it so it doesn't need to be refrigerated.

Touring

I rented a car for a couple of days to have a look around. The island is basically a volcanic desert with only a few places where they appear to have successfully turned the volcanic soil into something fertile. Among these was an area with vineyards spread across a broad valley. The largest natural attraction on the island is Timanfaya National Park, in the center of the Montañas del Fuego, a still active volcanic area with vast, sharp-edged lava flows. In the tourist center at the top of a hill chickens were being cooked for the restaurant over an active volcanic thermal vent.

Salt ponds at Salinas de Janubio

Driving along the coast I saw large salt recovery ponds at Salinas de Janubio that have been in operation since the 19th century. The square ponds themselves make an interesting mosaic of subtly different colors resulting from various microorganisms in the water. The ponds also support a variety of bird life that thrives in the saline environment.

Repairs

Finding a replacement for the failed Iridium GO! turned out to be a challenge given my remote location. I stopped at the well-stocked chandlery at the marina and asked whether they could source at least one, ideally two,

Iridium GO! units so I'd have a backup. They were skeptical but said they would make some phone calls to their suppliers and see whether any were available in Spain. They called me back the next day and said they had two units sitting on their counter that had arrived by plane that morning. The price was astronomical, more than twice what I would have paid in the US, but I really had no choice. A working Iridium GO! for position tracking, email and downloading weather forecast files was essential to my voyage. After their call, I went to the chandlery right away and bought them both. They said they were the last two in Spain, a fact I confirmed later when I contacted some chandleries in mainland Spain and asked whether they could get one. After swapping the SIM card out of the failed unit, I quickly had a new one up and running. As my voyage concluded, that one was still working and the spare unit is still in its box in a locker on *Phywave*.

In addition to replacing the failed Iridium GO! I also had some work done to repair damaged places on the luff tape on the mainsail. My theory was that rolling the sail on the boom stresses the points on the luff tape at the battens because that's where the damage occurred. There are many benefits to a boom furler for the mainsail, but careful rolling and reefing is necessary to protect the luff tape. Doing that was a matter of practice at keeping the correct tension on the halyard while rolling the sail up inside the boom. Having the sail under load (full of wind) made this process harder even though Schaefer maintains that it should be possible to reef the sail at any point of sail. Wear on the mainsail luff tape would be a recurring problem on this voyage.

With the local touring and sail repairs, I stayed in Rubicon a few days longer than originally anticipated. To make up for lost time, and stay more or less on schedule, I planned to make the next ocean passage all the way to Cabedelo, Brazil, a great circle distance of about 2,500 nm, or about 20–25 days en route. My route would take me just west of the Cabo Verde Islands, also another popular starting point for boats crossing west to the Caribbean. In the event a tropical storm popped up after I left Lanzarote, Mindelo in the Cabo Verde Islands would give me a place to seek shelter until the storm moved on.

8

Onward to Brazil

I left Rubicon Marina at the south end of Lanzarote Island at about 0840Z on October 21, motoring southeast into the channel where the winds were forecast to be stronger than on the west side of Fuerteventura Island. After I had motored for five hours, the winds built sufficiently to the point I could start sailing. That continued for several days, with generally downwind sailing with occasional shifts that put the wind on the starboard quarter or beam. The boat sails better with the wind from those directions, so I took advantage of those conditions when available.

With all the downwind sailing, I decided to get more adept at setting the whisker pole that wings out the genoa headsail to catch the most wind. It's a little awkward to set the pole mainly because I have the dinghy strapped down to the foredeck; it's in the way when handling the pole. The pole itself is mounted on a track on the front of the mast. To set it, I must unclip the end fitting attached to a bail at the foot of the mast, then use a line running through blocks to lower the end of the pole sliding on the mast track. I then walk the end I unclipped from the bail out to the bow where it can be clipped into one of the genoa sheets at the genoa clew. With the boat rolling around, this procedure can be slow and unstable. The pole is free to swing around until it is clipped in on both ends.

Once the pole is clipped into the genoa sheet, it's then a simple matter to return to the cockpit, release the genoa furling line, pull out the sheet and trim it to position the poled-out sail as desired. The pole is great at keeping wind in the sail as the boat rolls around with passing seas.

Any time I was outside the cockpit and on the deck, I would always wear my inflatable life vest, which has a tether that can be clipped into various points on the boat to keep me from becoming detached from the boat if I fell overboard. The grab bars, granny bars (around the base of the mast) and pulpit are the best places to clip in. Going forward to the bow, my only option is to clip into the jacklines running the length of the boat. These lines are strong but are not very taut, so a fall overboard clipped into a jackline would likely leave me dragging in the water alongside the boat.

When sailing solo there is no "man overboard" drill. Even though I had a waterproof PLB (personal locator beacon) in a pocket on my life vest, falling overboard and becoming detached from the boat while far from land, or from other boats, would pretty much be a death sentence. To evoke a famous line from the movie *Apocalypse Now*: "Never get out of the boat."

Jibing (or gybing) the boat means turning the boat so the wind is coming from the other side of the stern but the boat is still sailing downwind. Moving the mainsail boom to the other side is one task I've mentioned before. It must be done in stages to keep the heavy boom from violently slamming across the boat. I have a boom brake that is designed to control that.

Sailing around the west end of the Cabo Verde Islands

Moving the whisker pole over to the other side when jibing was a challenge because I have a staysail on *Phywave*, a sail on a second forestay a few feet aft of the main forestay. When initially setting the whisker pole, I had to choose which side of the staysail I would set it on. When jibing I had to furl the genoa, go back to the bow, unclip the pole from the sheet, then go back to the mast and hoist the track end of the whisker pole far enough up the mast so the free end would swing around behind the staysail to the other side. With the boat rolling from side to side, this became a bit of a timing game. I had to lower the track end of the pole when the boat rolled and swing the pole so it was on the other side of the staysail. If the dinghy wasn't in the way, I could more easily walk the free end of the whisker pole to the other side. Anyway, once the pole was on the correct side of the staysail the procedure involved for unfurling the sail was the same as described above.

Given the steps and work involved in jibing, I tried to keep sailing with the wind on the starboard or port side of the stern as long as possible. With wind direction constantly shifting it can get a little crazy trying to follow all the shifts to maximize boat performance. I was glad I wasn't racing where that certainly would be an objective. Even so, over the first days after leaving Lanzarote I averaged a boat speed of 5.2 knots. If I could average 5 knots or more, I was happy; that's 120 nm in a 24-hour day. With the genoa poled-out, I could get a boat speed of 6–7 knots with a 15-to-20 knot wind sailing downwind.

On this passage the ocean seemed particularly empty. I occasionally had a group of dolphins swim alongside the boat. One morning a school of flying fish came across the bow. They'd pop up and fly for several meters just above the water before dipping back in. Of course, there were a few cargo and tanker ships passing by, and commercial fishing vessels of 30 meters in length. No small fishing skiffs.

I usually left the companionway leading from the cockpit down into the cabin open at night. One night a seabird, I don't know what kind, flew into the cabin through the companionway, looking for a free ride, I guess. A bird can make a mess on a boat, so I had to trap it under a bucket, slip the bucket lid under the bucket, then release the bird off the stern. Waking up in the middle of the night to capture and release a bird wasn't fun. From then on, I kept the companionway closed at night.

My next routing decision was whether to go west of the Cabo Verde Islands or through them. I was trying to minimize the miles I'd have to sail through the doldrums often found in the intertropical convergence zone

An approaching rain squall

(ITCZ) that is typically located a few degrees north of the equator in the Atlantic Ocean this time of year. I decided to go just west of the Cabo Verde Islands then turn almost due south for Cabedelo, Brazil. There was no tropical storm activity in the forecast so there was no reason to stop at Mindelo to seek shelter.

Rather than sail through the Cabo Verde archipelago, I decided to sail west around the western end of Santo Antão Island. It was a lucky move. Sailing maybe 10 miles offshore, I was able to pick up a solid 3G data signal on my cellphone for a few hours. That let me catch up on email I didn't receive on the boat's Iridium GO! email account but also let me download an important document that was too large to download on the low-bandwidth Iridium GO! satellite link. That important document was the waste permit for my voyage to Antarctica issued by the NSF.

The day before leaving Lagos I received the other important document I needed to sail to Antarctica—a letter from the EPA approving the Initial Environmental Evaluation (IEE) I had submitted. My IEE was a detailed 25-page document that explains the purpose for my expedition of one to Antarctica, where I planned to go while there, what I planned to do at those locations, how I planned to protect the environment and wildlife, and how I was prepared to handle emergencies with the aim toward being self-sufficient. The waste permit application was similar except much shorter and focused on how I would handle waste produced by my expedition.

For both documents I had to explain in some detail my proposed use of an aerial drone (UAV), both its operational use and how I would recover it, on both land and water, if something went wrong and it crashed. Recreational drone use is not allowed on the tourist ships visiting Antarctica (under IAATO rules) for good reasons. Imagine putting 100 tourists ashore on some penguin colony island and 20 of those tourists want to launch drones—it would be total chaos! It would be especially chaotic when you consider that most of those tourists would not be skilled drone pilots. Getting permission to use my drone in Antarctica for recreational purposes is a rare thing that could only happen with a private expedition, not an IAATO-sanctioned tour.

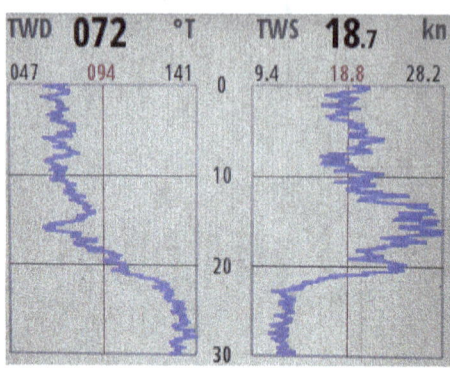

Rapidly changing wind direction and speed with a vertical scale in minutes

I now had all the approvals I would need to take *Phywave* to Antarctica as an expedition of one. It was just a matter of sailing there—not so simple—but at least I was sailing west and south in the right direction.

I had to submit the same documents and get the same approvals when I flew my plane to Antarctica in 2014. The EPA and NSF were accustomed to dealing with yachts visiting Antarctica; issuing permits for my flight was a first for them. Ultimately those documents were much simpler than those for a yacht, but the experience of creating them, and getting them approved, gave me a correct format for the documents I needed to submit to get permission to sail there.

Turning south after passing Santo Antão Island, I had some good downwind sailing for a few days. As I crossed 10 degrees north latitude things changed dramatically. As I mentioned, the ITCZ is located at these latitudes. The sky got gloomier, the wind shifted to the east and in the middle of the night I was surrounded by thunderstorms. One storm eventually hit me, the wind speed rapidly rising above 30 knots, with torrential rain and heavy waves. I scrambled to reduce sail, getting soaked in the process, then just hung on as the storm moved over and past me. It came in so fast I was really not ready. I had set my high-wind alarm at 35 knots (gale-force winds)—it was going off almost continuously. Of course, everything is more difficult and unnerving when it's a pitch-black night.

That was the first of three such episodes, though two occurred during daylight. I've also had heavy rain with little increase in wind. Curiously, my radar did not show much for thunderstorms, unlike the rain squalls, which it showed in detail, when I was crossing the Atlantic eastbound. The boat's radar is designed to show things on, and just above, the water; i.e., at low elevation angles. Thunderstorms, being much higher, don't register except when their rain is falling intensely.

I'm happy to say that as I sailed farther south, I believed I was getting clear of these storm patterns. The southern sky the morning of November 4 was looking more promising, and hopefully I would soon have some sunshine and steadier winds.

Crossing the Equator

At about 0623Z on Thursday, November 10, 2022, I crossed the equator southbound. I was now officially in the Southern Hemisphere. It was an hour before dawn so I waited until the sun was up for a little ceremony giving a dram of whiskey to Neptune for continued safe passage as I had done at other significant milestones on this voyage. I made a short video of this one, which I posted on my YouTube channel. A pilot friend of mine who was in the navy and knew the equator-crossing traditions, said I had now been promoted from

Close encounters with large ships sometimes occurred

a "slimy pollywog" to a "Trusty Shellback." Of course, being solo, there was no hazing by Trusty Shellbacks on board, something that other yachts with experienced crew may organize for the pollywogs.

Thursday also marked the day the sailing weather finally turned favorable. For the preceding several days I had 13-to-15 knot winds from the south requiring me to sail upwind. With those winds I couldn't really sail my desired course of 210 degrees; I had to sail off to the west, which was problematic because I anticipated ocean currents that would also push me west, perhaps too far west to make it around the eastern bulge of the Brazilian coast. For that reason, one guidebook said to cross the equator no further west than 28 degrees west longitude. I ended up crossing at about 29 degrees 50 minutes west. But that day the winds finally rotated around to the southeast, becoming the trade winds I had expected. I was now comfortably sailing a beam reach on the course I wanted, making good speed. The current push west was no longer an issue. The weather forecast models I used were also wrong about when the winds would rotate. I was glad the reality had finally arrived in spite of the forecast.

Just north of the equator is the São Pedro e São Paulo Archipelago (St. Peter and St. Paul Archipelago), a small group of rocky outcroppings in the ocean far from anywhere. Even so, it has an occupied Brazilian outpost for maintaining the navigation light and, I suppose, research activities. It's a curious place, so I made a diversion in my sailing route to pass very close by and get some great photos, especially of the waves crashing against the rocks, erupting in geysers of water higher than the top of the lighthouse. There was

St. Peter and St. Paul Archipelago

also a boat there, tied to a mooring buoy. I'm not sure if it was a supply boat or just a fishing boat. Before I could even see the place over the horizon, I heard radio conversations on marine channel 16 in Portuguese, I assume between the boat and the shore facility. It's a rare, faraway place you can't see or get to via any tourist conveyance, so that's the main reason I made a point of sailing past there.

Cabedelo, Brazil

I arrived in Cabedelo on the morning of November 14, 2022, completing my second Atlantic crossing. Since leaving Norfolk, Virginia, on August 2 I'd crossed the Atlantic twice, landed on three continents, visited five ports, and put 6,880 nm under the keel of *Phywave*. I was stern-tied in Marina Jacaré Village, a small, friendly marina on the east bank of the Paraíba River. It's a pleasant location but very isolated. The Immigration and Customs offices I had to visit were miles away to the north at the Port of Cabedelo, while the Port Authority (navy) I also had to visit was in João Pessoa, several miles to the south.

With the assistance of paperwork prepared by Nico, who owns the marina, yacht crews usually take taxis to these locations, which must be visited on both arrival and departure. I rented a car to make it all easier and gave rides to other cruisers who also had to go to these offices. The nearest ATM is a 25-minute walk from the marina, the nearest supermarket even farther. Getting clean diesel also requires a trip to a nearby gas station with jerry cans. I didn't know what the rental car place would say when I returned the car with a faint odor of diesel inside. With running around prepping the boat for the next passage I really didn't have as much chance to enjoy the place as I had hoped. After many of the chores were done, I eventually had a few days to relax.

Jacaré is an old, fairly undeveloped area situated on the riverbank about four miles south of Cabedelo and five miles north of João Pessoa, a much larger and more stylish city with high-rise condos overlooking seemingly endless expanses of white sand beaches. With an international airport, it is an up-and-coming city in Brazil. Highway BR320 runs north–south down the center of the peninsula from the industrial Port of Cabedelo through Jacaré into João Pessoa and further south. The ocean (beach) side of the highway is where the new developments are happening, with upscale shops and condos, while the western side of the highway facing the river is run-down and impoverished in many places, including the neighborhood immediately around the marina. Nonetheless, Jacaré is where all the pleasure boats are moored or docked, both local boats and visiting boats.

Phywave stern-tied at Marina Jacaré Village

There was a restaurant/bar at the marina open for lunch and dinner. It was the best place to eat within walking distance, so I ate there often. Most of the patrons were people off the boats in the marina. Of the 14–16 boats in the marina (which could hold maybe 30 boats) only about eight boats had people staying on board. Two boats left while I was there, leaving a small group that hung out in the restaurant/bar, including an English father-son crew who had arrived two days before I did from Mindelo in the Cabo Verde Islands. They had damaged sails and luckily found a competent sailmaker to get them fixed. They were headed for Cape Town.

Our group included Tom from England and his girlfriend Hannah, a Canadian, who were sailing a large custom-designed catamaran, *Artemis*. Tom had been seriously injured in the past and was now a paraplegic. In 2021, with other crew, he had sailed *Artemis* across the Atlantic from Europe to the Caribbean. With Hannah, and a few others at times, they had sailed from the Caribbean to Cabedelo. They planned to head south to the Beagle Channel and Tierra del Fuego where I might see them again at some point.

Tom got around in a motorized scooter. He had designed the catamaran to accommodate his disability with a flat main cabin floor that led to the aft pontoons. By positioning a ramp from the end of the boat's pontoon onto the dock, he could roll up to the dock and onto land. He had also equipped the boat with motorized winches and sail furlers, and a set of mast-top cameras so he could watch from above as he maneuvered the catamaran into a marina. Hannah was new to sailing but had quickly learned what to do so she could handle lines and other things on deck Tom couldn't easily access. Tom had also installed a Starlink antenna—the first cruiser I encountered who had one. I was very impressed with the download and upload speeds he was getting and pretty much decided I would add one when that became feasible.

Tom was having problems with his boat's batteries and needed to buy some replacements. Since I had a car, I volunteered to take him around to the shops. Once he had propelled himself out of the scooter into the passenger's seat, it was up to me to disassemble the scooter and stow it in the trunk. With instructions from Tom, I finally got reasonably adept at disassembling and reassembling it. But Hannah was the expert; watching her do it was amazing.

I sometimes thought of Tom and Hannah during my voyage when things seemed to be going badly. I reminded myself of how Tom managed with his limitations and thought to myself, "You've got nothing to complain about."

I would gather with Tom, Hannah and other cruisers for dinner and drinks at the marina restaurant, talking late into the night about sailing, the places we had visited and many other things. It's one of my fondest memories of this voyage.

On my original sailing route, I had planned to stop in Uruguay. Now that I was in Brazil, I was considering other options. I thought about sailing directly from Cabedelo to Puerto Williams, a 3,500-nm passage, by far the longest so far on this voyage. To break that up, I finally decided to sail from Cabedelo to Mar del Plata, Argentina, about 2,400 nm away. Mar del Plata offered a better marina than those available in Uruguay and was not as far off my main route as the ports in Uruguay were. From Mar del Plata I would have about 1,200 nm remaining to Puerto Williams, but perhaps more importantly, Mar del Plata would be a good place to jump on a favorable weather window for passage along the coast of Argentina. The weather along this coast often includes very challenging wind and sea conditions, famously given the nickname "Roaring Forties" by early sailors centuries ago, referring to 40 degrees south latitude. I had already contacted a marina operator at Mar del Plata who was happy to welcome me there, and happy to email me in English since my Spanish is limited.

9

Mar del Plata

I left Marina Jacaré Village on Tuesday morning, November 22, and made my way north along the Paraíba River for a few miles before turning seaward in the narrow, marked channel passing the north end of the peninsula where the town of Cabedelo is located. The tide had just reversed direction so I was slowed by a building tidal flood current.

The first day and a half out from Cabedelo the winds were light and variable, often headwinds, so I tacked several times trying to make useful progress. By Wednesday night the winds settled in from the northeast so I could set the boat up for a port side broad reach and make good progress. With winds in the 15-to-18 knot range, I was getting boat speeds of 6–7 knots, which is good for a boat like *Phywave*. Before that day I had sunny conditions and was able to recharge my batteries from the solar panels, primarily, and from the wind generator. In direct sun I found the solar panel could produce 20–25 amps. It takes 20 knots of apparent wind for the wind generator to produce 8–10 amps.

After a few days the sky turned overcast with scattered cloud buildups and intermittent light rain showers. A squall line was looming 6 miles to the east. I was still making good progress south, but I expected more cloudy, volatile weather over the coming days. I would definitely be using the generator that night to recharge the boat's batteries.

Sunset sailing south

The first week of sailing from Cabedelo was challenging: the strongest winds and roughest seas I have encountered since beginning this voyage. There was a strong high-pressure system sitting off the coast of Brazil creating gale-force winds and 3-to-4 meter seas. There were continuing warning messages about it day after day in the weather forecasts I downloaded. Rather than go close along the coast where the winds might be weaker, as some of the routing algorithms suggested, I opted to stay far offshore and skirt the gale area by sailing due south rather than following the coastline westward. The wind forecast showed somewhat weaker winds farther east. Though this would lengthen my passage to Mar del Plata, dealing with less wind and no nearby shoreline with its possible hazards made the longer passage worth it.

For five days I had 25-to-30 knot winds on the port beam or slightly aft, gusting to over 35 knots during frequent rain squalls. The seas were running at 3 meters, making for a very rolly ride. It took effort for me to move around the boat and prepare meals. I had three reefs in the mainsail and just a small triangle for a headsail (more than three reefs) to try to balance the helm. I was making good speed but not exactly in the direction I wanted to go. I tried to take this in stride as a preview of rough conditions I was sure to encounter farther south.

On Friday afternoon, December 2, these conditions finally moderated, pretty much as the forecast predicted, and the wind backed toward the north. The high wind–high seas warning messages in the forecast were now gone. I gradually turned off my southerly heading toward the southwest. The sky was finally clear enough that I saw the sunset for the first time in nearly a week.

On December 4 I jibed over to a starboard tack and set a course over ground (COG) of 235 degrees, which would take me straight to Mar del Plata, about 900 nm away. The forecast called for a stretch of dead air (no wind), which I'd have to motor across. I hoped no difficult weather systems would pop up on my route during the eight days it would take to get to Mar del Plata.

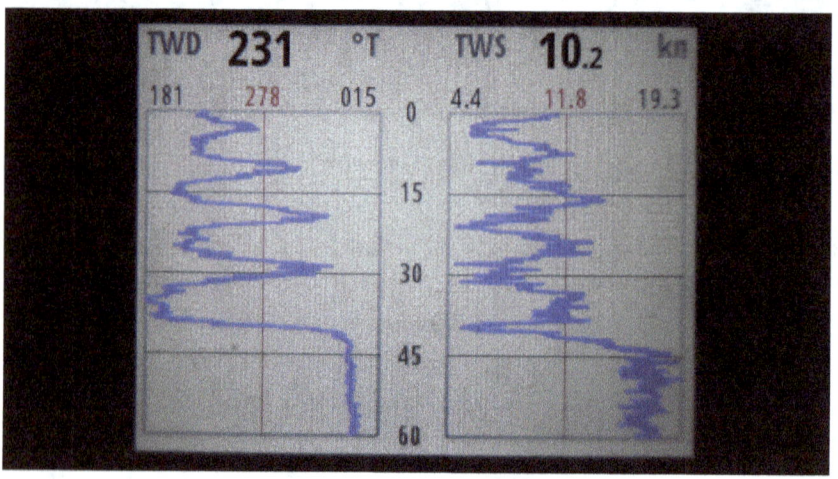

Very sudden shifts in the wind direction and speed were common

I occupied myself by reading, actually rereading, novels stored on my iPhone that I read years before. They seemed like new books, the stories vaguely familiar, but the details long forgotten. I also read the cruising guidebooks I had for going south along the Argentine coast, through the Le Maire Strait and into the Beagle Channel westbound. The one covering the southern coast of Argentina was sparse and out-of-date so not particularly helpful.

Besides reprovisioning and resting, one of the main reasons for the stop in Mar del Plata was to assess the weather forecasts for this 1,200-nm passage to Puerto Williams. The Argentine coast is subject to fast-moving cold fronts with very strong winds (pamperos) that roar unabated across the flat plains (pampas) of Patagonia from the Andes Mountains. I certainly had my experiences with these winds when I flew my plane through Patagonia in 2013 and 2014.

Swing bridge at the entrance to the YCA marina

I wanted to avoid these cold fronts/squall lines if possible, but if I couldn't, I'd have to heave-to for a while. While heaved-to the boat would drift more or less downwind at 1 to 2 knots. Every boat heaves-to differently. I had experimented with *Phywave* a week before but with only 15 knots of wind. Two reefs in the mainsail, no headsail and the rudder tied down hard to lee seemed to balance the boat with a drift of about 120–135 degrees off the wind direction. I didn't know how well this setup would work in the 40–50 knots of wind I might expect from a pampero. Typically, the front passes in 12 hours, though sometimes it may be longer. At least the winds would generally be out of the west, so the heave-to drift direction would be out to sea and open water rather than toward the shore, which would be definitely be a hazard. There were also a few anchorages where I might have been able to take shelter with enough warning. Generally, though, it's better to take my chances in open water rather than attempt an uncertain run to an anchorage. When it's closed up tight, the boat's not going to take on water, so it's a matter of finding a configuration where the ride is reasonably stable until the front passes.

Passing through the Le Maire Strait would be a separate challenge that involved finding the right wind–tidal current combination. I discuss that in more detail later.

I arrived in Mar del Plata on Tuesday morning, December 13, after several days of variable winds. For the final 12 hours I had wind right on the bow, so I had no choice but to use the engine to make tangible progress and arrive at the marina during daylight hours.

I had an odd experience with my boat name when I was arriving at Mar del Plata. In choosing *Phywave* as the name of my boat I really didn't think about how others who speak another language would say it. Ten miles out from the Mar del Plata harbor, harbor control started trying to make contact on VHF radio channel 16 with a boat called "fee-wah-vay." They kept calling the boat but it never answered. After several minutes it dawned on me that I was "fee-wah-vay." I called them back using my pronunciation of *Phywave*.

Yacht Club Argentino (YCA) has a marina that can accommodate boats the size of *Phywave*, so that's where I was headed. I had contacted them a few weeks before to reserve a place. After entering the harbor there is a yellow pedestrian swing bridge that must open for access to the mooring berths. Outside the swinging bridge I was surprised to be met by two dinghies from YCA that tied *Phywave* to a mooring buoy for about 30 minutes until the dockmaster could come out and lead me to my berth. While the marina generally had European-style stern tie berths with pilings, the place they had for me was a side-tie to a long pontoon. It was easy to dock with them handling lines. It was also easy to back out when I left.

I originally planned for Mar del Plata to be a short stop of a few days to reprovision the boat. However, late in the passage from Cabedelo I had a serious failure—the U-bolt that attaches to the clew of the mainsail broke so that when the sail was fully deployed the clew was flying free—not good. I had to roll in the sail to the first reef to keep it under control. Even so, the tension on the clew along the foot and leech of the sail was lost. It wasn't possible to attempt a repair or even investigate what had happened at sea since the boom is high above the cockpit, and I would have had to use a telescoping ladder I had on board to climb up there to look at the clew attachment U-bolt. I wasn't going to try to set up the ladder while rolling around at sea. When I was finally tied to the dock at YCA I climbed up there and found that one side of the stainless steel U-bolt that's tied to the clew had sheared off, resulting in the clew slipping off the bolt. It's a substantial U-bolt so I was really surprised it sheared off the way it did. Once at the dock I was immediately engaged in trying to find a fix. Just getting the boom furling drum apart to remove the broken U-bolt took an instruction video sent to me by Schaefer, the boom manufacturer.

I hired a local sailmaker to help me resolve the problem. Since a replacement U-bolt was not available locally, we used a temporary fix with a soft shackle made from Spectra line, strong stuff that we thought would suffice until I could get the replacement U-bolt from Schaefer installed. The upside, I supposed, if there was one, was that I knew the Schaefer furling boom construction much better than before. I hoped to get this bush fix in and be on my way within a week. From the blogs I'd read by other cruising boats, it was routine to periodically have to fix broken things as a voyage progresses. Maybe I'd been lucky before that point in having no major problems.

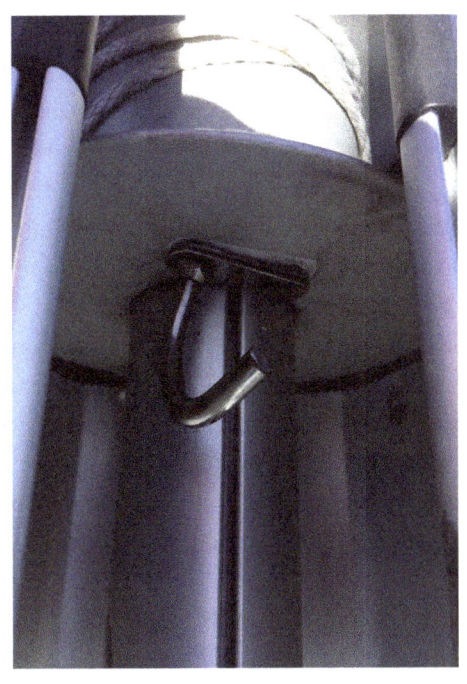

Broken U-bolt in the Schaefer boom

The marina at Mar del Plata is not in the greatest part of town. For some reason, none of the ATMs would accept my Chase debit card, so I was there several days with no Argentine pesos in my pocket. My Visa credit card worked in restaurants and shops, but I was pretty sure I would need pesos to pay the sailmaker in cash for helping with the boom repairs.

Argentina is a country with significant economic turmoil. It maintains an official rate for currency exchange, but everybody knows the black market rate is almost 50% better—i.e., more pesos for a dollar. From my experience flying in many parts of the world, where I had to pay US cash for drums of aviation fuel, I developed the habit of traveling with a substantial amount of cash in new US$100 bills. These are most valuable when dealing with a private money exchange.

I had to track down a private money exchange somewhere in this town since the banks only offered the official exchange rate. Facing a similar problem, some other cruisers told me where to find a money exchange business near the marina. Arriving there, I saw they posted the official rate in the window, but when I presented my US$100 bills across the counter, they gave me the black market rate.

I decided to take a break from living on the boat and booked a couple of nights in an ocean-view room at a hotel that was walking distance from the marina. The hotel also had fast Wi-Fi, unlike the marina, so I could update all the apps and charts on my iPads and iPhone and download several more books.

I found a large supermercado (supermarket) for provisions, but it was far enough away from the marina that I had to use an Uber to transport the pile of supplies back to the boat. I had a long list of things to buy since I was, in part, shopping for the passage to Antarctica as well. The shops in Puerto Williams, the jumping-off point for sailing to Antarctica, apparently had just basic provisions. Puerto Williams is a small town, population about 2,200, so no supermercados. Even though this supermercado in Mar del Plata was a large store with full shelves, there wasn't much variety on these shelves—they were full of the same items: a thousand cans of tuna, for example. Of course, I was used to American and European markets where the food shopping variety is extensive. I was incrementally adjusting my diet on this voyage based on what was readily available in these foreign markets.

Since my next official landing point was going to be in Puerto Williams, Chile, I had to clear out of Argentina by once again visiting Immigration, Customs and the Prefectura Naval (Argentine Coast Guard) as I had done on my arrival. These offices were several blocks away from the marina but a reasonable walking distance. As I expected from reading the guidebooks, the Prefectura Naval gave me an email address where I was to send an email every day reporting my latitude/longitude position, speed and course, and whether all was well aboard. This is a classic position report format for ships at sea. As I left Mar del Plata, I adopted this routine, trying to send the position report at the same time each day.

My visit to Mar del Plata seemed like a very brief stay in Argentina, a country I had visited several times before. My first visit was in 1981 when I was working for Harris Corporation in Quincy, Illinois as a systems engineer. Harris sold TV and radio broadcast transmitters and antennas around the world. On one occasion I was asked to accompany the Harris South America sales guy to Buenos Aires to make an engineering presentation designed to convince the government to buy a large number of AM radio transmitters. During the weeklong trip we were wined and dined by our hosts, who even took us on a side trip to Mendoza, famous for its Malbec wines.

Glacier on Lago Argentino

I returned again in 2011 to join a two-week voyage across the Antarctic Circle on a Russian research ship named the *Vavilov* that had been converted into a small cruise ship. The ship departed from and returned to Ushuaia. It was a great trip with several stops on islands along the Antarctic Peninsula and landings on the massive continent itself. A lively group of other passengers made it a really enjoyable trip.

That was my first experience in Antarctica. In 2014, of course, I flew to Antarctica in my own plane, N788W. While flying south I stopped at several destinations in Argentina including Iguazú Falls, Buenos Aires, Comodoro Rivadavia, Río Gallegos and El Calafate. The town of El Calafate is on Lago Argentino, which has several glaciers coming down to the water's edge. I remember well taking a tour boat to see these glaciers.

In spite of its economic and political difficulties, I had enjoyed my visits to Argentina over the years. With many other places in the world to see, this voyage in *Phywave* may likely have been the last time I visit there.

10

To Tierra del Fuego

I left Mar del Plata on December 20, about noon local time. For the first few days I had great following winds and made good progress but eventually the wind shifted to the south and I was sailing into a headwind, trying to tack back and forth across it. This process was aggravated by a strong countercurrent that took me more than a day to figure out. At first it showed up as a north-setting current. I thought it might be an offshoot of the well-known Falklands Current, although I was too far west to encounter that. When I would try a port tack, sailing to the southwest, the current would push me north; my actual course over the ground (SOG) was almost due west—almost no progress south. I tried to make the best of this but it was very frustrating. Some hours later I noticed the current rotating to an east set, then a south set, then start rotating back to a north set. Very weird. After watching this happen over 24 hours, I concluded the current was following the tide changes, with a north set on ebb tide. It never occurred to me that tidal currents flowing away from the land would turn and flow north and south along the coast. That said, I started this voyage not knowing much about how ocean currents work; I was getting a live-fire education, surprised the two guidebooks I have for sailing this coast, although discussing currents, don't mention this phenomenon.

Headwinds and currents continued to impede my progress south over the next several days. Watching the weather forecasts for the crossing from Puerto Deseado to Bahía Thetis on the eastern tip of the island of Tierra del Fuego,

I decided to anchor for a day so I could make the crossing in a little better weather window. I chose to anchor at Bahía Oso Marino, about 10 nm south of Puerto Deseado. Puerto Deseado itself, located near the mouth of a river, has a complicated entry with high tidal currents and not many good facilities to accommodate visiting yachts. At Oso Marino I had the entire bay to myself. The holding in sand for the anchor was great; it needed to be because there were 20–30 knot winds blowing through from nearly all directions. I'm glad I had a Spade anchor that's good at resetting itself.

While anchored, I poured the remaining diesel from my jerry cans into the main tank, something that's almost impossible to do while at sea unless the water is dead calm.

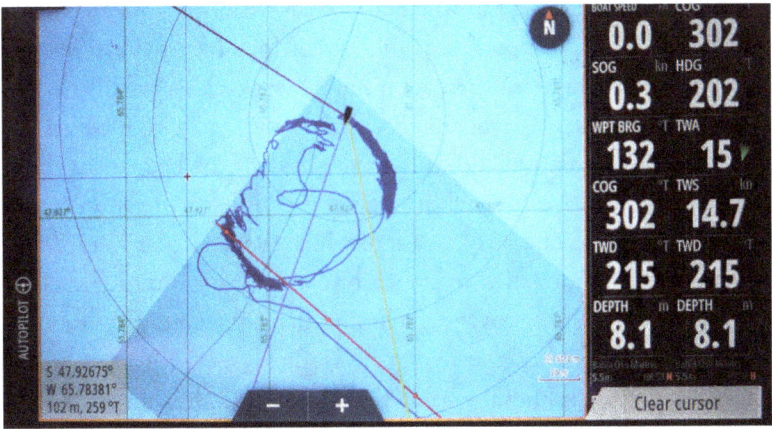

Swinging at anchor in Oso Marino when the wind shifted 180 degrees

Leaving Oso Marino at around 10 a.m. local time, I was contacted by a member of the Prefectura Naval in Puerto Deseado who wanted to know my intentions, where I was going, and other relevant information. I gave him the details he asked for, and at his request, agreed to add his email address to the daily position report emails I had been sending to the Prefectura in Mar del Plata. All yachts transiting Argentine waters are required to do this. A good thing, I think, that they keep track of where boats are in case of a problem.

After leaving Oso Marino I continued to work my way south into light and sometimes contrary winds. The forecasts had not been particularly accurate. I was trying to avoid the very strong westerly windstorms that are common in this part of Argentina, the Patagonian coast. For several days I had been sailing across the infamous "Roaring Forties," the area between 40 and 50 degrees south latitude. The next day, likely, I would pass south of 50 degrees south latitude, into the "Furious Fifties." These descriptive names were bestowed by the earliest European mariners for a reason. I was trying to avoid experiencing the reason firsthand. I chose to anchor again around the east entrance to the Strait of Magellan to wait for more moderate winds and seas before crossing to Bahia Thetis.

I had more equipment issues since leaving Mar del Plata. One of the deck-mounted blocks (pulleys) that controls the sheet (control line) for the mainsail failed. I had one spare so I was able to get going again, but it was my only spare. My brother Jim, who was coming to Puerto Williams in January to join an Antarctica cruise, would be bringing me a couple of spare blocks and the replacement U-bolt for the boom.

More seriously, I suppose, was the loss of four of my diesel jerry cans overboard in what was a really freak episode. I was tacking the boat, moving the genoa from port to starboard. For a time during this process, the sail and sheets violently flap in the wind as the bow of the boat turns through the wind and before I can winch in the sheet. While the sheet was flying it caught under the end of 2" × 6" board to which the jerry cans were attached. The board itself was attached to stanchions with heavy-duty cable ties that had held fine during this voyage, including through some very rough seas. Before I could even react, the flying sheet quickly yanked the board right off the stanchion, breaking the cable ties and leaving that end of the board hanging over the side. The seas were rough but I went forward to try to grab the board, with the sheet still yanking on it, to try to pull it back on board. It was no use. The forces from the sheet and the weight of the board with three full 20-liter jerry cans attached were too much for me; I couldn't drag it back aboard. I had to let it fall over the side where in a half a minute the weight and heavy seas broke the cable ties holding the other end of the board and it fell away, certain to sink. I didn't think that if I turned the boat around, I would have a realistic chance to recover them, especially with the rough seas. Surprisingly, one of the three full jerry cans somehow detached itself from the board and stayed on deck. I was able to grab that one and bring it into the cockpit so the total loss was four jerry cans and the mounting board. I would just have to make do with six jerry cans instead of ten for extra diesel going forward, unless I could find some more jerry cans in Puerto Williams.

While at anchor in Oso Marino, inspecting the boat, I discovered the furling line for the genoa had chafed almost all the way through. If it had broken while at sea, the genoa would have unfurled with no way to bring it back other than to release the halyard and try to lower the sail to the deck. This would have been difficult alone at sea since it's a huge sail. I replaced the furling line with another about the same diameter, which should be adequate.

The boat was as ready as I could make it for the crossing to Bahía Thetis and Le Maire Strait, which I expected to be the roughest passage so far.

I haven't mentioned much about wildlife, partly because I don't know much about the birds and other wildlife I was seeing. Of course, the albatross is the most common bird hanging around the boat while at sea. There are a few different varieties. For a time, a couple elected to use my bowsprit as a perch. An albatross following your boat is generally considered a good omen but beware treating them with disrespect, as Coleridge's "The Rime of the Ancient Mariner" warns.

Commerson's dolphins

New to me were the Commerson's dolphins. They are unmistakable, being almost all white with a black dorsal fin and head. I first encountered them after leaving Mar del Plata. Like other dolphins, they will swim alongside the boat, even under it, experiencing the bow wake as something different from what they typically experience in the ocean. I was able to get some short videos of them in action. As I was coming into Bahía Oso Marino there must have been a hundred or more playing around within 50 meters of the boat. Truly a rare sight.

Hanging at Anchor

After leaving the anchorage at Bahía Oso Marino I thought I had a weather window to make it to Bahía Thetis, straight south across Bahía Grande, before west gale-force winds moved in. That weather window closed down, so I sought an intermediate point to anchor where I could wait for three or more days for the gale to blow through. Even a marginal anchorage would be better than three days hove to at sea in gale-force winds. Unfortunately, there were no harbors, bays or coves suitable for small yachts, and no easily accessible ports, along this part of the Argentine coast. One of my cruising guidebooks was *Patagonia & Tierra del Fuego Nautical Guide* by Mariolina Rolfo and Giorgio Ardrizzi, commonly known among cruisers as the "Italian book" and regarded as the bible for sailing those waters. It had a brief reference to a charted anchorage a yacht had previously used, situated 2 nm north of Cabo Virgenes at the east entrance to the Strait of Magellan. That yacht had anchored there for similar reasons, to avoid the worst of a westerly gale, because the anchorage is immediately to the east of (in the lee of) a very tall coastal escarpment. This serves to block the worst of the gale winds from the west, leaving the water mostly flat and relatively calm.

I decided to make for that anchorage, arriving January 1, 2023, around 1900Z. I set the anchor and put out 55 meters of chain, expecting it to still be windy. It was still windy, but not nearly as bad as being on the open ocean. The holding ground there for the anchor was very good. The winds were typically 10 to 20 knots, but I had gusts of 30 knots or more. There were no waves, only occasional swells, but I could look east to the open ocean only a mile or so away and see much more turbulent waters.

Life swinging around an anchor in gusty winds is not much fun. Every creak and groan of the anchor chain during a strong gust is unnerving, making me wonder if something would fail or the anchor would drag. I used a so-called bridle on the anchor chain consisting of a chain hook that was hooked on a link in the anchor chain and attached to a heavy 3/4" line. The line was then secured to a bow cleat. Once the chain hook was set, I let out a few more feet of chain so the hook and heavy line were taking the load of the pulling chain instead of the windlass. This left the windlass without a load because the part of the chain out to the hook was slack. This is a common technique for anchoring that should always be used (though most sailors don't), especially if high loads on the chain are expected.

Anchored in the lee of this cliff, sheltering from strong winds

Le Maire Strait

The gale ended the evening of January 4 after four nights at anchor. I planned to leave the anchorage on Thursday, January 5, at 0900Z and sail 180 nm southeast, directly to Bahía Thetis, with an estimated arrival time on the evening of January 6. Bahía Thetis is a bay on the west side of the north entrance to the Le Maire Strait where it's advisable to wait for a suitable combination of wind and current in the strait. The tidal currents through this strait can be quite strong, and as tidal currents, they reverse direction twice in a 24-hour period. When you have a situation of wind blowing in the opposite direction of the current flow, the opposing forces can sometimes create huge standing waves that can be dangerous. They have damaged and sunk boats. It's a situation that must be avoided.

Reviewing the weather forecast as I sailed southeast, it appeared there would be a wind from the north on January 7, blowing in the direction I wanted to go. If I could time my arrival at the north end of Le Maire Strait during an ebb tide and ahead of a south-setting current, I would have the wind and current flowing in the same direction I wanted—south. I was going to try to make the passage south when the south-setting ebb tide began at High Water (HW) slack at 0906Z on January 7. Timing was everything there. If the wind forecast held, I expected I could make it into the Beagle Channel to a protected anchorage called Puerto Español in Bahía Aguirre before nightfall. From there it would only be less than two more full days along the Beagle Channel to Puerto Williams, assuming no strong contrary winds. I expected to motor most of the way west along the Beagle Channel unless I got a relatively rare easterly following wind or a wind from the north.

However, I had good wind and was sailing fast toward the north end of Le Maire Strait. I needed to slow down so I would get there at the right time on January 7. I did that by reducing sail. Normally in a sailboat you're trying to make the most of the wind and sail as fast as possible, but in a circumstance like this, slowing down was the better strategy. Given the forecast, it also meant I wouldn't need to anchor at Bahía Thetis to wait for a suitable wind/tide combination. That combination was forecast and I could sail right through.

My timing did not work out precisely but it was close enough. Contrary to the tide forecast, I initially encountered a weak north-setting current. It eventually faded to ebb tide, then the south-setting current I expected arrived, about one and a half hours after it was predicted to arrive. I was already a few miles into the strait when it went to ebb tide. However, the north wind was

In the Beagle Channel looking back at Le Maire Strait

only about 10 knots directly on the stern, not enough for efficient sailing, so I was motoring rather than sailing. A light wind of 10 knots is typically not a big problem when blowing opposite the current. I passed a larger sailboat motoring north, having no apparent difficulty with the wind and current combination.

I continued past Bahía Buen Suceso, another good anchorage to wait out rough weather on the west side of the strait. Farther on, I finally turned the corner at the south end of the strait and headed west toward Bahía Aguirre where the anchorage at Puerto Español is situated at the west end of the bay. I was now officially in Tierra del Fuego proceeding west down the Beagle Channel. After I had anchored in Puerto Español, two other sailboats showed up to join me. I didn't bother to launch the dingy and go ashore to visit a small home along the shore as they did. I saw smoke from the home's chimney so I guess someone must have been living there.

Puerto Español with a small home

Puerto Williams, my destination on the Chilean side of the Beagle Channel, was more than 70 nm west of my anchorage in Puerto Español, too far to go in a single day. That passage would have been mostly motoring because the wind forecast showed little wind or a light headwind. I needed an intermediate anchorage somewhere. There were many available, but I wanted to stay on the Argentine side of the Beagle Channel since I hadn't yet been cleared to enter Chile. From talking to other cruisers, however, I learned that staying on the Argentine side wasn't really an issue since boats navigating the

Beagle Channel could choose an anchorage on either side with apparently no problems.

Bahía Harberton, a famous place that tourists from Ushuaia can visit by road, was one possibility, though cruisers and guidebooks noted substantial kelp in the bay which can be problematic for setting an anchor and cleaning it off once it's pulled up. Just west of Bahía Harberton is Bahía Relegada, which I found in the Italian cruising guidebook. The notes about the anchorage were favorable, especially in the east arm of the bay, so I decided that would be my intermediate stop before Puerto Williams.

Heading west along the Beagle Channel

Bahía Relegada

Heading west, I was mostly motoring, with occasional short periods of 20-knot winds from the north that made for good beam reach sailing. It seemed like a long day as I arrived at Bahía Relegada in a sublime late afternoon light. I was captivated by the mountains and scenery as I proceeded down the famous Beagle Channel which has so much mariner history. I had my own history with this place, beginning when I took a cruise to Antarctica on the *Valvilov* in 2011. I once again saw the abandoned ranches and sunken ships in this channel I remember from that voyage. In 2013 and again in 2014 I flew over the Beagle Channel en route to Antarctica. It was time to reflect on how far I had come since leaving Norfolk just five months before. I was less than two days away from Puerto Williams, the jumping-off point for the voyage across the Drake Passage to Antarctica, certainly the most challenging sailing I would experience on this solo voyage to seven continents.

Bahía Relegada was a peaceful place, well-protected from wind and waves, with a few cattle grazing in nearby pastures and no other boats anchored there. I spent a restful night, looking forward to the next day, when I would finally arrive at "Antarctica Central," the Micalvi Yacht Club in Puerto Williams.

11

Puerto Williams

I arrived in Puerto Williams on Monday morning, January 9, after anchoring twice on my way west through the Beagle Channel, which came after my passage south through the Le Maire Strait. The last leg from Bahía Relegada to Puerto Williams took less than three hours, arriving there in late morning and rafting up to another boat at the Micalvi Yacht Club. I had to contact the Chilean Armada (navy) on the VHF radio as I approached to inform them of my arrival. I had previously told them about what time I would be there. One of the first steps on arrival was to have the health inspectors visit me before I left the boat to make sure I wasn't sick with any disease I could spread to the local inhabitants. They needed an approximate arrival time to schedule that visit.

Puerto Williams competes with Ushuaia in Argentina for the title of southernmost town. Puerto Williams is certainly farther south by a few miles but Ushuaia would argue it's too small to be considered a real town with a population of only about 2,500 people.

One of the advantages of a small town is that everywhere you need to go is within walking distance. Upon my arrival, health inspectors came to meet me at Micalvi to complete some paperwork to ensure I wasn't ill. I can't remember if they asked anything about COVID vaccinations, but I had my yellow WHO international vaccination card and COVID vaccination cards with me just in case. I couldn't leave Micalvi and go into town until the health check was completed. Following that, I had to visit Immigration,

Sign at the entrance to Micalvi Yacht Club

Customs and the Armada offices for the usually clearing-in steps, a stamp in my passport and filling out various forms. Another large sailboat had arrived that morning just before me. I found myself following that crew around town as they walked to these offices and completed the same steps of the process.

The fundamental work of preparing for the next sailing leg to Antarctica was challenging in Puerto Williams because there really wasn't a port or great resources for fuel and provisions. The Micalvi Yacht Club is situated at a (deliberately) sunken military ship in a channel of the river. There are no docks or pontoons to tie to, so the only choice is to raft to other boats. During the austral summer, when many boats are using Micalvi, the boats may be routinely rafted six or seven deep. If your boat is in the outside position, to get to shore you may have to climb over six other boats—a real pain. The unspoken protocol is that you must walk across another boat's deck forward of the mast. Unless your boat is at the end of the raft, you also have other people walking over your boat to get to their boat. That is certainly annoying and limits privacy.

Power and water are additional issues. There are some electrical sockets along the passageway on the ship but you have to string a long extension

Phywave, with the heavy aluminum boom and American flag, rafted in among other boats

cord from there to where your boat is rafted. Of course, when a boat wants to leave the raft, along with untying the boats, these electrical connections need to be undone, then redone. Water is available by a really long hose attached to a water line on the ship. Everyone uses that same hose. I never got a clear answer on how good the water is, but I saw other people filling their boat water tanks with it so I assumed the water was OK to drink.

Long ago someone should have come up with a plan to add finger docks of some sort to solve the problems with rafting so many boats. Maybe somebody did and they never implemented it. Anyway, given the rafting situation this really isn't a great place to bring your boat if you intend to get fuel and provisions and do Chilean paperwork for sailing to Antarctica. I saw other boats, regular charters to Antarctica, get fuel and provisions in Ushuaia, a much larger town with more dock space, then come to Puerto Williams only for the Chilean entry paperwork and the permit to go to Antarctica, an approved sailing itinerary called a zarpe. They're tied up at Micalvi for maybe half a day, then leave.

Others avoid the Micalvi rafting hassle by anchoring in the river nearby. This leaves them more exposed to the weather and means a trip ashore in the dinghy anytime they want to do something in town. The advantage is not having to climb over other boats and preserving their privacy.

The famous sailor's bar in the Micalvi ship closed long ago—nobody could really tell me when with certainty. I was looking forward to having a pisco sour in the bar when I arrived, and the good times and camaraderie of hanging out there with other sailors. Sadly, that scene, still described in the Tierra del Fuego cruising guides, is long gone and with it one of the reasons to endure the hassles of rafting at Micalvi. I was invited to an Argentine-style BBQ (asado) at the Cedena sailing school across the river from Micalvi, which came closest to a sailor's gathering while I was there. An asado is really a carnivore's feast with lots of slow-roasted meat and some potatoes.

I had been to Puerto Williams before, briefly, in 2013 during a reconnaissance flight I had made to 60 degrees south latitude toward Antarctica. I stopped at the Puerto Williams airport on my way back to Punta Arenas to refuel my plane with a rotary hand pump from a tank of fuel I was carrying as cargo. As I explained in my 2015 book, *Flying 7 Continents Solo*, I decided not to try to actually land in Antarctica that year. I returned in 2014 to complete my flight to King George Island in Antarctica.

Fuel

The only way to get diesel fuel is to take your fuel cans (jerry cans) to a gas station a half mile away from Micalvi, fill them up and take them back. At that point it's necessary to climb over all the boats again with the heavy fuel cans to get them to your boat. In a word, it's ridiculous, but everyone seems to accept this way of doing things. If you're lucky, someone with a dinghy in the water will help by taking the heavy fuel cans back to your boat so you don't have to carry them over the string of rafted boats.

There is a hand truck at the club that people use to carry the full fuel cans from the gas station to Micalvi. Being in the "no expense spared" mode, I went to the tourist office and asked if there was anyone in Puerto Williams who would rent me a car or truck. Yes, a couple of people. The next morning Fernando showed up at Micalvi with a beat-up old truck with a few problems he explained, like the trick to starting it. I handed him some cash, he gave me the keys, and away I went. No paperwork. Now I was more in my element, driving around a little remote foreign town in a funky old truck. I transported my full fuel cans from the gas station back to Micalvi easily and did the same for other cruisers facing the same problem. I was also able to line up a dinghy at Micalvi to transport the fuel cans back to the stern of my boat. Given I was in the middle of a raft, I really couldn't get my own dinghy off the foredeck and in the water very easily.

Fortunately, I was able to find some additional 20-liter jerry cans at a shop in Puerto Williams to replace the ones I had lost overboard sailing south. The new ones were not as heavy-duty as the ones I lost, but they would do for the voyage to Antarctica and beyond. I was lucky to find them.

Boats rafted together alongside sunken ship at Micalvi Yacht Club

Provisions

Not surprisingly, the two largest food markets in Puerto Williams, Simon & Simon and Sotito Supermercado, are still pretty small compared to supermercados in places like Ushuaia or Mar del Plata. Getting provisions from these shops back to the boat is a hassle similar to moving the fuel cans, though the bags of provisions are lighter and easier to carry. I again used my rented truck to pick up provisions and take them back to Micalvi, then completed several trips from the truck to my boat, climbing over all the other boats in between mine and shore.

The fresh produce in these markets was very limited. Mostly what they had were things with a longer shelf life like onions and potatoes. There was an abundance of frozen meat—steaks, hamburgers, chicken—but without a freezer on *Phywave* I'd have to accept that they would thaw and be good for maybe a week to 10 days. There was also lots of canned fish, mainly tuna, with a variety of labels. Fresh bread and empanadas made daily were some of the best things available.

Restaurants

While in Puerto Williams I think I ate at every restaurant that was open. There are only three or four, some with variable and uncertain operating hours. The food was actually pretty good, with pizza, steak and chicken dishes, and a selection of beers and Chilean wines. After having fed myself during the long passages that preceded my arrival in Puerto Williams, I was happy to have restaurant food I didn't need to prepare myself and that wouldn't draw down the provisions on the boat.

Money

Chilean pesos were available from the ATM at a small bank. After being frustrated when trying to get cash at the ATMs in Mar del Plata, I found my debit card worked in this ATM, so I had all the cash I needed. The mercados, the restaurants and the fuel station all took my Visa card without a problem. There were fees to pay at the Armada office for permits that, oddly, required both Chilean pesos and US dollars.

Touring

Puerto Williams is located on Isla Navarino, which turns out to be a popular destination for hikers and mountaineers interested in a really remote, end-of-the-world outdoor experience. The mountains called Dientes de Navarino are a particular attraction. When I took a flight leaving Puerto Williams for Santiago (via Punta Arenas), the plane was full of these folks and their piles of outdoor gear.

While I had the truck, I took a drive east with some cruiser friends along Y-905 to the end of the road, literally. After a few miles of asphalt, it turned to gravel, wound along the shoreline, then inland, finally emerging again along the shore, ending at a place called Caleta Eugenia. There were a few houses and barns there, and fishing boats pulled up on the beach, but not much else. We walked around for a bit along the shore, then drove back to Puerto Williams. It was good to get out of town on a sunny afternoon. I wish I had made a similar drive west along Y-905 toward Puerto Navarino where there is a ferry that crosses to Ushuaia. I think that would have been more interesting than going east.

The Silversea cruise line had recently established Puerto Williams as a new cruise ship port and an alternative to Ushuaia, which had been the main port for cruises going to Antarctica. While I was there, a new pier was under construction, large enough to accommodate the Silversea cruise ships and others that were sure to follow. Silversea arranges private charter flights from Santiago to Puerto Williams to bring their passengers to the ships. I watched a few of their cruise ships come and go, and I certainly encountered them on my way to Antarctica. That year they had at least three ships making the voyage to Antarctica. I heard a rumor that Silversea was also planning to build a large hotel in Puerto Williams to help with the logistics of getting passengers to and from their ships. Now that a few years have passed, it would be interesting to see what impact all these changes have had on a little town like Puerto Williams.

Antarctica Zarpe

By Saturday, January 14, all the fuel, water and provisions were on board *Phywave*, finally. I even found a lavandería to do my laundry. The weather forecast suggested going to Isla Lennox on Tuesday, January 17, anchoring for the night, then setting off across the Drake Passage on Wednesday. The Armada will only issue the zarpe one day before departure, so that meant on Monday I needed to be back in the Armada's office to get that. The process was easier than I expected. I thought my US expedition documents (the IEE and waste permit included in appendix H) would be carefully examined to make sure they complied with regulations. Instead, the young Armada woman at the counter simply went through these documents page by page, taking a photo of each page with her cellphone. Those pages, all in English, could have really said anything. Fortunately, I had remembered to get them printed while I was in Cabedelo after receiving approval of the documents by email from the EPA and NSF. The paper copies were essential for the zarpe process. I wanted to bring a printer with me on this voyage, but the small laser printer I wanted in the US was not available due to COVID-caused supply chain issues. I eventually would buy one later in my voyage.

Now faced with my imminent departure, exactly how I would get my boat out from the rafted string is a problem the denizens of Micalvi know well. They had set up a group chat on WhatsApp that connected everyone who was there. Sending out a message that a boat needs to leave will summon the sailors to handle all the various lines tying boats together. I asked them to handle my departure and they told me what I needed to do. It all went smoothly. I decided to first move *Phywave* to the outside end of the raft of boats on Monday afternoon at high tide. I then had an easy departure early on January 17 by just disconnecting a few lines tied to the boat next to me.

12

Antarctica

I left Puerto Williams on the morning of January 17, headed for Isla Lennox as an intermediate stop before crossing the Drake Passage. This one-day delay lined up with the weather forecast I was now seeing. Isla Lennox is about 40 nm southeast of Puerto Williams via water, so I found myself motoring in light wind back east along the Beagle Channel, passing abandoned structures and a half-sunken ship. Along the way there is a very small fishing hamlet called Puerto Toro with a pier. Boats returning from Antarctica have sometimes sheltered in Puerto Toro since this pier is the first man-made structure where they could be tied up. Puerto Toro is not connected to Puerto Williams by a serviceable road. Excluding Antarctic research stations in Antarctica, it is the southernmost permanently inhabited place on earth—about 20 people live there year-round.

By the time I reached the anchorage on the east side of Isla Lennox the wind had kicked up to 20 knots, making anchoring a little more challenging. To anchor in the wind, it's necessary to turn the boat into the wind and essentially bring the boat to a stop to drop the anchor. Of course, after bringing the boat to a stop the wind will start pushing the boat backward while falling off to one side or the other. When I ordered *Phywave* I made a great decision to include a chain counter. As I mentioned before, a chain counter is a display at the helm that not only has buttons to lower and raise the anchor but also shows how much chain is deployed. With the bow falling off to one side,

Armada station at Isla Lennox

the anchor is being dropped toward the side of the boat rather than directly in front of the bow. I usually initially drop a chain length that's twice the water depth before I start backing up to set the anchor while also letting out more chain. It's definitely a two-handed operation. Ideally, I want to back up directly downwind from where I dropped the anchor, but with the bow falling off to one side or the other, that really isn't possible. There's no choice but to accept this. Once the anchor starts to bite and the chain stretches out, the bow will swing back into the wind and the process of backing up to set the anchor can be completed. Finding a place to drop the anchor at Isla Lennox was also a bit of a challenge since there were broad rafts of kelp covering the bay. Kelp should be avoided when possible because it can impede an anchor from properly setting in the bottom mud.

I ended up staying two nights at Isla Lennox when a forecast gale warning for the Drake Passage came up for the day I planned to leave. That forecast was removed the next day so I left the anchorage on January 19.

Charting Issues

When I headed east out of the anchorage, I experienced one of the common nautical charting problems that can occur anywhere in the world. As I was making my way down the channel between two small islands, I could see that I was about in the middle of the channel. However, the position of my boat shown on the chartplotter was far over to one side of the channel, almost on the shore of one of the islands. How could the chartplotter be so wrong in showing my position when it was using satellite GPS latitude and longitude coordinates?

The explanation is a little involved but very important for sailors to understand. Over the years (centuries), increasingly refined mathematical models have evolved to represent the earth's surface. The current model is an oblate spheroid (a sphere squished down a bit at the North and South Poles) and designated as WGS84. WGS is an abbreviation for World Geodetic System. It was preceded by WGS60, WGS72, and others. Of course, every time the model is changed, the location of a latitude/longitude position relative to physical points on the earth also changes.

The WGS84 model and datum are the basis for the latitude and longitude coordinates displayed on any GPS device. The various GPS satellite constellations—there are now several—are actually datum-agnostic, but WGS84 is the agreed-upon datum used when the satellite signals are converted to latitude/longitude coordinates. Everyone gets WGS84 coordinates so they can drive, fly, sail, hike, etc. using them. Everyone is happy, right? Wrong.

The problem comes when you plot WGS84 coordinates on a map or chart that wasn't drawn using the WGS84 datum and coordinate system. It will show an incorrect position relative to the physical features on the chart. This problem is especially acute with nautical charts that have been drawn many years ago using who-knows-what datum, map projection, coordinate system, etc. Modern boats like mine are all equipped with chartplotters, moving map displays like a satnav map used in a car. However, the electronic charts the chartplotter uses are often derived from these old paper nautical charts without correcting them to WGS84.

That was the problem I was encountering leaving Isla Lennox. It also occurs, to a greater or lesser extent, throughout Tierra del Fuego and Patagonia. The Pacific is another place where the nautical e-charts can be far off. Through a somewhat convoluted process, tech-savvy cruisers are now georeferencing satellite imagery and loading that into their chartplotters. Not only does it accurately display their boat's position relative to islands, reefs, sandbars, etc., it also shows other information like submerged coral heads as dark shapes in the water. Unlike nautical charts, however, the satellite images don't show any depth soundings, which are still important. Realistically, both the nautical charts and satellite images are needed. It seems chartplotter makers should pick up on this satellite data source as a product and make it easy for people to load satellite imagery into their chartplotters. Maybe they're working on that.

The second charting issue involves Antarctica itself. Before leaving home I purchased the most recent British Admiralty paper charts for the areas of Antarctica where I planned to go. Of course, to understand where your boat is relative to the land or underwater hazards it's necessary to take the GPS coordinates and plot them by hand on the paper charts. It's a relatively slow, potentially error-prone process, and it has the same position error issues I described above. I bought the paper charts as a backup because the standard Garmin/Navionics e-chart coverage available for my chartplotter does not include Antarctica. After some online research, I had come across another nautical charting app called iSailor that runs on my iPads. As I mentioned before, the iSailor app did have chart coverage available covering the Antarctic Peninsula. When I compared the charts in iSailor with the Admiralty charts, they had identical information, so it was clear the paper charts were the basis for the e-charts in iSailor. Of course, this gave me a moving map display on my iPad but not on the chartplotters at the helm or nav station. I ended up plotting positions and courses around islands in Antarctica using iSailor, then entering those coordinate positions into my chartplotter at my helm so I could steer using them. I could also set the iPad showing the iSailor charts near the helm and watch it while steering. I had a waterproof case for the iPad to protect it from the weather when using it this way. This setup was not as good as having the e-charts on my chartplotter, but good enough.

Drake Passage Southbound

With light winds, I motored for much of the first day after leaving Isla Lennox. From then on, the crossing was a mix of light and variable winds, sometimes using the engine to assist so I could make tangible progress. That was followed by 20-to-25 knot winds in a perfect direction to get the boat up to 6–7 knots.

I saw several cruise ships on the AIS going both north and south following the same route as I was, more or less. Some were close enough I could see them visually. The waters of Antarctica, as defined by the Antarctic Treaty, begin at 60 degrees south latitude. I crossed that latitude line late on January 21. Even though icebergs can be found at latitudes farther north, I became more vigilant for ice as I crossed this boundary line.

Penguins on an ice growler approaching Deception Island

The last 24+ hours approaching Antarctica were a stay-awake marathon on ice watch using the radar and my eyes. I was determined to arrive at Deception Island and anchor during daylight hours, meaning I had to keep my speed up. As the wind faded and crazy uncharted ocean currents both assisted and slowed my progress, I made occasional use of the engine to maintain my speed. Ultimately, I made it across the notorious Drake Passage from Tierra del Fuego to Antarctica in a little over four days.

Every sailor imagines the glorious first landfall at a new island or continent, the first glimpses of the highest peaks, the mountain slopes, the coastlines and the towns. I've already experienced that a few times on this six-month voyage, particularly when I arrived in the Azores. By the way, landfall to a sailor is when land is first sighted, not when first going ashore. Think of sailors centuries ago navigating with the crudest instruments across vast stretches of ocean; sighting land would be the big moment, not wading up onto the beach.

Alas, I was denied my big landfall moment arriving in Antarctica. The relatively warm north winds pushing over the cold Antarctic water created fog. As far as 100 miles out from the first islands of the Antarctic Peninsula (Smith Island and Snow Island), the visibility was less than 2 nm. Huge cruise ships passed by me within a few miles and I never saw them. I sailed past Smith Island and Snow Island, easily close enough to see them but saw nothing, just

Small cruise ship in the fog entering Neptune's Bellows

fog. Getting close to Deception Island the visibility collapsed to less than 1/2 nm. Another cruise ship passed me that far away going the opposite direction, but I couldn't even see an outline in the mist. It was a little spooky.

The entrance to the water-filled Deception Island caldera is a very narrow passage known as Neptune's Bellows. I wondered, "Are my e-charts accurate enough? Will I be able to find this entrance in the fog?" Well, I found it, and as I approached, a cruise ship called the *Fram* was also just starting through. I had only to follow them while coordinating our positions using the VHF radio. Passing through Neptune's Bellows, and inside the caldera, visibility improved considerably. I was finally motivated to grab my camera and take photos; it is a spectacular place.

The anchorage I was heading for is a place called Stancomb Cove in the northwest corner of the Deception Island caldera. It felt great to have gotten here, definitely the "Mt. Everest" of my project to sail solo to seven continents. Of course, I still had to "climb back down" by crossing the Drake Passage northward back to Puerto Williams and civilization. The northbound voyage is actually harder than southbound for several weather/sailing reasons I discuss later.

I had a cake mix on board. I thought I would bake a cake to celebrate my arrival, but then I thought it was premature. I didn't want to tempt Neptune's ill will with such a presumptive gesture. I decided to wait until I returned to

Puerto Williams for this celebration, when I have again escaped and transcended the icy grip of these winds, these waters and my own mistakes.

Stancomb Cove

Stancomb Cove is the best place to anchor for small private yachts like mine. It's reasonably well-protected from the winds and offers pretty good holding for the anchor. There was one other boat anchored there when I arrived on the afternoon of January 23. The depth of the cove bottom was pretty uneven, ranging from 25 meters to less than 10 meters. I motored around until I found a good spot to drop anchor with an 8-meter depth. I initially put out 50 meters of chain, eventually increasing that to 60 meters when the winds blowing through the cove increased to 40+ knots, with blowing snow—basically a blizzard.

I stayed a week anchored in Stancomb Cove. On the second day I took the dinghy to the beach, wandered around for a while and took photographs. There were resident sea lions lounging on the sand in the sun. I especially wanted to get a photo of me with *Phywave* in the background as evidence of arriving on my fourth continent. I brought a tripod to the beach and used the timer on the camera to accomplish this.

One day that week Barry Kennedy's boat *Gringo* showed up in the cove. Barry is a very experienced Antarctic sailor. In preparing my IEE for visiting

***Phywave* at anchor in Stancomb Cove**

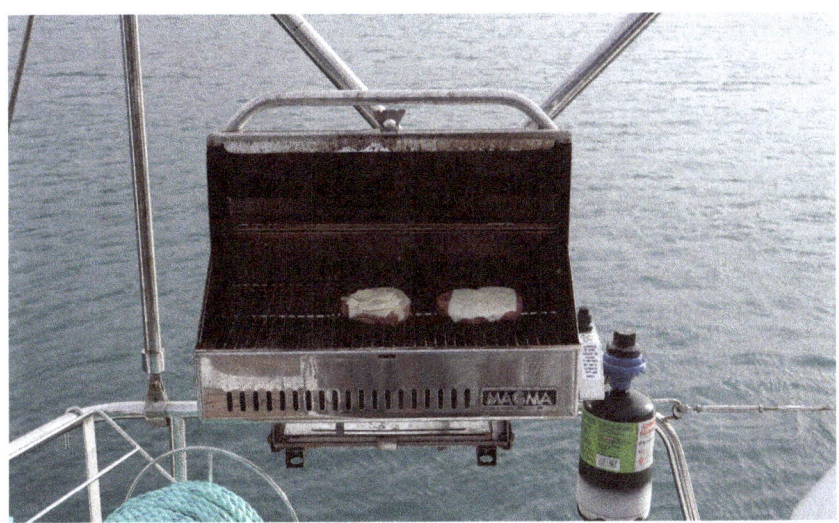

Cheeseburgers on the grill

Antarctica, I had reviewed his IEE submissions from prior years to get an idea of the acceptable format. Somehow, Barry had heard I was sailing solo, a very rare thing in Antarctica. He came over to *Phywave* in his dinghy with his notebook computer to show me some Antarctic anchorages where it wasn't necessary to set lines to shore. Setting shore lines is a challenge for a solo sailor since no one is left on board to keep the boat maneuvered in place when taking a line ashore in the dinghy. It can be done but it is tricky.

At that point I felt "out on a limb" being in Antarctica and was reluctant to venture farther south along the peninsula. I had fundamentally accomplished my primary goal of sailing to Antarctica solo, so it seemed going farther would just increase the risk. Barry was a great guy for offering his advice on anchorages; in retrospect I wish I had taken him up on his offer of information and been courageous enough to sail farther south. I also had a very solid anchor set in Stancomb Cove; I hated to give it up for something unknown and likely more tenuous. Instead of talking about anchorages, we talked about flying over a glass of whiskey. Barry is a helicopter pilot who works in Alaska firefighting during the summer.

On the beach in Stancomb Cove

Having made the fundamental decision not to sail farther south, my attention turned to planning a departure date to head back north to Puerto Williams. Of course, it is all about the weather, so I was downloading forecast maps twice a day and communicating by email with Magnus Day, an Australian sailor with extensive Antarctic sailing experience I had retained to help with interpreting and advising me on weather forecasts around Antarctica.

Kayakers from a cruise ship

While I was anchored in Stancomb, a few cruise ships occasionally came by and anchored outside the cove in the caldera where deeper water is found. Those ships had the courtesy to contact the small yachts anchored in the cove and let us know they would be launching large Zodiac boats to take their passengers on shore excursions, including hiking and kayaking. For a time, the cove turned into an "Antarctic holiday camp" with all these tourists on the beaches, hiking the surrounding hills and paddling around in kayaks. This would last for a few hours in the afternoon until finally the Zodiacs would collect everybody brought ashore (hopefully) and take them back to their ships. After all the Zodiacs, kayaks and other gear was stowed, the ships raised their anchors and moved on to their next intended anchorage.

Blizzard in Stancomb Cove

Listening to these cruise ships coming and going on the VHF radio, I was surprised to learn they had to have reservations for particular anchorage locations, and there was some confusion about where anchorage 1 versus 2 was actually located. The wild, free-form cruising one might expect in Antarctica, which I experienced on the small cruise ship in 2011, apparently was no longer the case. From a safety perspective, it makes sense to have coordination between these large ships vying to take their passengers to the same interesting places for the same experiences, but it certainly erodes the spontaneity of it all. Later I heard that cruise ships had to anchor and wait for a slot to take their passengers ashore at very popular places like Port Lockroy farther south along the Antarctic Peninsula. It was a strategy to keep these places from being overrun with tourists.

It reminded me of my early days backpacking in the Sierra Nevada Mountains in California. As a teenager I enjoyed mountain climbing and backpacking along the eastern slopes of the Sierras from Mt. Whitney all the way north to the Minarets near Mammoth Mountain. In the early days of backpacking, it was possible to just head off up a trail and camp at whatever lake looked appealing. As backpacking became more popular, that had to change. The National Park Service (NPS) and Forest Service (USFS) started requiring reservations to camp at particularly popular lakes. For me, this was a game changer. The freedom to go where I wanted, when I wanted, was lost. Eventually, I also lost interest in backpacking partly for that reason.

The beauty of Antarctica

Heaving-To in the Drake Passage

Initially motoring then sailing, I departed Stancomb Cove and Deception Island on January 30, heading northwest and passing Smith Island and Snow Island, which I could easily see under clear skies, unlike before.

Not surprisingly, the weather forecast changed dramatically after I left Deception Island. I continued to sail northwest, trying to put in substantial westing because I knew the winds and currents in the Drake Passage would push me east as I got farther north.

Two days north of Deception Island I had a significant equipment failure. While tacking the boat (moving the sails from one side to the other) I lost control of the heavy Schaefer boom. It slammed against the shrouds while pulling on the main sheet with substantial force. The force was enough to completely break apart one of the blocks that controls the main sheet. This was the second time one of these blocks had failed. The main sheet rigging that Allures provided with *Phywave* was designed for conventional booms that are much lighter than the Schaefer furling boom. Given that, I guess it was not really surprising the Schaefer boom could exceed the design limits of the main sheet block system.

I could not start sailing again until I replaced the broken block, which turned out to be a challenge. In the rough, cold seas I was experiencing, I had to remove the old standup block and fit the new block, which entailed removing small parts and replacing them. It can not be done while wearing gloves. It took almost an hour with my bare hands to get this done. Fortunately, I could reach the broken block by unzipping a dodger panel, so I didn't have to go out on deck to finish the replacement. It still left me with cold, numb fingers and hands. It was not frostbite but it still took a few weeks after I returned to Puerto Williams for my hands and fingers to feel and flex like normal.

I ordered *Phywave* with a boom brake that is meant to control the speed at which the boom can move. I failed to have the boom brake line tight while I tacked the boat, leading to this incident. I resolved to more conscientiously lock down the boom brake at all times. My tacking/jibing procedure thus became a two-step process: I would first center the boom with the main sheet and then lock down the boom brake line. Then I would turn the boat and let the main sheet and boom brake line out as the sail filled. I no longer let the boom fly across the boat from one side to the other in one action, even with the boom brake engaged to slow down that motion.

My timing for crossing the Drake Passage northbound didn't work out very well. A weather system with high winds and waves was forecast to move through the northern part of the Drake Passage, north of 60 degrees south latitude, on Friday, February 3, then move farther east on Saturday. With that in mind, I left Deception Island on Monday thinking I would sail slow, north and west, and come in behind it, sailing north on Saturday with the better weather that was forecast.

Well, the weather system slowed down and didn't peak until Saturday, February 4. In addition, I neglected to consider the wave forecast, which had ocean swell heights peaking above 6 meters on Saturday afternoon. All this meant I really didn't want to continue north into high seas until late Saturday or early Sunday. It also meant I should have left Deception Island several days later than I did, like Thursday or Friday.

Given those circumstances, I needed to slow down and delay south of 60 degrees south latitude to let the worst of the weather system pass north of me. As a described before, the way to do that in a sailboat is a technique called "heaving-to." In this case, I stopped the boat by a reefed configuration of sails and locked the helm hard to port so the boat wants to turn to port, but it can't because of the sail set, so it stops moving forward. The boat lies with the bow about 45 to 50 degrees off the wind and just drifts backward at 1 to 2 knots to the northeast. Heaving-to is an old, time-tested technique for safely riding out high winds and seas.

Part of the reason for heaving-to is that I really had no useful direction to sail. Going south would have taken me farther from the bad weather but farther from my destination. Going north would have taken me closer to my destination but closer to the worst of the weather. Going east or west wouldn't have improved my situation. So, to paraphrase from the famous movie, sometimes doing nothing is a cool hand. I hoped that delaying 48 hours would give me a better weather situation when I started sailing north again.

Return from Antarctica

I returned to Puerto Williams from my voyage to Antarctica on February 10, with *Phywave* safely rafted up at Micalvi. At that point I was pretty sure I had become the first person to both fly and sail solo to Antarctica.

The voyage south to Antarctica was relatively smooth sailing. The voyage back north across the Drake Passage turned out to be brutal. The few days I spent heaving-to to remain south of the stubborn storm at my north was not enough. I eventually had to start moving north to avoid getting caught by the next weather system moving in from the west. The route map shows the crazy zigzag path my boat took returning north compared to my route going south.

As the seas from the west moderated a bit, I was able to make steady progress. That came to an end when I had another serious equipment failure. While I was trying to get some sleep, the furling line on my genoa headsail snapped in winds blowing at 30+ knots, causing the entire sail to roll out and send the boat ripping along at high speed, essentially out of control. After considering various ways to get the sail down, including dropping it with the halyard, I was able to climb out on the violently bouncing bow, frigid seawater splashing over me, and attach a new line to the remaining line on the furler drum. With that additional line I was able to get the sail rolled back in. I think I earned my sailing stripes with that one. The furler line was now an ad hoc combination of two lines connected with a carabiner. I didn't have a replacement furler line on board or the motivation to reeve a new line back on the drum. As such, the genoa was no longer available to me, so sailing slowed down significantly. Eventually I passed the latitude of Cabo de Hornos (Cape Horn) where I was technically out of the Drake Passage and back among the islands of Tierra del Fuego.

To break up my return voyage to Puerto Williams, I decided to anchor at Isla Picton where there is a great natural harbor and an outpost for the Chilean Armada. My initial attempt at anchoring there resulted in so much kelp on the anchor that I instead chose to tie to a small mooring buoy available near the Armada outpost. It took me several attempts to pick up the mooring but eventually I snagged it. I had a restful night with basically no wind. When I dropped the mooring the next morning, I realized that somehow the mooring line had gotten fouled in my propeller. I don't know if this happened while the boat was drifting around at night or if I inadvertently drove over the mooring line when I tried to leave after dropping it. Anyway, I was stuck, unable to go anywhere. Although I had a dry suit, gloves and boots to go into cold water on

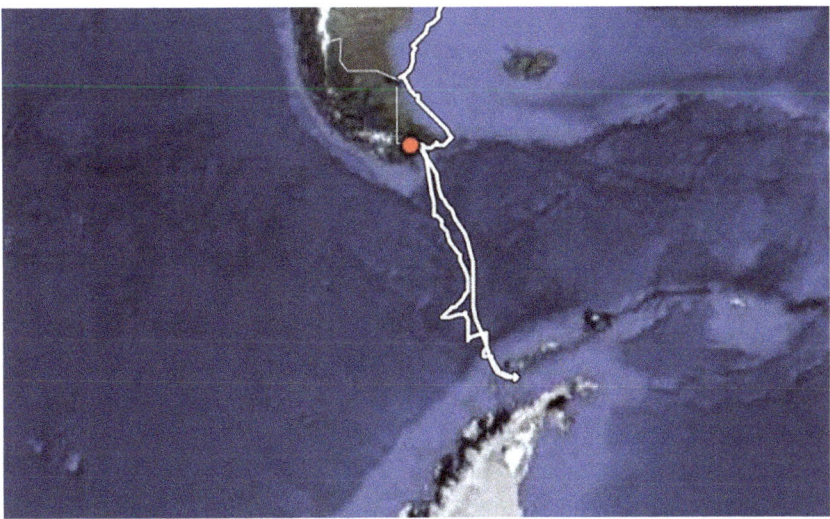

Sailing routes south and north (zigzag) to Antarctica

board, at the time I didn't carry any scuba diving gear on board so I couldn't go under the boat to cut the line free. I contacted the man at the Armada outpost at Isla Picton by VHF radio and told him my problem, that I needed a diver to cut me free. He told me a navy patrol cutter was coming the following day on a regularly scheduled supply visit to the outpost. The cutter would have divers on board who could help me. The cutter did arrive the next day, but not until late afternoon. I was hoping they'd get there in the morning so I could move on to Puerto Williams that day. The Armada divers did cut the propeller free, followed by me dropping the anchor, resigned to spending another night at Isla Picton.

From Isla Picton I had contacted Lalo, the OCC port officer at Puerto Williams, by email with my arrival time. He was monitoring my VHF radio conversation with the Armada, which must be notified of the arrival of any boat or ship. As I approached Micalvi, Lalo came out to greet me in his dinghy with another sailor who climbed aboard *Phywave* to help with the mooring lines to once again raft up with other boats. Lalo was making a video of my arrival with his cellphone and later interviewed me from his dinghy after I had rafted up. A solo voyage to Antarctica is very unusual, so he wanted a video record of my accomplishment, which he later sent to me via WhatsApp.

When I reflect on my return voyage from Antarctica, I see it as a cascade of equipment failures, poor decisions on my part, and bad luck. It was a relief to finally be back at Micalvi even though I don't particularly like the place. I was happy to visit my favorite restaurant and enjoy the pisco sours they make just the way I like them.

To celebrate my successful but difficult solo voyage to Antarctica, I also baked the French vanilla cake with vanilla frosting I had considered making at Deception Island. I almost never use the little propane oven on the boat but it was ideal for this. I invited sailors on neighboring boats to come over and share the celebration cake.

Problems with the Power Distribution

While at Isla Picton a substantial electrical problem cropped up. The cold, moist climate of Tierra del Fuego results in substantial condensation inside a boat. While I was sleeping in my bunk, water drops would form on the ceiling above me and drip on my face. That was annoying, but the bigger problem was condensation running down the surfaces inside the boat and into critical electronics, causing corrosion and eventually short circuits.

In building their boats, Allures installed a separate computerlike network to control the operation of all the electronics in the boat. The network is made by a French company called Scheiber. Using a convenient touch screen at the nav station, I can turn various systems and components on and off by sending signals via the network to remote power units located throughout the boat. Normally, this is a very efficient way to distribute and control 12-volt power. However, it does rely on the Scheiber network hubs and other modules to operate correctly.

While at Isla Picton I noticed that the light switches were working erratically. The gauges showing fuel and water tank levels on the touch screen no longer appeared. More seriously, my ability to turn on the chartplotters, radios and autopilot no longer functioned from the touch screen. I could still turn them on by finding the appropriate power module for each—often located behind a panel installed with screws—and manually pressing a switch to supply them with power. It was a very troubling situation I had to get resolved once the boat was back in Puerto Williams.

I contacted Vincent Mauger in technical support at Allures. After telling him the problems I was experiencing, we concluded that the communication links of the Scheiber network must be shorted out somewhere. He gave me advice on how to systematically disconnect sections of the network to isolate the location of the short. It took some time to do this, but I eventually identified a network signal distribution hub as the source of the problem. Pulling it out and opening it up, I discovered the copper tracings on the circuit board had been corroded by condensation and shorted together. I used a small flathead screwdriver to scrape away the corrosion. By reinstalling the hub after that I got the network working again, but clearly that was only a temporary solution. I needed a replacement hub, and as I additionally discovered, a replacement power distribution unit located next to the hub had also shorted out due to corrosion. It would have been unwise to continue my voyage with such a bush fix in place, so I arranged for Allures to send replacements to my home on Bainbridge Island where I would soon return.

Taking a Break

After my victory in sailing solo to Antarctica, and because I had been on the boat and sailing since the preceding August, I decided to take a break and return home for a while. Leaving the boat at Micalvi with Lalo agreeing he would check on it from time to time, I flew out of Puerto Williams on Monday, February 20, and arrived at my home on Bainbridge Island, on February 22. It happened to be colder when I arrived at home than it was in Antarctica! I was not sure how long I would be home but several weeks for sure. I had a list of things to bring back to the boat and a tall stack of mail to go through. Being that time of year, I had tax returns to prepare and file and a few other time-sensitive things that needed attention.

The next leg of my voyage would be from Puerto Williams north through the canals and fjords of Patagonia to Puerto Montt, which would be my departure point for crossing the Pacific. The scenery along this route is apparently spectacular—I remember flying over part of it when I flew my plane a couple of times between Puerto Montt and Punta Arenas. In my initial naïveté about the area and the sailing conditions, I assumed I could sail this solo with many anchorages along the way. Having now spent a fair amount of time in Puerto Williams and discussed this passage with very seasoned sailors in the region, I came to the conclusion that doing this trip solo would be very difficult, with potentially serious damage to the boat if things went wrong. Although people have done it solo, the experienced sailors I talked to wouldn't try it solo themselves. There are many narrow anchorages where shore lines are needed to secure the boat. Setting shore lines solo is a challenge, as I described before. It's something I've done in the past but in settled weather with no real wind to push the boat out of position once I leave in the dinghy to connect the lines to shore. In addition to the anchor, the shore lines stabilize and hold the boat's position and orientation.

The weather conditions along this route are also particularly unfavorable during this time of year, with very volatile, gusty, wet weather and mostly headwinds. Very little sailing can be done; most of the passage is done by motoring. I've expressed before how I dislike running the engine due to the noise.

Taking all these factors into account, I decided I would not try to do this passage solo. With that decision made, I further decided to hire a crew to take *Phywave* to Puerto Montt, a crew from Australia a friend recommended with many years of experience doing Antarctic charters and sailing the waters of Tierra del Fuego and Patagonia. The plan was for them to take *Phywave* to Puerto Montt while I was home for a break.

This decision meant I wouldn't be able to claim sailing around the world solo because I would miss crossing a few degrees of longitude (roughly between 67.62 degrees and 72.93 degrees west). I can make up for that gap at the end of my voyage by sailing across the Caribbean to Florida. A solo circumnavigation was still possible. As with flying around the world, sailing around the world means crossing all the longitude lines (meridians) and, for some, crossing the equator twice.

Of course, my core objective was sailing solo to seven continents. Having a crew take the boat along an inshore route from Puerto Williams to Puerto Montt in South America doesn't compromise that goal. As I began my break, I had sailed solo to four continents with three to go—Australia, Asia, and North America. I left from North America, so I couldn't yet count that one until I'd sailed there from someplace else. There's nothing official about any of this. I'm pretty much deciding myself what it means to sail solo to seven continents. It's a great adventure regardless of how it's described.

13

Puerto Montt

When I left Puerto Williams on February 20, I was pretty burned out on sailing and living on the boat. The preceding seven months had been intense sailing, for me at least, covering more than 12,000 nm, two Atlantic Ocean crossings and landings on four continents, culminating in a challenging solo voyage to Antarctica and back. I was due for a break.

I originally planned to be at home for six weeks, that timing meant to line up with meeting the delivery crew I hired to move my boat from Puerto Williams to Puerto Montt. In retrospect I realized six weeks would not have been long enough for a number of reasons.

There was a problem with the first delivery crew I hired. That crew consisted of an older Australian sailor with extensive sailing experience in Tierra del Fuego and Antarctica as well as his home waters; that sailor's adult son, also very experienced in these areas; and the son's girlfriend, sailing experience unknown. I thought this was a good choice. As it turned out they did a very poor job of planning the voyage. They booked outbound flights from Puerto Montt that left them only about five weeks to complete the trip. Similarly, they only brought about four weeks of provisions with them. It was not nearly enough time or provisions given the highly variable and difficult weather that's encountered along this route, weather that would certainly delay them at various times. After going only 80 nm in two days and getting pinned down by bad weather for about a week, they abandoned the voyage and returned to

Puerto Williams in *Phywave* with a variety of complaints (excuses). I encouraged them to refuel, reprovision and change their outbound flights to provide more time, but they chose to walk off the job instead. Given this sailor's reputation, I expected him to be trustworthy, complete the job I hired him for and do what he promised to do. Clearly it was a mistake to rely on him.

Mauro and his crew in Puerto Montt

When I contacted him later, he refused to refund the money I had paid him to make the delivery. He used that money for plane tickets from Australia to Puerto Williams for the three of them. In response, I refused to reimburse him for about US$3,000 he spent on fuel, provisions and other expenses in Puerto Williams. For refusing to refund the money I paid him to deliver my boat to Puerto Montt as promised, less what he paid for expenses, he proved himself to be not only untrustworthy but also dishonest.

Fortunately, I was able to hire a replacement delivery crew within a few weeks of the Australian crew's failed attempt. Mauro Carrizo is a Chilean captain in Puerto Williams with his own boat, *Serendipia*, he uses for charter trips to the canals and fjords of Tierra del Fuego and south Patagonia. When

I first arrived at Micalvi in Puerto Williams in January, *Serendipia* was the boat I tied alongside. Mauro's family was on board at the time—his young daughter handed me an Oreo cookie across the railing. It was a nice welcome to Micalvi. Mauro gave me a fair, all-inclusive price for taking my boat to Puerto Montt along with two crew members he would hire. Mauro and his crew left Puerto Williams on April 15 and arrived in Puerto Montt on May 11, taking just 26 days to make the voyage and conclusively demonstrating there were no problems with *Phywave* (which was among the Australian's excuses for not completing his delivery). If you are thinking of taking a charter cruise in Tierra del Fuego or southern Patagonia on a sailboat, I can highly recommend Mauro. His website is *https://www.serendipia-sailing.com/en*.

Having to hire a replacement crew delayed my schedule about six weeks, but it was an additional six weeks at home I needed. It really took that long for me to feel re-energized about getting back to the boat and sailing across the Pacific. It also opened up an opportunity that I hadn't expected.

Starlink

When I left *Phywave* in Puerto Williams, I had a long list of things I needed to bring back. One of them was a Starlink dish. I had friends on yachts who were using Starlink dishes with great success in Patagonia, Brazil and other parts of South America. I decided to buy one and temporarily set it up at home to see how well it worked.

I bought the Starlink Global Roam package. The dish itself is just 12" × 20" and easy to set up. The hardware cost about US$700 but the "best effort" global service plan is US$200/month. "Best effort" means "you get what you get" in terms of speed. At times at home I got a download speed of greater than 100 Mbps, more typically 30–50 Mbps. Not super-fast but certainly adequate and still vastly better than the Iridium GO! I was then using on board. The Iridium GO! is pathetically slow (with a speed of less than 2 Kbps) and uses a restrictive Iridium internet portal that supports a very limited number of apps. It's really impractical to use for anything more than text emails and downloading compressed weather forecast GRIB files. The Roam service plan is a month-to-month plan, so I can stop and restart the service (and monthly cost) to suit the way I intend to use it.

I wouldn't want Starlink for a permanent installation at home since I have an optical fiber connection providing as much data speed as I'm willing to pay for. Instead, my plan was to take the Starlink dish back to the boat, assuming I could get it through Chilean Customs without too much drama.

Large suitcases packed for return to Chile. The Starlink dish is in the center

Many people have modified the Starlink disk antennas to suit particular purposes. There are a number of videos on YouTube of people removing or disabling the motors in their dishes and mounting them horizontally on the top of RVs, vans and boats. Apparently the Starlink satellite constellation is now dense enough that this works about as well as the motor-steered dish and obviously would be mechanically much simpler, with less wind resistance. I was considering doing this but was hesitant because it involves cutting the plastic shell and resealing it into a new horizontal mount of some kind. Given it's going to be on a boat with big waves—I've had waves break over the whole boat, flooding the deck and cockpit—having it be watertight is an important criterion. Some ad hoc mounting work would be required at the boatyard in Puerto Montt where my boat was headed.

There was also the issue of using it offshore since the service plan says land only. There is supposedly a geofence so it won't work when the boat is about 12 nm offshore, or so they say. However, I've heard reports of people using Starlink while crossing the Pacific on yachts, so it remained to be seen if the geofence really kills service offshore or if a different plan would provide service.

I originally bought the Standard dish, which is designed for home or portable use. It's not really intended for use on boats. After that purchase Starlink chaos began. While I was at home, they significantly lowered the price of hardware and airtime plans for their Maritime package. The Maritime package consists of a larger flat dish. A bigger antenna aperture results in a narrower radiation beam, more gain, lower sidelobes and wider pointing angle range; i.e., a better antenna. It is also designed to be mounted flat and pointed straight up, making it more rugged than the Standard dish, which is on a motorized pole mount and not meant to be used in motion. With the big price reduction, I decided to return the Standard dish for a full refund and buy the Maritime package instead. I had a good place to mount the big dish on *Phywave*'s aft arch. The only real downside was that it draws two to three times more power than the standard dish—always an important consideration on a modern sailboat that relies on electrical power and battery storage for just about everything from navigation to radios to the autopilot. Inconveniently, all Starlink dishes were powered by 120 VAC, which meant I would need to use an inverter to power it from the 12-volt batteries on the boat. Of course, the boat is already equipped with a large inverter, but I rarely turned it on. I didn't want to use it just to run Starlink, so instead I bought a small sine wave inverter to run Starlink only. The small inverter has a convenient on-off switch to stop the power drain when I'm not using Starlink. Others have gone a step further and used various components to power Starlink directly from the 12 volts on the boat, bypassing the 120 VAC power supply. Making that conversion involved more work than I wanted to do.

Starlink installation

With the big Starlink dish and its components, and the other gear I already planned to bring back to *Phywave*, I had three big suitcases I needed to get to Chile as checked luggage. I shuffled things from one to another until they all weighed about 50 pounds. Fortunately, I was flying on Delta to Santiago, in the Delta One cabin, so two bags flew for free and the third cost me US$200, still vastly cheaper and simpler than trying to ship them to Chile. Even so, for someone who has flown commercially, and in my own plane, all over the world for years with nothing more than a single small carry-on duffle bag, all this luggage felt like a hassle to move around. Upon arrival in Santiago, I was directed to the Customs inspection line where my poor Spanish served me well. After some back and forth, and using Google Translate, with the Customs agent, who became visibly frustrated trying to understand the purpose of what was in my cases, "para mi velero!" I explained, she waved me through.

Rather than try to get all the gear on the local flight in a small plane to Puerto Montt, no doubt with high excess-luggage charges if they'd take the bags at all, I decided to rent a car and drive to Puerto Montt from the Santiago airport. It was the right move. The big cases fit easily into the car. It was a pleasant two-day drive south with an overnight stop in Chillán. I found very pretty countryside along the way, driving first through vineyard country followed by farms and managed forests in hills farther south. Having flown over this part of Chile in my own plane three times, it was interesting to see it from the ground level.

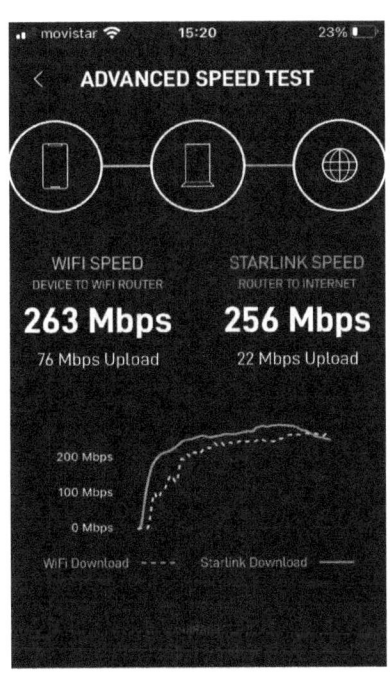

Starlink speeds in Puerto Montt

Progress in Puerto Montt

By agreement, Mauro and his crew had left *Phywave* in the Club Náutico Reloncaví marina. Upon arriving by car at the marina, the first task was to get the three large cases down the gangway to the floating docks (muelles) and unpack them. Fortunately, everything inside seemed to have survived the long flight from Seattle, including the big Starlink dish. After unpacking them, I gave away the empty cases since there wasn't any room for them on *Phywave*.

I expected to be at Reloncaví at least another three to four weeks getting various maintenance tasks done, including application of new antifouling bottom paint and, of course, installing Starlink. The marina at Reloncaví is really nice compared to what I'd experienced recently at Mar del Plata and Micalvi. I looked forward to getting *Phywave* ready for the next chapter in this solo voyage to seven continents.

Hauling *Phywave*

I was most curious to see how well the Starlink dish would work, so in the first few days after arriving I spent my time getting the dish mounted on the arch; running the cable through a new hole I drilled in the deck, with a waterproof gasket fitting; and mounting the power supply, router and small inverter to power the Starlink components. I connected the inverter to a 30-amp circuit breaker I had already installed for the Icom IC-7300 SSB radio.

The dish itself was mounted to a post welded onto the stern arch next to the solar panels. A Starlink-provided pipe mount I brought with me slid perfectly over this post. The mount is normally intended to be held in place by set screws. I don't rely on set screws to hold anything—they too easily work loose—so I drilled a hole through the mount and the pipe and through-bolted it using a long stainless steel bolt and locknut I brought with me from home.

The installation fired right up with download speeds greater than 200 Mbps. I was very pleased with it. I planned to keep my Iridium GO! account active for a while as a backup until I could see exactly how reliable Starlink would be at sea.

Next on the list was hauling the boat out of the water and putting it on blocks on land (called "on the hard" in the boating world) so new antifouling

New antifouling paint on *Phywave*

paint could be applied. When it came out of the water I was surprised at the fairly poor condition of the paint. The boat had only been in the water for a little over a year. I was even more surprised that the zinc anode on the hub of the propeller was completely eaten away. A zinc anode is meant to be slowly eaten away by the natural electrolysis process that occurs when a boat is in salt water, and that is meant to happen before corrosion can start eroding other metal fittings like the propeller or thru-hull fittings. Normally the zincs would be replaced when they're about 50% gone. On close examination, there was no corrosion on the propeller, and the hull zincs were still in good shape. I replaced the propeller hub zinc with a spare I had, but I would have to keep a closer eye on it in the future and replace it sooner if needed. It really should not have been eaten away completely in a year.

Since I really hate sanding and painting, I hired a local contractor to do the antifouling paint. After the entire hull was sanded, two coats of antifouling paint went on. There were rain showers off and on but the painters got some lucky breaks with dry weather to complete the job.

After the boat was out of the water for about 10 days the travel lift came to pick it up and put it back in the water. I drove it back to the same marina berth where it was before. The two travel lifts they have at Reloncaví are small compared to others I've seen, so I needed to disconnect both backstays to allow the lift to drive close enough to the center of the boat to pick it up. I've never been comfortable with the backstays off, especially with some strong winds blowing across the marina, but there was still plenty of tension holding the mast up from the shrouds and forestays. Still, not ideal; I was happy to reconnect the backstays once the boat was back at the dock.

It's pretty uncomfortable staying on a boat when it's on the hard, especially if there's no place to plug in and get power. A ladder is also needed to get from the ground to the deck. I used the telescoping ladder I have on board which I also used to access the Schaefer boom. However, instead of staying on the boat while it was on the hard, I booked a cabana at Cabañas Tungulú very near the marina on the hill overlooking the Tenglo Channel and beyond—a fantastic view. It was a very pleasant respite that spoiled me, I think. Life on the boat was a downgrade by comparison.

Engine and Fuel

There was still a lot to do. Next came changing the engine oil and filter, along with the paper filters in the Racor primary diesel fuel filters that are ahead of the fine secondary fuel filter on the engine. I also needed to sort out the many jerry cans (bidones) of diesel left on board by Mauro and his crew, a few just partially full, five of which were added by Mauro after I left the boat in Puerto Williams. Some of that fuel looked pretty dirty, with small bits of what looked like rust at the bottom. I'm not sure where Mauro got that diesel but I decided to discard it. Money is not an issue and there's no reason to invite problems crossing the Pacific by using diesel of dubious origin. Of course, I have a separate funnel filter I use to put diesel into the main diesel tank from the jerry cans, a funnel filter I actually used to carry on my plane. Once I had the diesel sorted out, I filled up the main tank and all the bidones I decided to keep. That gave me a total fuel load on departure of about 850 liters. Since the next leg would be almost entirely sailing—and hopefully I wouldn't get becalmed too long in the Pacific—that fuel load should be much more than needed, certainly more than most people would carry.

Mainsail and Boom Repairs

After the engine maintenance was completed, I turned to repairs on the running rigging and sails. I still hadn't raised the mainsail yet so I didn't know its exact condition, but I expected batten replacement and minor sewing repairs would be needed. The canvas bimini and panel connecting it to the dodger had been damaged by high winds sailing south in the Atlantic, so they also needed some patching and sewing work.

There was a sailmaker at Reloncaví who helped me take the mainsail down and carry it to his loft a few hundred meters away. All the sails on *Phywave* are Hydra Net sails, which I chose for their outstanding durability. However, the strong Hydra Net core is covered with other material that had been damaged by UV exposure. Patches were required to fix that. There was also damage to luff tape around the places where the battens end. This is essentially the same damage I noticed and had fixed in Lanzarote. The sailmaker there used Kevlar to patch the torn places because it is strong and very thin. The sailmaker at Reloncaví didn't have Kevlar, so he just used regular Dacron sailcloth to patch the luff tape. This turned out to be a big mistake as I discuss later. Anytime a patch is used on the luff tape, especially thicker material, it causes more drag raising or lowering the sail in the very narrow hinged tack used with the Schaefer boom. Ideally, the luff tape should be a continuous piece that is tightly sewn so there are no edges, like patches have, to peel back

With Curtis and Kate on Chiloé Island

as the tape is moved up and down the track. As my voyage progressed, I was learning more about the difficulties and limitations of the Schaefer system.

As I discussed in chapter 9, the U-bolt that holds the clew of the mainsail had sheared off. The Spectra line I used to replace it had been in there ever since, even during my tough voyage to Antarctica. I had a replacement U-bolt brought to me in Puerto Williams, but there was no practical way to do the replacement at Micalvi, which requires completely disassembling the end of the boom. In calmer conditions and tied to a dock at Reloncaví, I was able to use the telescoping ladder and climb up on the boom, disassemble the drum, replace the U-bolt and get it all back together the way it should be. It was gratifying that the bush fix using the Spectra line had actually worked quite well through all the rough conditions since Mar del Plata, but I was happy to have the boom back together the way it was designed.

My stay at the Reloncaví marina stretched from my original estimate of four weeks to six and a half weeks. The repairs to my mainsail took longer than expected and were followed by a week of bad weather offshore I didn't want to bash into. Even though I wasn't making progress on my voyage I was comfortable there with a rental car. I also got to spend time with some good friends, Curtis and Kate, whom I first met in Puerto Williams. They are sailing *Sweet Ruca*, funding their travels with a great YouTube channel called Sailing Sweet Ruca that had more than 110 episodes at the time. They put a lot of effort into producing high quality videos of their adventures. They even interviewed me for an upcoming episode because my mission to sail to seven continents solo is unique and I'm in the same demographic (old) as many of their viewers. On one of our excursions, we took the ferry across to Chiloé Island for the day to have a look around and stop for a seafood lunch at a restaurant overlooking the sea near the town of Ancud. *Sweet Ruca* would also be heading across the Pacific to French Polynesia but not leaving Puerto Montt until August. I may see them again somewhere down the line. It's not unusual in the cruising community to once again encounter a boat and crew you first met some time before.

14

Patagonia to the Marquesas

I was finally underway again, sailing north along the coast of Chile toward the southeast trade winds, a westward flowing river of wind that would take me across the Pacific toward French Polynesia. I expected to pick up those winds somewhere around 15–20 degrees south latitude, maybe farther south.

I changed my intended destination from my original planned route. I was going to skip Rapa Nui (Easter Island) since I already spent a week there in 2013 visiting the moai and other interesting archaeological sites. The anchorages there are also renowned for being problematic, with no real protected coves or harbors. A boat is exposed to the open sea and rolling swells most of the time. Changing wind directions move from one side of the island to another, so it's usually necessary to move the boat every few days to stay on the lee side.

I was also skipping the Pitcairn Islands group (four islands). Though I've never been there, it has the same issue with poor anchorages that are open to the sea.

Finally, I was late getting going on that leg so to pick up time I'd reduced the number of stops. I decided to sail to the Gambier Islands atoll in French Polynesia, weather permitting. The anchorages of this archipelago are in the lagoon inside the outer reef forming the atoll. As the 16th-century mariners discovered, it's a bad idea to sail there directly from southern Chile and risk getting becalmed in the high-pressure region that usually dominates that part of the South Pacific. The better strategy is to sail north along the coast of Chile to pick up the trade winds, as discussed before. It's the long way around, though, so I estimated around 4,200–4,400 nm to Gambier, a passage of 35–40 days, which would have been my longest by far. Once in the trade winds I expected it to be pretty smooth downwind sailing with consistent 15-to-20 knot winds on the stern. One caveat to that is the climate transition from La Niña to El Niño weather patterns that was occurring at the time. In El Niño years the southeast trade winds tend to be weaker and more variable than in La Niña years.

Exit formalities from Chile at Puerto Montt required me to visit three separate locations for Immigration, Customs, and the Armada office at the port. Since I had already turned in my rental car at the airport, I had to use an Uber to go to these various places a few miles apart and away from the marina. Like they did for my voyage to Antarctica, the Armada issued a zarpe to me, this time for a voyage to French Polynesia. They would only complete the exit formalities the day before I intended to leave. They wanted me to stay at the marina until I actually left, not wander around town after officially exiting Chile. With all the exit stamps and zarpe in hand, I was ready to go.

I left Reloncaví marina on July 7 at first light, around 1200Z. The route to the ocean winds around islands and through various channels where many floating aquatic farms are found. I'm not sure if they're for fish or shellfish—mussels, oysters and clams are popular here. However, they are not lit, or marked on the nautical charts, so unless you're a local and know where they are it's treacherous to navigate these channels at night.

I'm happy to say my work on the boat in Puerto Montt, especially cleaning and redoing the antifouling paint, paid good dividends. Motoring at 1,750 rpm I was getting a boat speed of nearly 6 knots. When I left the boat in Puerto Williams I was getting around 4.5 knots at that power setting. I also think replacing the zinc on the hub of the propeller may have helped. Its cone shape would definitely assist smooth water flow around the propeller, improving its efficiency.

I stopped for an overnight anchorage at Puerto Abtao, about 30 nm west of Puerto Montt, to wait for the ebb tide passing through the Chacao Channel which leads to the ocean. The flood and ebb currents through the channel can be fast, up to 9 knots at times, so it's essential to pass through westward on the ebb tide. Motoring through the channel on the evening of

July 8 I enjoyed a speed boost from the ebb current of over 6 knots, a total SOG of more than 12 knots. Once through the channel, I had to work my way west and north around a tight little low-pressure system that had popped up. Winds around low-pressure systems blow clockwise in the Southern Hemisphere.

Then it was a matter of sailing north for the next several days and getting into the trade winds as soon as possible. At least the weather was improving compared to Puerto Montt, where it was rainy, cold and windy much of the time, with maybe one nice day per week. It was the austral winter so this weather was not unexpected. I was sailing under mostly clear skies to that point, a welcome change I hoped would continue.

Turning the corner and sailing north

One morning I was up early to adjust sails. The stars and moon were brilliant against the deep darkness of the open ocean at night; my old friend, the constellation Orion, was hanging upside down over the eastern horizon waiting for the orange glow hints of the emerging dawn. It was going to be a good day.

Sailing North

The wind and current continued to be favorable as I proceeded north along the west coast of South America. I was reminded of when I had flown along this same coast in my plane in 2013 and 2014. I pulled up the photos I had taken on those flights on my computer. Several great memories emerged: making new friends, the amazing sights of Chile's string of volcanoes, the Atacama Desert and flying over the Nazca Lines in Peru.

Along this stretch much of my sailing was downwind. Fortunately, the autopilot on my boat has a mode where it can be set to maintain a given angle to the wind instead of maintaining a fixed course. This autopilot mode will steer the boat so it always maintains that angle. Sailing downwind, it's important to ensure there isn't an accidental jibe where the boom swings across the boat. By setting the autopilot to maintain a downwind angle to wind of say 165 degrees, for example, it will ensure the boom always remains on the same side of the boat. Even though the boat's heading will wander around to maintain this wind angle, out on the open ocean those changes don't make much difference as long as you're still headed in the right general direction.

Rough waters

I thought that once I crossed 20 degrees south latitude and entered the usual trade wind zone the winds would become steadier and more reliable. That wasn't the case. For several days the wind direction had varied over 50 to 60 degrees and wind speed ranged from 7 knots to 25 knots. The forecast didn't reveal any of this. I hoped that as I moved farther west and north the winds would steady.

I also expected to pick up a following current, the Peru Current, but that hadn't happened yet either. The boat speed through the water had almost always been greater than the SOG, indicating a contrary current. The SOG is determined by GPS position fixes, so it's very accurate. The boat speed through the water is calculated using a little paddlewheel spinning on the bottom of the boat, which is less accurate and can be wildly wrong, or stop altogether.

Often the paddlewheel will get fouled with bits of weed or other things in the water that inhibit it from spinning freely, so it usually reports boat speeds that are too low. It's unusual for it to be too high. If the paddlewheel calibration is off, I can adjust it but I need a measured course in still water, or to run the course in both directions, to calibrate it. That's not going to happen at sea. For the meantime, I decided to live with it. The SOG is the one that ultimately matters since that tells me how fast I was getting to my destination.

Looking at longer range weather patterns along my route, it appeared that the El Niño weather pattern might require changing my destination from Gambier Atoll to the Marquesas. I wouldn't know for a few weeks but at that point it looked like I would encounter difficult weather and contrary winds by turning south to Gambier at 23 degrees south latitude. In contrast, the Marquesas were in the middle of the trade winds I was now joining. The Marquesas were farther away than Gambier but closer in terms of time if those wind patterns held. It felt ironic to be considering a change in destination to the Marquesas after considering and rejecting other South Pacific destinations. I might have first heard of the Marquesas in the Stephen Stills song "Southern Cross." A great song.

I'd had one failure since leaving Puerto Montt. The top fiberglass batten in the mainsail broke. I had spare batten material that I inserted in the batten pocket, but it needed to be cut to the right length with a hacksaw. This can

Sailing downwind with the genoa winged out on the whisker pole

be a little tricky if you do it while in place, holding the batten with one hand with the saw in the other hand and holding on to the boat with your third hand. My dad, who was in the navy in World War II, said sailors have a rule: "One hand for yourself, one hand for the ship." What if the ship needs two hands? If you're in the navy you get another sailor. That wasn't an option on *Phywave*. I decided it would be less convenient, but safer, to mark the batten length, pull it out and take it back to the cockpit to cut it.

With the batten cut to length and inserted in the batten sleeve, the next step was to push a strap attached to the sail into the batten pocket. The strap has Velcro on one side and wraps around the end of the batten, which is then shoved deep into the batten pocket where the opposite piece of Velcro is located. Usually, this system is sufficient to hold the batten in place, but as I mentioned before, on this voyage I'd had problems with the battens working their way loose. I started sewing them in when I was in Horta as described in chapter 4.

Otherwise, all was well on *Phywave*. It was just a matter of turning the miles, day after day, week after week.

Squid Boat

Crossing the Atlantic it was common to find dead flying fish on the deck, even in the cockpit, when I first came up the companionway in the morning. I've seen these flying fish spend a fair amount of time airborne, skimming across the water, so it was not a great surprise to see some of them end up on my boat. But I didn't know what was up with all the squid that started showing up on the boat in the Pacific. I found out later they can sort of fly, but before that I assumed they were getting tossed up by the waves that routinely hit the hull of *Phywave* and broke over the deck. Most are less than 6 or 8 inches long and don't weigh very much. Water could easily toss them onto the boat. However, one day a really big one landed on deck, about 18 inches long with tentacles, weighing over a pound. Somehow it got wedged under the headsail halyards. I tossed it overboard and hoped for a short, intense rain squall to wash away the bloody mess it left. After a few days the dead flying fish were also back, increasing the diversity of the seafood menu I was inadvertently gathering. Even though some friends suggested it by email, I was not inclined to eat any of this stuff. It looked gross and I had no idea if eating it hours after it left the seawater and died was even safe.

Squid on my deck

Many cruisers fish while at sea. They may have poles and reels, or they may simply drag a line with bait off the stern of the boat. I've heard stories and seen photos of impressive fish caught this way. Of course, once caught they need to be cleaned and fileted, most easily done with a table mounted on the boat designed for that purpose along with the sharp knives to filet the fish. I used to fish as a kid but never had any interest as an adult—way too boring and inactive. I will say I've enjoyed sashimi on other people's boats while at anchor in a few places, so I was able to enjoy fresh fish on occasion without doing the work.

I passed 80 degrees west longitude on July 21, 840 nm due south of the Galapagos Islands, a very interesting place I visited for a week in 2007. From my position there remained about 2,950 nm to Nuku Hiva in the Marquesas Islands, about 24 days averaging 5 knots. My boat trip log said I'd already sailed 2,450 nm since leaving Puerto Montt, so this would turn out to be a 5,400-nm passage when I finally arrived there, more than twice as long as the longest passage I made in the Atlantic Ocean.

Long Days Downwind at Sea

I was approaching the first anniversary of my departure from Norfolk, Virginia, where I topped up the fuel tank and had stayed overnight. I had set off eastward the following morning, August 2, 2022, headed for the Azores. It was time to reflect on where I had been and how far I had come.

Before this trip, I'd sailed for many years but in relatively protected waters removed from the ocean, like around Puget Sound and among the channels, islands and harbors north of there. This was my first excursion offshore, my first time being underway alone at night, but fortified by naïveté and blind faith, I had sailed on into the night, asleep in my bunk with the autopilot in command. It's only water out there, a vast ocean, nothing to run into, I had told myself. That first night was peaceful, the second night I was awakened by a brief, intense rain squall that had me scrambling up on deck with my headlamp on to reduce sails. By the time that was done the squall had moved on and I put the sails up again.

Since those first days of my voyage, I'd learned a lot about sailing, especially ocean sailing. I've had so many adventures that the past year seemed compressed; how could all those things have happened?

Aside from the three-month break I took at home that spring, I'd spent most of the other nine months alone on *Phywave*. I've landed on four continents (Europe, Africa, South America and Antarctica) and in six countries (Portugal, Morocco, Spain, Brazil, Argentina and Chile). The boat's trip log said I'd sailed almost 17,000 nm, a distance that was increasing each day. On the current passage I'd sailed about 3,200 nm from Puerto Montt with 2,200 nm remaining to arrive at Nuku Hiva in the Marquesas Archipelago.

I was sailing west across the Pacific into a setting sun, a common sailor fantasy now real, though I still saw the clouds above me as a pilot would see them, not as a sailor would. With thousands of hours flying solo in my small plane all over the world, I don't think that will ever change. I wouldn't want it to change.

The days on that passage seemed much the same, flowing together with no distinguishing features, the trade wind direction and speed finally steady, a sky that suddenly clouded over then just as quickly brightened to brilliant blue, seemingly at random, followed by nights lit up with a moon waxing full. That sky was the upper half of a world that has the hypnotic, twisting rhythm of the waves beneath. And me in between.

West of Home

On August 11 I sailed west of 122.5 degrees west longitude, which is not important except it's the approximate longitude of my house on Bainbridge

Island. At that point I was happy to note any arbitrary scrap of progress, no matter how insignificant.

There have been many movies with a scene of an 18th-century sailing ship becalmed in an ocean somewhere, drifting around a dead-flat sea, its canvas sails hanging limply from the yardarms in forlorn anticipation of new wind. The crew sits around on deck in whatever hint of shade they can find, or construct with spare sails, as an intense, merciless sun beats down on them. Though there's no breeze to be found on deck it's better than being in the stifling, rank atmosphere below deck. Some kill time whittling or scratching scrimshaw while others sit with their backs against a bulkhead, sweat dripping down their faces, eyes closed, as they try to fill their thoughts with images of home. Some occasionally dip a ladle into a wooden bucket of seawater and pour it over their heads, the brief evaporative cooling lasting seemingly seconds.

One seaman happens to notice a seabird fly by, barely flapping its wings to gain loft. He looks to the top of the mainmast where a pennant is gently stirring. No, it can't be, it's just another tease from Zephyrus. But as he watches, the pennant begins to lift and slowly wave. Others notice him and also look skyward, each with a flicker of hope their windless oblivion is ending. Then the topmost skysail fills with a resounding "whap." Now everyone is looking up as the sails begin to fill with wind from the top down. The crew jump to

Anchored in Baie de Taiohae

their feet; a cheer rises as the ship slowly begins to move through the water. The officer on deck steps up to the helmsman who simply nods that he has steerage. The officer gives an order to turn the ship to take best advantage of the rising wind. The crew gladly scrambles up the masts to adjust sails. Their long drifting nightmare in the doldrums has come to an end.

That was me for a few days as the wind speed fell below 5 knots and its direction wandered over a 50-degree range. The southeast trade winds at that latitude, even much farther south, should have been solid in direction and speed. But that was an El Niño summer, renowned for lighter, variable trade winds. I had firsthand evidence of that. I had to work my way progressively farther north than I ever expected to get around a large patch of dead air hundreds of miles across encroaching from the south. Of course, unlike the 18th-century ships I have "iron wind," an engine I can use to keep making progress. But the engine is loud, and its heat adds to the already 32+ degrees Celsius ambient temperature outside. It's even hotter in the cabin.

I've had to use the generator more than I expected to charge the batteries. The mornings are often filled with low clouds. The sun doesn't rise high enough in the sky to provide much illumination for the solar panels on the stern arch until late in the morning. At that point good charging current would begin and could have lasted until late afternoon except, sailing west, the sails would shadow the solar panels. I found that sailing south in the Atlantic

Phywave **anchored in Baie de Taiohae**

worked out better for solar charging because the sun moved across the beam of the boat and kept the panels illuminated most of the day.

Some wind finally returned as I passed the point 1,000 nm east of Nuku Hiva. From there my revised estimated arrival time was August 20 or 21, depending, as always, on the winds.

Landfall—Je Suis Arrivé!

On the afternoon of August 20 I anchored in Baie de Taiohae on the island of Nuku Hiva in the Marquesas Islands group in French Polynesia after a 5,400 nm, 45-day passage from Puerto Montt, Chile. It was by far the longest passage I'd done, or would need to do, to complete my solo voyage to seven continents and my solo circumnavigation. I dropped anchor among several other boats in the bay. It was a bit rolly, with small swells occasionally coming through the opening of the bay from the ocean. One nearby monohull sailboat had set bow and stern anchors to keep their boat pointed into the incoming swells and reduce side-to-side rolling.

The following morning, I had to go ashore to complete entry formalities for French Polynesia. I had alerted the OCC port officer, Kevin Ellis at Yacht Services, to my arrival. He assisted me along with a few other newly arrived cruisers with the process. Since I was at anchor, it was the first time I had to clear-in to a country using my dinghy to get ashore. As I did in Antarctica, I used my spinnaker halyard to lift my dinghy off the foredeck, where it was strapped down during passage, and then dragged it around to the stern. With it tied by the swim step, I muscled my 6-hp Yamaha outboard motor, weighing more than 60 pounds, out of its stern locker and onto the transom of the dinghy. I then connected the gas tank, primed it and crossed my fingers it would start. Luckily it did start with no drama—not always a sure thing after it had been bumped around at sea during all the days since I last used it.

With Kevin's help, the clearing-in paperwork with the Gendarmerie (police) was quickly done. I was authorized to stay in French Polynesia for up to 90 days. Since French Polynesia is a department of France, the visitor visa rules are pretty much the same as those used in Europe. Some cruisers get long-stay visas and stay here for months, even years. After exploring a few local shops and getting cash at the ATM while ashore, I had my first restaurant meal and beer in a long time!

I planned to stay there about a week to add to my provisions, top off diesel reserves and fill the propane tank I'd been using (the second one was still full). When I'm in a place with resources it makes sense to fill up everything—I'd need it eventually. I'd run my watermaker for a couple of hours while motoring in there so I was set for fresh water. It's always better to run the watermaker while far offshore rather than in a harbor because the seawater is cleaner. In Nuku Hiva I could also get laundry done and dump accumulated garbage from my passage. With chores completed, I was hoping I would have some days to relax, look around and maybe rent a car for a day to tour the island.

Unfortunately, I lost six weeks from my original schedule for various reasons, six weeks I certainly would have liked to have back so that I could take a more leisurely island-hopping route across the Pacific to Australia, which would be my fifth continent. As it was, I needed to keep moving. From where I was, I planned to sail southwest to Rangiroa in the Tuamotus island group and anchor inside the atoll for a couple of days. Then it would be on to Huahine, my last stop in French Polynesia. Having been to Tahiti (Papeete) and Moorea several times over the years, I had no desire to return. These places are crowded with cruising boats and tourists engaged in all sorts of loud, annoying water activities. The locals have also imposed increasingly tight restrictions on where cruising boats can anchor at these islands, as well as at Raiatea and Bora Bora. It's a long-simmering conflict that has seen cruising boats and dinghies sometimes damaged by vengeful locals.

From Huahine I planned to sail directly to Savusavu, Fiji. I really wanted to stop in Tonga (Vava'u), a country I've never visited, and it was on the way to Fiji, but I didn't think I'd have time. It was important to have the boat in a secure location in Australia for the tropical storm season which traditionally begins in November. As I've indicated before, "traditionally" is becoming a broken word when it comes to weather. Climate change is eroding weather patterns that sailors have relied on for centuries.

Exploring Nuku Hiva

After my 45-day, 5,400-nm passage from Puerto Montt, Chile, to the Marquesas I was looking forward to a well-earned break from sailing. My week in Baie de Taiohae was certainly a break from sailing but unfortunately not the relaxing, restorative interlude I hoped it would be.

Typical small grocery store on Nuku Hiva

The bay is reasonably well-protected on three sides but is subject to a fairly continuous swell from the south that will roll the boat back and forth depending on how large the swell is. Even the catamarans I saw at anchor, which are generally less susceptible to this, were rolling around. It wasn't seriously uncomfortable, mostly just annoying.

The swells, and wind waves that sometimes pop up, can make for a bumpy ride in the dinghy from *Phywave* to the place on shore where cruisers can tie up with the other dinghies. I won't call it a dinghy dock because it's just a concrete wall with a couple of ladders and a chain along the top where dinghies can be tied. There isn't a lot of space, especially since local fishermen tie their boats to the same wall, with some using stern ties to buoys. It's easy to get tangled up with the stern ties, as I did once, while coming in with a dinghy.

Dinghy dock (wall)

With not much space for the dinghy, the normal process with two people would be to nose the dinghy to the wall and have the forward person grab the ladder or chain and tie the dinghy to it while the other person keeps the engine running to push the dinghy against the wall. However, being solo, I'm necessarily sitting in the back running the motor, so I have to swing the dinghy sideways to grab the ladder or chain, a challenge in a crowded space.

I'm explaining these details to point out that taking the dinghy to shore was a hassle. Of the seven days I anchored in the bay, I only took the dinghy in on four days. While I was there the bay had only about two dozen boats at anchor, and only about a third of those had people on board. The others were anchored long-term (it's free) while the crews went off somewhere else, even back home for a break. I've seen photos of the bay with more than 50 boats, most with crew on board. That would have made for a vastly more crowded dinghy landing wall than I experienced.

Waterfall on Nuku Hiva

There is a gray sand beach near the dinghy landing that people occasionally use to land their dinghies. I tried that one day instead of the wall. It was more work and sand got everywhere. Even with small swells breaking on the beach it was still some work to push the dinghy out past them to get going back to *Phywave*. Later someone told me there are sometimes small hammerhead sharks in those waters. Great! Apparently, they only come around early in the morning for a wild chum-feeding frenzy when the local fishermen are cleaning and cutting up their catch and throwing the scraps in the water.

Taiohae is the administrative capital of the Marquesas, but even so, there isn't a lot there. Beyond the government buildings there is one really good hotel with 20 bungalows (and no vacancies), a handful of guesthouse/pensione-type places, four or five restaurants, three very small grocery stores and a variety of tourist shops and tour companies. The grocery stores were barely adequate to reprovision the boat, but I could get fresh eggs. In Puerto Montt I bought food for several months, so I really just needed to replace fresh food I had consumed en route to the Marquesas.

The best day I had on Nuku Hiva was Friday, August 25, when I rented a car, had lunch at the upscale four-star hotel with an amazing view of the bay. After lunch I drove around a good portion of the island to see 500-year-old archaeological ruins and small villages nestled at the heads of the many bays around the perimeter of the island. Driving on narrow paved roads up and over steep forested ridges provided spectacular views of the lush forest and tall waterfalls plunging into the deep valleys.

On my first day ashore, I met a couple from Austin at lunch who were sailing a nice 44-foot catamaran. They had arrived in the Marquesas from Panama, as I recall, and had spent two months anchored in Baie de Taiohae. Of course, they knew every place in the town and shared that information with me. However, I didn't see nearly enough in the town, or on the island, to justify staying there that long, especially in an anchorage that was sometimes rolly. Some folks just love to hang out on their boats and have made a lifestyle of it. I guess I'm not among them, instead pursuing my sailing mission.

When the end of my week at Nuku Hiva came, I didn't hesitate to up anchor and move on.

15

French Polynesia

I had no particular desire to visit Papeete or Tahiti, where I had been before, more than once, but sailing circumstances forced me to change my mind. The day after I left Nuku Hiva I had a serious problem with my mainsail; I could only raise it halfway.

I've explained before that the mainsail luff tape, sometimes called a bolt rope, is a rope sewed into the luff (leading edge) of the sail. It was once again giving me problems. The rope fits into a narrow track that is attached to the mast with hinges so the track can rotate. It's critical that the luff tape easily slides up and down the track as the sail is raised and lowered (reefed). Over time the sailcloth that wraps around the luff tape had gotten worn, in some places split open. The first repair on this was done in the Canary Islands, where the sailmaker used Kevlar film to patch over worn places along the luff tape. That worked pretty well since the Kevlar doesn't add much additional diameter to the luff tape. Increasing the diameter of whatever is wrapped around the luff tape, of course, would make it more difficult for it to slide in the narrow track.

The sailmaker in Puerto Montt also attempted to patch the luff tape but didn't have Kevlar film so he used conventional Dacron sailcloth, much thicker than the Kevlar film. This seemed to slide OK when we put the sail back on in Puerto Montt, but the hoisting and reefing action on the sail during the passage to the Marquesas eventually caused the Dacron cloth to bunch up around the luff tape, making it difficult to move the sail up and down the track. I saw what was happening and tried to cut back the bunched-up Dacron but that really didn't work. Finally, the jam got so severe the luff tape jumped out of the track, causing further damage to the cloth covering, essentially shredding it in places. This happened at the third batten down from the top, so I could only raise the main sail that far. It would have been crazy to try to continue my voyage as originally planned with such a major problem with the mainsail.

I decided I needed to pull the sail off, get rid of all the luff tape patches, and have luff tape entirely resewn to the sail. The sail itself was in very good shape. The only sailmaker that I considered competent and equipped to do this work, Tahiti Sails, was in Papeete, the capital of French Polynesia on the island of Tahiti. With that reality, I changed my routing and headed straight for Tahiti, sailing through and bypassing the Tuamotus, which was a great disappointment. I didn't know how long this repair would take and to what extent it would affect my plans to get to Australia by November. I did know that people leave boats needing serious repairs to their hulls, and other repairs, in Papeete for extended periods. The worst case was that Tahiti Sails couldn't make the luff tape replacement and I would have to box up the sail and ship it back to the manufacturer in the US for repair. I'd hand the sail over to Tahiti Sails when I arrived and hopefully have their assessment soon thereafter.

After my 770-nm passage to Tahiti with half a mainsail, I anchored in a place called Venus Point just a few miles north of Papeete, a quiet anchorage protected from east winds, with only two other boats there. This was unlike the area inside the reef around Papeete itself, where there were a large number of boats anchored or on mooring buoys, some derelict, and two large marinas which are perpetually full. The glut of boats in Papeete is another reason I didn't want to go there. Since there was no space in a marina for me, I had to have the boat hauled and put on the hard so I could take down the mainsail and have the repairs done. I didn't want to anchor out with the other boats and try to remove the sail and manage the repair process by commuting to shore in my dinghy.

Oh well—the good and bad come with the mission I set for myself. I booked an ocean-view room at a nice hotel and a rental car so at least I could make the best of the time while I was stuck there.

I had visited Tahiti in 1986 on my first excursion to the South Pacific. I had flown to Fiji first, where I spent a week at the Musket Cove Island Resort and Marina on Malolo Island off the west coast of the main island of Viti

Levu. I remember it was a very short flight in a very small plane from the main international airport. That was long before I became a pilot myself in 1998.

From Fiji I flew to Papeete and took the ferry across to a resort on Moorea where I spent several more days before returning to Papeete for my flight home. The bar on the ferry had a sign reading "Free beer tomorrow." I thought that was clever at the time but I've since seen that sign in many other bars.

I returned to Papeete in 1999 for a cruise on a relatively small cruise ship (700 passengers) run by Renaissance Cruises, which went bankrupt in 2002 after the attacks on 9/11 undermined the cruise industry. It was a millennial cruise, the idea being to cruise across the international date line on December 31, 1999, and then be in the next century. It didn't quite work out that way but it still was an enjoyable cruise where I tried parasailing and riding a WaveRunner for the first time. I also met a few interesting people including a woman who had stayed in the same short-term rental apartment in Paris on the Quai des Grands Augustins where I had stayed a few years before. It was definitely a "small world" encounter.

Papeete

It was an active 10 days in Papeete.

I had the boat hauled out and put on the hard at Technimarine so I could remove the mainsail for its repairs. It's a big sail so I normally have one other person help me take it off and put it back on. Doing it alone with the boat at anchor would have taken five times as long. It also would have been risky—a sudden gust of wind could have pulled the sail off the boat and into the water where recovery would have been nearly impossible. Even if I got it flaked (folded) and tied in a bundle, I'd have to carry it ashore in the dinghy. Of course, to put it back after repair would have been the same risky process in reverse. Though expensive, hauling the boat was the only viable option. I did take advantage of it by having the bottom power washed. It's amazing how fast sea life latches onto a hull.

It really is not comfortable to stay on the boat when it's out of the water—you can't use any sink drains because normally they discharge straight into the water. Boatyards are also hot, noisy, dusty places with sanding, scraping and painting going on all day. Hanging out there is no fun.

Given that, I booked a room at the Hilton Hotel Tahiti on the waterfront, a pretty nice place and convenient to where I needed to go in Papeete.

Phywave on a travel lift in Papeete

It was connected to a shopping mall with a huge Carrefour supermarché where I bought everything I wanted to provision the boat for the passage all the way through to Australia. It was also just a 10-minute drive from downtown Papeete with its wide variety of good restaurants. The pool and sunset views from the hotel over nearby Moorea were pleasant distractions from everything happening with the boat, my schedule and my route. Staying at the Hilton was the relaxing, restorative interlude I wanted at Nuku Hiva but didn't get. A hot shower every day? It had been months since I had anything close to that luxury.

I rented a car during my time in Papeete. Since there wasn't any Uber-type service available, the car made it easy to run around to the marine chandleries and pick up a few things I needed. There was even a big Ace Hardware store near the boatyard where I found, of all things, Coleman gas canisters that fit the Magma grill mounted on the port pushpit of *Phywave*. I left the US with three canisters and had only one-half of one remaining, never seeing them

View from my room at the hotel

anywhere else I've been, until then. I bought several so I could start grilling again. I also did some touring, driving the coast road around the perimeter of Tahiti Nui and stopping at a quaint beach restaurant for lunch. During the drive I had some spectacular views of the steep, forested interior of the island.

With the sail repaired, repairs I hoped would last until at least Australia, I had the boat dropped back in the water and drove it inside and outside the reef south past the airport to Marina Taina, where there is a fuel dock. The route inside the reef to Taina runs past the ends of the runway at the international airport. Because of this, it's necessary to report a boat's position to Papeete Port Control when approaching the ends of the runway in case there is a landing or departing aircraft that would consider the height of the mast to be an obstacle. It also provides space in case the plane has an emergency that could put it in the water. Having a boat sitting off the end of the runway would only compound that emergency. In fact, as I was going south to Taina I had to stop and wait for a departing plane for this reason.

I filled the main diesel tank and any empty jerry cans at Taina so the boat had more than enough fuel for the passage to Australia. In fact, I didn't expect to use much fuel, as easterly winds continued to prevail along my planned route.

Onward from French Polynesia

What about my route then? I had to bypass Rangiroa and head straight to Papeete for sail repairs. The next stop would have been Huahine. But with the time burned going to Papeete and the days I spent there, any visit to Huahine would have had to be a short one. Making the effort to drop the dinghy in the water, mount the engine and then reverse the process for just a day or two ashore didn't seem worth it, so I eliminated the stop in Huahine.

After Huahine I had planned to stop at Savusavu on Vanua Levu Island in Fiji where they'd just completed a great new marina with a restaurant, fuel dock, etc. (Nawi Island Marina). After the extended stay in a hotel in Papeete, and taking on full fuel at Taina, taking a break in a marina became less important. It also was a bit out of the way from my direct course to the Torres Strait and ultimately to Darwin, where I wanted to leave the boat during the tropical storm season. Darwin is also most efficiently positioned

Many boats anchored or moored at Papeete

One of the derelict boats around Papeete

for the ongoing voyage to an Asian port somewhere for my sixth continental landing. From that landing it would be passage across the Indian Ocean and around the southern tip of Africa.

Considering all the variables, I changed my plan and decided to sail to Vava'u in Tonga for a short stop because I'd never been there, unlike Fiji. It would also give me a chance to reassess crossing the Coral Sea to the Torres

Strait at the northern tip of Australia. Vava'u is also a pretty well-protected place, popular with cruisers, where people feel comfortable waiting out tropical storms.

The sun setting over Moorea

The usual route for transiting the Torres Strait begins at a point just south of Bramble Cay. As might be expected, it is a heavily traveled route with lots of big ship traffic and strong currents. It's far from ideal for a small boat, especially sailing solo, where keeping an active watch for ships full time for the 40+ hours of the transit is not very feasible.

In browsing some cruiser forums about the Torres Strait I read others describing an alternate route, a shortcut that crosses the Great Barrier Reef (GBR) beginning at Raine Island and continues northwest for about 120 nm to Thursday Island, where the Torres Strait passage is made. Yes, you're right if you guessed Thursday Island is between Wednesday Island and Friday Island. The Raine Island passage is described in an obscure book by Ken Hellewell written some 20 years ago. I thought I'd have no chance of locating a copy, so I was surprised when I found a Kindle version on Amazon. It has specific GPS coordinates and mini-chart extracts for the entire route, which necessarily maneuvers through a myriad of coral reefs in the GBR. It even identifies a few anchorages he successfully used when he made the passage himself, although one is now off-limits as a Marine Protected Area in the GBR marine reserve. With no ship traffic nor strong currents on this route, and a much shorter distance, it certainly seemed like the better route to get through to Thursday Island and the Torres Strait.

The Raine Island passage entrance, some 2,500 nm from Vava'u, now became my target following the stop in Vava'u. If the weather reasonably cooperated, and nothing significant on the boat broke, I expected it would work out for my schedule. However, if things went slowly, I might skip Vava'u and continue straight on to Raine Island.

With this route now decided, I left Papeete on September 15 and sailed west past Moorea toward Tonga. Papeete would therefore be my exit point from French Polynesia. The process of leaving French Polynesia did not go as smoothly as entering at Nuku Hiva. First, a sailor has to go to the custom house to complete their paperwork. The Customs house (Direction des Douanes) is not conveniently located but rather in an industrial area a few miles from the center of Papeete in a place called Motu Uta. When I entered at Nuku Hiva, Kevin Ellis should have mailed the customs forms I completed to this main office, or should have told me to do it, but he didn't. Consequently, the customs people had no record of me entering which delayed things a bit. I did have my own copies of the paperwork I could show them. Next, I had to go to the Immigration office at the main airport to clear out of French Polynesia. Again, this was a few miles from the center of Papeete. I had furnished them with advance notice by email that I was leaving, but when I arrived first thing in the morning at their office, they had no record of being notified. I had to wait there for almost an hour while they figured out what to do. Given all the boats coming and going in French Polynesia, I was surprised their process was so screwed up. Eventually it all got done and I drove back to Papeete to turn in my rental car. The agent there took me to the boatyard where I could reboard *Phywave* for its launch.

It was disappointing not to spend more time in French Polynesia. It is an iconic sailing paradise that fills calendars with photos of clear turquoise water, white sand beaches and palm trees. These days, that is offset by often crowded anchorages, noisy Jet Skis and unhappy local residents who view cruisers as interlopers, only tolerated because they spend money ashore. The government of French Polynesia is aware of the situation and routinely imposes restrictions on where cruising boats can anchor. Cruisers are well-advised to stay current with the changing regulatory environment.

Rack of lamb at a restaurant in Papeete

As I steered a course on my route north of Moorea the seas were choppy with a strong wind on the beam. That sea state finally calmed and the winds became more consistent as I cleared Moorea, reached the open ocean and settled in for the 1,450-nm passage to Vava'u.

16

Vava'u, Tonga

Tonga is a country with 171 islands stretching from north to south across about 185 nm. The capital is Nuku'alofa, on one of the southernmost islands, but the most popular stop for cruisers is the Vava'u island group at the northern end of the island chain. The main town in Vava'u is Neiafu. There are also

Busy mooring field at Neiafu

Mango Café with dinghy dock

many outlying villages, resorts and anchorages, making it ideal for cruisers who want to spend weeks there exploring. It has a large seasonal humpback whale population; swimming among the whales is one of the main attractions for tourists.

After my unplanned stop in Papeete, I had a fairly uneven crossing to Vava'u—periods of no winds followed by 4-meter waves with 8-second intervals and 30-to-35 knot winds. To take a break from these conditions, I heaved-to for a while north of Palmerston Atoll and let the boat drift westward.

Wind and rain greeted me as I finally maneuvered through the outlying islands of the Vava'u group into the narrow channel that leads to Neiafu. After tying up to the commercial dock, I spent a couple of hours going through the Customs and Immigration clearing-in process, which required getting local currency from an ATM. There were only two ATMs within walking distance of the Customs dock and one of those wasn't working. The local currency there is the Tongan pa'anga, commonly abbreviated as TOP.

After clearing through Immigration and Customs, I was faced with finding a place to put my boat. Neiafu is located on Port of Refuge, a well-protected but fairly deep harbor with abundant coral heads, making anchoring there a tricky proposition. To accommodate the many yachts that come there, a few companies have installed moorings. Moorings are basically very heavy weights, like a big block of concrete, sitting on the bottom. The blocks are attached to heavy-duty lines or chains with loops that are pulled to the surface by a buoy or float of some kind. Attaching the mooring lines to the bow cleats on a boat provides very secure holding even in strong winds, assuming the mooring is in good condition (they need periodic maintenance).

I faced a couple of issues after clearing in. I contacted the two companies by radio that had essentially all the moorings and both told me they were all taken because the previous week was the Vava'u Blue Water Festival and a lot of boats showed up to participate. The second problem was that it can be difficult to pick up the mooring lines when sailing solo, especially if it's windy. It's necessary to maneuver the boat as close as possible to the mooring buoy, then leave the helm and try to fish the mooring loops out of the water with a boat hook while the boat is now drifting away because no one is at the helm. Of course, after grabbing a mooring loop you have to be ready to quickly get it tied to something on your boat. Just trying to pull on it with your boat hook is a good way to lose your boat hook. I have a clever hooking device with an attached line that I can put on the end of my boat hook that solves that problem, but not the problem of the boat drifting away.

Catholic church in Neiafu

Fortunately, some longtime friends I had never actually met solved both problems. I've followed a Swedish couple named Lars and Susanne Hellman on their boat *Sea Wind* for more than 18 months after I first spotted them going to Antarctica in 2021 and wanted to keep track of where they anchored. Since then, we've traded many emails and I've followed their posts on Facebook and YouTube.

I knew they were already on a mooring in Neiafu so I sent them a quick email asking if there were any open moorings near them. Lars immediately

With Lars and Susanne

responded and said he was headed to town in his dinghy and would look around for open moorings on the way. Fifteen minutes later, as I was pulling away from the commercial wharf, Lars came alongside in his dinghy and said he found a great mooring very close to town that just opened up. He not only led me to it, but when we got there, he fished the mooring loops out of the water and put them around my bow cleats. *Phywave* was hooked up and secure! Lars and Susanne are amazing people. I had them over to my boat that evening and opened a great bottle of red wine I bought in the Algarve that I'd been saving for a special occasion. They had preceded me to Puerto Williams, Antarctica and Puerto Montt, so we knew a lot of the same people in these places and shared many stories about similar experiences.

The morning after I arrived was Sunday, October 1. I was relaxing in *Phywave*'s cockpit with a cup of coffee when I heard music coming from the nearby Catholic church. The beautiful voices of the choir had found their way across the water to me and *Phywave*, a wonderful start to a peaceful morning and my first day in Tonga. I remember thinking I was going to like my time there.

My mooring buoy was right in front of Mango Café, a short 200-meter dinghy ride from my boat. It had a large, newly constructed dinghy dock and a stairway leading up the bluff to the main street in Neiafu where all the shops and markets were located. Though there were other restaurants in town a short distance away, Mango Café was a key place for cruisers to gather. I ate there several times during my week in Vava'u. Having such easy access, I sometimes came ashore more than once a day, which allowed me to see everything within walking distance and eat at all the restaurants around town.

Though I had loaded up with enough provisions in Papeete to last me until Australia, I still wandered into the three or four small markets in Neiafu to see what they offered. I was delighted to find bacon! What these shops may have depends on the larger developed countries with which they primarily trade. In the case of Tonga, it's New Zealand, so meats of various types were readily available. Of course, I needed to stock up on things that naturally don't last very long, like bread and lettuce for lunchtime sandwiches.

Several large catamarans came and went during my week there, I imagine charter operations of some sort. They could look impressive at night with blue lights running up their masts and illuminating their decks. Typically, when a boat is at anchor, or on a mooring buoy, it will turn on its anchor light, which is a small omnidirectional light situated at the top of the mast. The purpose is to mark a boat's position so that other boats that may be entering the anchorage or mooring field at night know where it is. I've always felt this single mast-top light was inadequate for this purpose, so I usually turn on my deck light as well, which is closer to the water but not visible in all directions. Having a set of deck lights, even a string of lights running the length of the boat, would be much better. I've seen other boats sometimes do this, especially boats whose crew were away for an extended period. No doubt, the lights on such unmanned boats were controlled by a photocell switch of some sort. There were a few boats with strings of lights like that anchored at Nuku Hiva.

S/V *Andiamo* Lost

A few days before I left Neiafu on October 6, a sailboat named *Andiamo* left Neiafu for Fiji. It was never heard from again. *Andiamo* was an older 38-foot boat with a well-experienced older couple sailing her. Apparently, from reports on the Boat Watch Facebook page, they were on a shoestring budget and their engine was not working when they left, nor did they have AIS or an EPIRB. An EPIRB is an emergency beacon that, when activated, transmits a signal to satellites with the boat's latitude/longitude position, sharing its location worldwide and alerting rescue services.

The passage from Vava'u to Fiji is not long, maybe three or four days of sailing for a boat like *Andiamo*. There were other boats making this passage, going both ways, so this was not an isolated or unusual passage. After *Andiamo* was several days overdue, the search and rescue operations at Fiji, Samoa and New Zealand went into action looking for her. They put out a maritime BOLO to alert all boats in the area to look for her. *Andiamo* is a fairly common boat name so there were a few false sightings of boats with the same name that turned out not to be the missing boat. A few months went by with no sign of the boat or crew. Ultimately, New Zealand declared *Andiamo* lost at sea with all crew on board.

Sailboat making for Neiafu as I was leaving

It was strange to be in the same area at the same time as the missing boat. It's only possible to speculate on what might have happened. Without a working engine, if the boat became becalmed, with no wind to permit navigation, the currents could have driven it onto a reef in the Fiji archipelago and destroyed it. It was foolish for them to depart Neiafu without a working engine. It illustrates the value of modern electronics, especially an EPIRB.

Still, in our modern, connected, technology-infused world, for a boat and two people to disappear off the face of the earth was bizarre and disheartening. It is a reminder that cruising the world's oceans is a serious endeavor, that things can go wrong putting lives in jeopardy.

Many cruisers, especially older retired people, begin their voyages with the somewhat mistaken belief that buying a boat and sailing the oceans is an inexpensive way to see the world. They buy old, worn-out boats that don't cost very much and try to fix them up themselves to save money. Often the amateur fixes are poorly done and the boat is less than seaworthy. They also avoid investing in modern electronics like AIS and an EPIRB, or a capable emergency life raft.

Compared to flying to remote places on commercial jets and staying in hotels, or sailing around on cruise ships, I suppose such a low-budget cruising approach to seeing the world can work, but it comes with heightened risks. Sadly, I think the loss of *Andiamo* may be a classic example of this.

Tonga Time

If you think crossing 180 degrees west longitude is crossing the international date line, you'd pretty much be wrong. The international date line is a politically hatched snake that slithers its way north–south across the Pacific Ocean. For example, in Tonga (officially, the Kingdom of Tonga) local time is GMT+13. The higher math I know says that's the same thing as GMT-12. Yes, but Tonga has very close ties to New Zealand. In fact, the shop and restaurant owners I got to know in Neiafu complained they couldn't find local

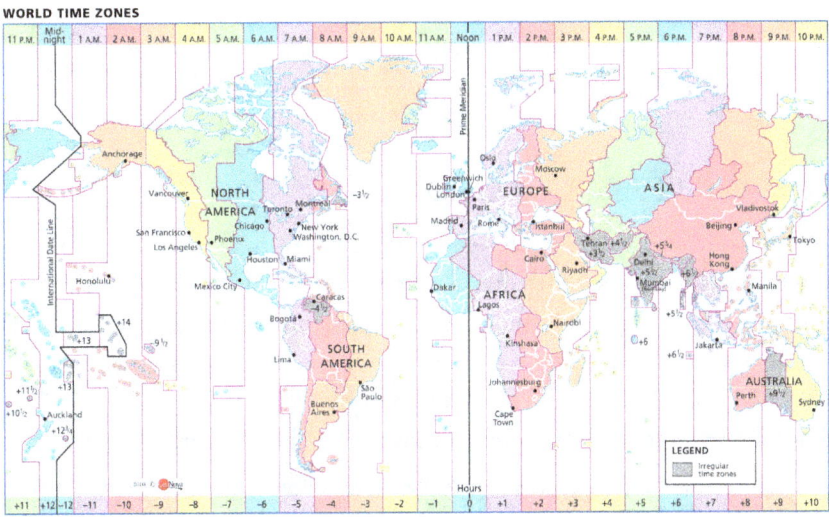

World time zone map

workers because they all went to New Zealand to pick fruit! Tonga wants to be on the same day as New Zealand so they invented GMT+13.

Then there are places that aren't satisfied with the even-hour differences set by standard time zones. They have half-hour differences, like in the Marquesas, and even quarter-hour shifts from an even hour difference ahead of or behind GMT. There can be no rational explanation for this except sheer bloody-mindedness.

When I was hitchhiking around Africa in 1975 with a backpack and guitar I got to know Swahili time in Kenya, on the equator. Zero o'clock was when the sun rose, consistently at about the same time every day. I remember bus schedules written in chalk on blackboards listing departures in Swahili time, which itself was an optimistic fiction because a bus rarely left until it was full of people, luggage, livestock, etc. It would drive all over town scooping up willing passengers to fill it before actually leaving for its destination.

On the boat I keep clocks and the log in GMT (UTC); the exception is my watch which is set based on my best guess at local time. The weather forecasts are all in GMT, so I need to convert to local time to understand whether the bad weather is going to hit me in the middle of the day or the middle of the night. Otherwise, it doesn't matter much what the local time is. The sun comes up, then goes down, called daytime; the rest, being nighttime, is routinely forecast to be dark. Then there's the morning you wake up and realize it's been tomorrow since yesterday.

I never flew on the supersonic Concorde, but I'm told you could take off from Paris at 10 a.m. and arrive in New York at 9 a.m. If you kept going around the world that way you'd never get old. We need to bring that back.

First World Flight Centennial

While moored in Vava'u I received an unexpected email that led to a phone call with Frank Goodell, a retired US Air Force general who was co-chairman of the First World Flight Centennial. The Centennial was being organized to commemorate the first flight around the world by a group of American military pilots in 1924 who left from, and returned to, Seattle in their primitive amphibious aircraft. When seeking funding for the event from Washington state, the then-governor, Jay Inslee, who is my neighbor on Bainbridge Island living two houses away, told Frank he should get me involved because I had flown around the world twice in my small plane. On the phone call Frank said he wanted me to participate in the Centennial and also wanted my help arranging for other small-plane pilots who had flown around the world to participate. I eagerly agreed. It was a great counterpoint to the world of boats and sailing that had so thoroughly occupied my time for most of the past three years. When I took a break from sailing and returned home after arriving in Darwin, I had a lot to do preparing for this event, as I discuss later.

17

Across to Australia

I left Vava'u on the morning of October 6, 2023, bound for Australia. At that point my fundamental goal was to get to Darwin before the beginning of the tropical storm season in the Southern Hemisphere, which historically begins on November 1 and ends in April. As I mentioned before, climate change is already eroding these well-established seasonal trends, as I would soon discover.

In originally planning my voyage, I had considered stopping in American Samoa or in Fiji or in Port Vila, Vanuatu. I had been to these places years before, so there wasn't much mystery remaining for me. They're nice places but, especially in the case of Fiji, very much havens for tourists, with multiple high-level resorts scattered around the islands. I'd visited both Port Vila and Pago Pago in my plane in 2011. Given the time I had to get to Darwin, more than 3,500 nm to the west, I really didn't have time to stop at any of these places even if I was interested in doing that.

Leaving Vava'u I had good winds for a few days headed for Fiji. I would need to stay alert passing through the Fiji archipelago with its many small islands surrounded by barrier reefs and narrow passages. Even though there are e-charts for my chartplotter showing these islands and reefs, some of them are not charted or surveyed to modern standards, so it's definitely prudent to give these features a wide berth when passing by them.

I sailed west through Oneata Passage on October 9 and crossed 180 degrees east longitude into the Eastern Hemisphere on October 10 at 0726Z.

I continued west then turned southwest through Kadavu Passage north of Kadavu Island. Once through this passage I had open water to my next waypoint south of Efate Island in Vanuatu where Port Vila is located. Part of the reason for passing close by Efate and Port Vila was the shelter they could provide as an intermediate safe anchorage if a tropical storm should suddenly appear in the forecast. I passed Efate on October 15.

As I passed Vanuatu, the Coral Sea remained between me and Australia. Furious naval battles happened there during World War II, resulting in several sunken warships that are marked on the charts, like the aircraft carrier USS *Lexington* and destroyer USS *Sims*. The Battle of the Coral Sea was a tactical draw with roughly equivalent losses of ships and aircraft on each side, but it is regarded as a strategic victory for the Allies because they stopped the planned Japanese invasion of Port Moresby on the south coast of Papua New Guinea. Later, in the fall of 1942, the Japanese tried to take Port Moresby overland along the now famous Kokoda Trail but were turned back and driven off the island by the Australian army.

The Coral Sea is aptly named because it has many widely spaced coral reefs scattered across it. While it's possible to weave a course through these reefs, I wanted to keep sailing life simple and avoid them altogether by setting a course that went north of Sand Cay in the Coral Sea.

Passing Efate, it is possible to take a direct route across the Coral Sea to the Torres Strait and onward to Darwin. After viewing the forecast, though, I had misgivings about taking that direct approach.

Weather Forecasts

I could download a number of weather forecast maps based on different forecast models, but the two I mainly used were the ECMWF model (known as the European model) and the GFS model (known as the American model). I tended to rely on the European model because it can offer higher resolution and seemed to have been a little more accurate when I compared the forecast conditions to the conditions I actually experienced. All the model forecasts tend to converge as you get closer to a forecast day and time, as might be expected.

The ECMWF and GFS models provide forecasts out to 10 days in the future. I usually wanted to see things that far ahead so I would have as much notice as possible of what to expect and could adjust my sailing route as early as possible. Because the boat is slow, it could take a long time to cover enough miles to get out of the way of bad weather. When I was flying my plane around the world, I didn't need such long-term warnings. My flight legs were typically only five to six hours long. I just needed suitable weather windows that lasted during daylight hours to keep moving forward. Otherwise, the plane and I were safe on the ground if bad weather arrived.

As I started out westward across the Coral Sea, I looked at the forecasts from the ECMWF and GFS models 10 days out, as shown in the screen captures here. The GFS model showed a typhoon moving southwestward over the Solomon Islands while the ECMWF model showed a benign low-pressure system in the same place. The websites I viewed that specifically track South Pacific tropical cyclones (typhoons) had no alerts about tropical depressions or waves that could develop into cyclones.

What to believe? If the typhoon was real, it was moving westward toward the Torres Strait where I planned to be about the same time it arrived.

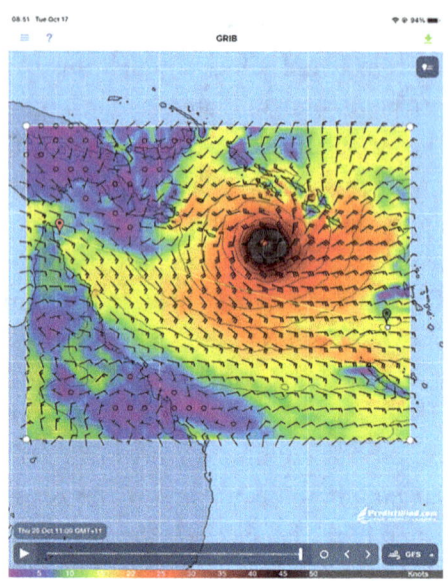

Coral Sea forecast with the GFS model

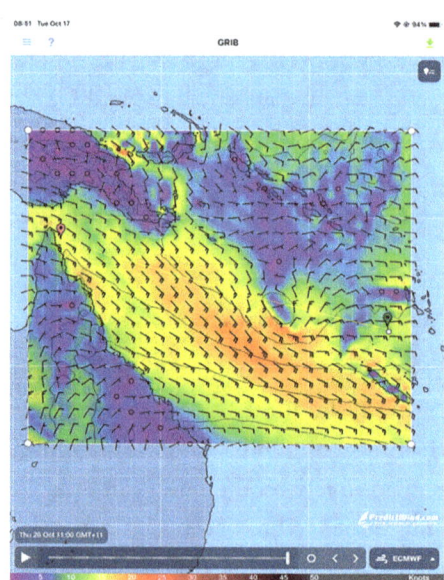

Coral Sea forecast using the ECMWF model

That was an untenable situation. Therefore, in case the GFS forecast was accurate, I needed an alternate plan. That alternate plan was to steer for a point just north of a tiny island/reef called Sand Cay, a course slightly south of the course directly to Torres Strait. From the Sand Cay waypoint I would be only about 200 nm from Cairns, Australia. That's about 1.5 days of sailing, so if I needed to run for shelter that would be my alternative. If no storm developed, I could still turn north and head directly to Torres Strait, and of course, alter my course at any time in that case. There was also the option to heave-to and just drift around south of the storm track, then resume my course to Torres Strait once it had passed.

As the days went by I eagerly downloaded each new set of forecasts as they were produced and posted every 12 hours. A typhoon that early, in October, would be rare. During the tropical cyclone season in that part of the Pacific most cyclones occurred between December and March.

Planning for contingencies like this, days in advance, was an aspect of sailing that I didn't experience when flying across the oceans. I was hoping the GFS-forecast typhoon would never develop.

Cairns, Australia—Continent Number 5!

The GFS-predicted cyclone did materialize but didn't move toward my intended route to the Torres Strait. Instead, it hit the north end of Vanuatu as a Category 5 cyclone, where it caused significant property damage and some casualties. Even though the storm was no longer a factor for me, I decided

Phywave in the marina in Cairns

to head for Cairns from Sand Cay anyway, mainly because I was tired of sailing. I also knew that if I cleared in to Australia at Cairns I would be free to anchor and go ashore wherever I wanted in Australia. There is always value to having that flexibility.

I was surprised when, more than 200 nm from Australia, I was overflown at a low altitude by a military-type aircraft. Shortly thereafter, I was contacted on marine VHF channel 16 by the border protection aircraft, which asked about my destination (Cairns) and the port I had last visited (Vava'u). Australia has a 96-hour advanced notification system for arriving yachts. I had submitted that advance notification but never got a reply that it had been received. Apparently, it was also not relayed to the people who operate the aircraft. Australia has set up a reasonable advanced notification system in theory, but from what I encountered it really didn't work very well. For example, there was confusion about exactly where to send an advanced notification, and then, as I mentioned, there was no confirmation that it was received. I think it was very much a case of the left hand not knowing what the right hand was doing. Once I got close to the marina in Cairns and contacted it by radio, it was the marina staff who arranged for the Immigration and Customs people to come down to my berth to clear me in.

To get to Cairns on the coast of the Australia I had to choose a way through the Great Barrier Reef GBR, the most extensive reef in the world, which runs along most of the east coast of Australia. I chose Grafton Passage as the most direct route to get from my position at sea into Cairns. It was also wide and deep, the passage most commonly used by large ship traffic, including cruise ship traffic, that comes to Cairns. Once through that passage, I turned west-southwest around the south side of Green Island and headed for the well-marked, but narrow, ship channel into Cairns. I was steering for Cairns Marlin Marina near the entrance to Cairns Harbor where I had already booked a berth. Like always, I had adjusted my speed on the open ocean so I would arrive at the entrance to Grafton Passage, and make my way down the ship channel to the marina, during daylight.

I arrived in Cairns on October 27, about 21 days after leaving Vava'u. The marina itself had many empty berths, so booking one was no problem. Cairns is on a river whose current contributes to the strong tidal currents. There was a strong outgoing ebb current when I arrived, so my SOG to the marina entrance was slow, and my turn into my assigned berth was a sloppy maneuver as the current kept trying to push me away from the dock. Thankfully, a marina staff member was on hand to take my dock lines and initially get *Phywave* tied up. Of course, I couldn't leave the boat and go anywhere until the Australian Immigration and Customs people had come down to the boat and completed the entry formalities. Those people arrived soon after I docked and efficiently completed their work. The real delay resulted from the "biosecurity" guy who checks for prohibited provisions. Australia is one of the few countries that makes cruisers surrender, and then destroys, a number of fresh food items including eggs, meat, vegetables and dairy products. About the only thing that's safe from being surrendered is canned food. They do this because they think these items will bring invasive species into Australia's geographically isolated ecosystem. I've asked people about this, and tried to find papers that offer scientific evidence of this risk, but couldn't find any. I suspect it's mostly guesswork by Australia, or a way to protect and insulate the economy, not the environment.

Once I finished all the entry formalities and surrendered a lot of food in a plastic garbage bag earmarked for destruction, I was free to leave the boat and enjoy a meal at a nearby restaurant and have a celebration mojito. I had landed on my fifth continent and officially crossed the Pacific Ocean! As before, achieving this milestone seemed anticlimactic, the celebratory moment diluted by the always-present realization that I still had a long way to go. Even though there was a long way to go, it seemed intermediate victories like this one should have resonated more significantly.

Reprovision, Refuel, Rejuvenate

Having come from Vava'u where there were only a few small grocery stores, I was delighted to find a large Woolworths supermarket within easy walking distance of the marina. Woolworths is a chain supermarket found throughout Australia. I took advantage of it, replacing many items I had to jettison because of the ridiculous "biosecurity" confiscation rules. I didn't have to buy provisions for a long passage, though, since Darwin is only about 1,250 nm from Cairns via the Raine Island shortcut across the GBR I had found.

The fuel dock for diesel was inside the main breakwater directly across from the marina, so I expected it would be easy to stop there to top off my fuel tank when I departed.

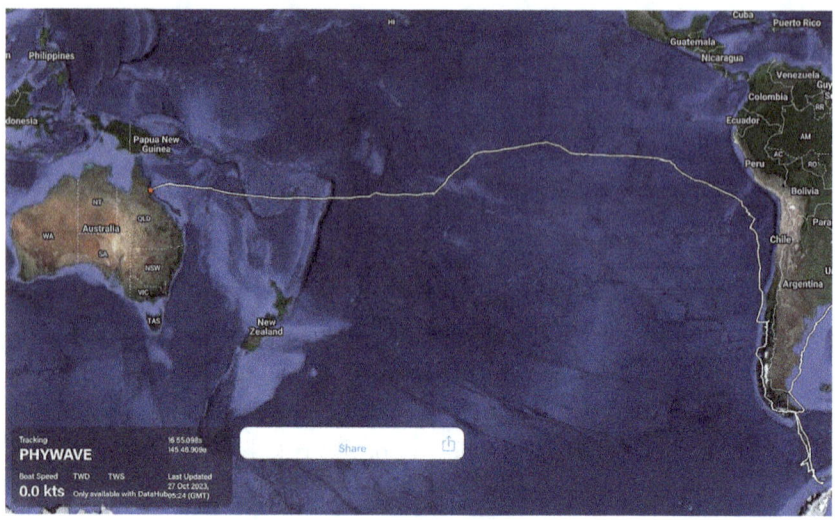

Route across the Pacific Ocean

I was comfortable in the marina, but there was also a large anchorage area on the other side of the main river, where Cairns is situated. There were many boats anchored over there that, of course, had to use their dinghies to come ashore for anything they wanted or needed, from provisions to fuel to a nice meal or drink in one of the many restaurants and bars.

There were also a few nice hotels along the waterfront near the marina. For a break from the boat, I decided to book a room at the Shangri-La hotel directly facing the marina—I could see *Phywave* from my room. I wanted to spend a couple of nights sleeping in a real bed and having some great hot showers. Being on the boat, it was difficult to think about anything except the boat, sailing and getting to the next destination because the boat was always right there in my face. Just having different walls to look at, and an ocean-view room, provided some space from all that.

The waterfront area abounds with good restaurants. I ate at several ranging from Italian to seafood to steak to Chinese. They were all an easy walk from my marina berth or the hotel, another luxury that being in the marina instead of being anchored across the river provided. With the few days I spent in Cairns, I ran out of meals to eat before I ran out of inviting restaurants.

Sailing North

I had booked the marina and paid for four nights but decided to leave a day early, on October 30, because the weather setup going north was more favorable then. After refueling at the fuel dock first thing in the morning, I made my way out through the narrow ship channel and turned toward Grafton Passage. I made some distance in that direction before realizing I should have chosen Trinity Opening, which passed through the barrier reef to the northeast, the general direction I wanted to go. It would have saved a few miles, but that really didn't matter much in the larger scheme of things. After getting through Grafton Passage to the open sea, I turned due north, headed straight for Raine Island.

18

The Great Barrier Reef to Darwin

Now that I had completed Australian entry formalities at Cairns, my next challenge was to sail north, cross the GBR, then sail west through the Torres Strait, a collection of narrow, shallow waterways connecting the Pacific and Indian Oceans.

From Cairns many yachts follow the inside route to the Torres Strait along the Queensland coast. This route is also an active shipping channel and full of islands and reefs. For me, sailing solo, it's a poor choice because I would have to stop and anchor somewhere every night to get some sleep. I'm much more comfortable far offshore where there's nothing to run into and I can let the autopilot drive the boat while I sleep.

Crossing the Great Barrier Reef

Leaving Cairns, I went back outside the reef at Grafton Passage and turned straight north toward Raine Island, 350 nm away, the point where I would start my passage across the GBR. As I mentioned, I first learned about this route from a book published some years ago by Ken Hellewell titled *Ken's Torres Strait Passage Guide*. The purpose of his book is to describe a shortcut from the Pacific Ocean through the Torres Strait to the Indian Ocean that

Raine Island with its tower

avoids going far north around the northern end of the GBR to join the busy shipping channels through the Torres Strait. The route he describes in the book is very detailed, with more than 30 GPS waypoints. After studying the charts, I decided I could come up with something much simpler that worked just as well. I chose route legs by trying to stay in water that was charted at least 20 meters deep. As I sailed this route, in fact, the shallowest depth I saw on the depth sounder was 19 meters. As a point of reference, that's more than deep enough to handle a huge cruise ship. The ship channel at Cairns, which I had just left, routinely handles such big ships and is dredged to a depth of only 12–13 meters. If charted depths as shallow as 10 meters were considered acceptable, my route across the GBR could be simplified even further.

Great Barrier Reef Route Waypoints		
Waypoint	Latitude (decimal degrees)	Longitude (decimal degrees)
0	-11.63630	144.10950
1	-11.65046	143.88968
2	-11.53255	143.73470
3	-11.38046	143.67806
4	-11.33867	143.56995
5	-11.28093	143.54342
6	-11.20801	143.35792
7	-11.12818	143.30280
8	-10.97783	142.98178

I set up my route waypoints in the chartplotter and instructed the autopilot to drive the whole route, which it did perfectly. I only had to adjust the sails when the course direction changed and the boat turned. Because the winds were light (10–12 knots), I motor-sailed part of the route to make sure I could get past the trickiest parts during daylight after starting from Raine Island at about 2150Z on November 1, or 0730 local time, with the rising sun.

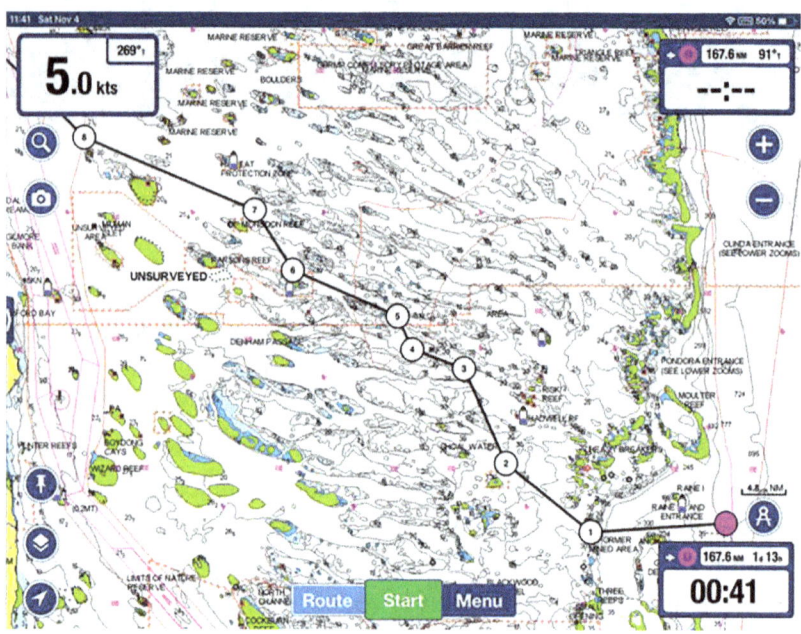

My route across the Great Barrier Reef

Crossing the reef along my route I didn't see any other boats. I saw breaking waves on the reefs facing the ocean but after that I didn't see any other reefs or even very shallow water. I did see the tower that was built long ago on Raine Island, but it was too far away to get a good close-up photo. In Ken Hellewell's book he says he anchored twice near partially submerged islands or reefs where he found shallow water and a sand bottom. Though I was following his route closely, I didn't see any of these islands, no doubt because they are little more than reefs that rise a few feet above the water level. Out of curiosity, I considered pulling off my route to see if I could find them but decided I'd rather push through and get across to the inside shipping channel while I still had daylight.

Waypoint 8 sits on a red line which marks the eastern edge of the inside shipping channel, so at that point I was home free regarding any reef hazards. On the chart at waypoint 1 there's a note that says "FORMERLY MINED AREA." Hitting a forgotten World War II mine and getting blown to bits would have been a spectacular conclusion to my voyage!

Torres Strait

By the time I had sailed west past the GBR it was after midnight, and I had a straight run of about 25 nm into and across the inside shipping channels. I decided to take it slow and use the opportunity to get some sleep, so I set the sails to give me about 4–5 knots. This would put me close to Cape York, the northernmost point of mainland Australia, and York Island around sunrise. I planned to stop near there and anchor to wait for favorable west-setting tidal currents in the boat channel running by Thursday Island. No ships were showing on the AIS in the shipping channels, so I was actually able to get a few hours of solid sleep, waking an hour before first light at 0600 local time.

York Island

I cruised past York Island early and realized, after rechecking the tide tables at Thursday Island, that there was a slack tide at 1035 following a west-setting flood tide. I could easily make that slack tide if I used the engine. I never want to hang around at anchor just killing time if I can keep moving.

The timing worked about right, though I was surprised to get hit with 3 knots of countercurrent in the channel west of the town of Thursday Island. It may have been an eddy current in the complicated channel.

I pushed on into the Arafura Sea, which at that point is very shallow, with depths of only about 10–20 meters. It's easy to see how a land bridge could have connected Australia and Papua New Guinea in the distant past. I got some useful wind on the stern, letting me wing out the mainsail and set the genoa on the whisker pole. That comfortable cruising west across the Arafura Sea lasted a few days, but I knew from the weather forecasts the doldrums were coming, and they were brutal. Except for some interludes with useful wind that lasted only a few hours, I had to start motoring even before turning south through the Dundas Strait toward Cape Don. The temperature rose, and with no breeze, I was getting cooked by temperatures of over 30 degrees Celsius.

The route to Darwin through the Dundas Strait passed Abbott Shoal, Rooper Rock and then the Howard Channel into Clarence Strait, which have their own challenging tidal currents. I had the predictions for the current speeds and directions, but with that long a route it's not possible to hit it all at the right time because the tidal current reverses every six hours, generally. I had to make some compromises in my calculations so they would average out reasonably well. As I wrote down my numbers, I remember sweat dripping

Thursday Island

off my head onto the paper, smearing what I had just written. I also started to develop a heat rash—a first for me. I was having fun now!

The water along that route was also shallow, about 20 meters, making the water a pretty turquoise over a sand bottom. With the excessive heat and humidity, though, it was like motoring across the surface of a giant hot tub. I did manage to hit the strongest current spot in the Howard Channel on time in the dark night, with a following current, and after that tried to figure out a place where I could get some sleep. I wanted to arrive at the entrance to Darwin Harbour, where several big ships were anchored, at daylight and reasonably well-rested because I would have to maneuver my way past them. From the Clarence Strait I had about 16 nm of sailing (motoring) south to the Darwin Harbour entrance. I pointed the boat in that direction, throttled back to almost idle so I was only going about 2–3 knots and went to bed, setting the alarm for around sunrise. There were no other ships around at that time. I counted on any that might come close to my course avoiding me as I slept. Keeping a consistent course and speed, even if slow, makes it easier for them to do that. Trying to get some sleep in busy waterways, or in areas with reefs or land that must be avoided, had turned out to be one of the bigger challenges of solo sailing.

Darwin

The timing worked out about right. I was still a few miles from the harbor entrance and big ships when I woke up an hour before first light. I could see the bright lights on the big ships in front of me and a faint glow of Darwin lights on the eastern horizon.

My final timing issue was entering the Cullen Bay Marina. The marinas in Darwin, and generally in the western Australia, are behind locks because of the significant tidal changes that occur there, sometimes 6–8 meters. However, the locks at the entrances to the marinas inhibit the normal exchange of water between the marinas and the sea, so marina water is relatively stagnant, promoting the growth of waterborne pests of various types brought in on the hulls of yachts arriving from foreign places. In the past, this has led to some highly polluted marinas resulting in substantial clean-up costs.

To mitigate the problem, Australia has an aquatic biosecurity group that requires yachts arriving from foreign locations to have their seawater systems treated with a chemical to kill the pests. I needed an appointment for this treatment that's done while my boat is tied at the pontoon just outside the lock into the Cullen Bay Marina, where I had booked a berth. I couldn't get an appointment until the afternoon of my arrival, so after making my way down the shipping channel toward the marina I diverted to the north and anchored in Fannie Bay for six hours. It's not well-protected but the holding is great in shallow water, about 3 meters deep at low tide when I was there.

Heading for the locks into Cullen Bay Marina

After enduring a quick rain squall that turned the boat around its anchor, I raised the anchor in the afternoon and motored about a mile to the pontoon, where the treatment was completed by a diver injecting the chemical into the seawater systems through the seacocks in the hull. It didn't cost me anything, but they told me they may start charging yachts for it in the future. Once the chemical was in the systems, I had to leave it for 10 hours. I couldn't start my engine and go anywhere with the boat. Ten hours ended at 1 a.m., but I was comfortable tied to the pontoon and wouldn't go through the lock into the marina until the next morning anyway. Personally, however, I could get off the boat and wander around, exploring the Cullen Bay area and having dinner at one of the restaurants there. I enjoyed crocodile carbonara that first night.

Behind the closing lock gates

Moving to my berth through the lock the next morning was a new experience made easier with a local sailor I met on the pontoon who offered to come by at 0800 local time to help me with mooring lines. *Phywave* was now securely tied up in berth A14 at the Cullen Bay Marina, where it would stay for the next several months.

I had a long list of maintenance tasks I compiled while sailing that I wanted to complete while there. Some could be done in the next two to three weeks, and others like repairs to the dodger and bimini, which had tears and

Phywave in Cullen Bay Marina

many corroded zippers that wouldn't move, would take longer. Just getting the dodger and bimini off would be a chore.

I would also be sending my mainsail away to an ace sailmaker in Sydney for a more permanent repair of the luff tape to replace the temporary patches I'd been living with. This job really didn't get done the way I wanted when I was in Papeete. I expected to fly home in early December and return to the boat in the spring to resume my voyage. I had a lot of weather research to do on how best to land someplace in Asia (for continent number six) and then continue across the Indian Ocean to South Africa.

Upon examining the mainsail track in some detail, I discovered that the narrow gap in the track where the sail slides just aft of the luff tape had been worn and widened, making it possible for the luff tape to slip free of the track. I had noticed this slipping happening while sailing to Darwin, and it limited me to raising the sail just to the point where this could happen. After I communicated this problem to Steve Majkut at Schaefer Marine, maker of the boom and track, he graciously shipped me, free of charge, a tube with replacement track sections and the associated aluminum mounting hardware. While in Darwin I tracked down a rigger and gave him the task of replacing the worn lower piece of track section with a new one.

I also had the rigger replace the end fitting on the whisker pole. The pin in the jaws that connects to the headsail had gotten bent and was very difficult to operate when reattaching that end to the bail at the base of the mast. I bought a replacement for this end fitting when I was back in the US, so I already had the required part on hand. After this damage to the whisker pole jaws, I came up with a new way to rig the pole with the genoa sheet. Instead of running the genoa sheet through the jaws on the whisker pole, which caused a lot of chafing on the sheet, I instead rigged a carabiner to the end of the pole to smoothly hold the sheet. This also allowed me to clip the sheet into the carabiner while standing at the base of the mast, then pull down and deploy the pole without having to go out to the bow. This technique proved to be much more convenient and safer, and it eliminated chafing on the sheet.

The Cullen Bay Marina office was willing to accept packages for me shipped to their address. In addition to the parts from Schaefer Marine, I ordered other things online such as a replacement for the Lewmar main cabin hatch that had been bent when the boom brake line caught under it.

It was the "wet" season in Australia: hot, humid, brutal weather I had first encountered as I sailed across the Arafura Sea to Darwin. I'm someone who really suffers in such conditions, so I couldn't stay on the boat. Instead, I booked a room in a nearby hotel where I could relax in the air-conditioning. I would get up early when it was a little bit cooler and spend maybe an hour or two working at the boat. By that point my tee shirt would be soaked with sweat and I would have to return to the hotel. The air conditioning and taking showers every day, something I couldn't do on the boat, eventually got rid of the heat rash I had developed.

Flying Across Australia in 2011

This was not my first time in Darwin or Australia. During my 2011 solo flight around the world, I flew from Bali, Indonesia, to Darwin, dodging massive thunderstorms along the way. I only stayed in Darwin a few days, happy to relax in a modern, English-speaking country after many weeks in places that were foreign to me. At the time, and perhaps still, the Australians were very paranoid about foreign bugs getting into Australia on a small plane or large commercial jet. Before a commercial flight could let people off, the Australian Border Force (ABF) insisted on spraying the cabin with an insecticide of some sort. This would have been the case for me too except I anticipated the process and had a can of Top of Descent with me, an approved insecticide for this purpose. As the name implies, I sprayed the inside of my plane with

Flying around Uluru (Ayers Rock) in 2011

it as I started my descent into Darwin. As I parked my plane outside the terminal to clear Immigration and Customs, I was approached by two guys who motioned to me not to open the door to my plane. I showed them the can of Top of Descent through my window and they gave me a thumbs-up to open my door. As I recall, there were several documents I had to file while in Bali in advance of my arrival in Darwin; in that regard, it was certainly the most elaborate entry procedure I experienced with my plane on that 2011 round-the-world flight.

From Darwin I flew down to Uluru (Ayers Rock) where I got some great photos of the rock by following a charted sightseeing route for planes. I stayed a couple of days there doing ground tours, then flew on to the Gold Coast Airport at Coolangatta. From there I left Australia and flew to Port Vila in Vanuatu, the end of my Australian flying experience.

19

Darwin to Lombok

I arrived back in Darwin, Australia, on April 19 after a long flight from Seattle and almost missing my connection out of Brisbane. Fortunately, Immigration for many incoming foreigners is done at a machine—you present your passport, pose for photo, take the printout, done. Many machines were available, no waiting. Customs was also quick—they didn't open any bags.

I had a lot of work to do to get *Phywave* ready to sail again—putting all the sails back on, topping off the diesel jerry cans, which I emptied to fill the boat's main diesel tank in December, topping off the water tank, buying provisions and arranging for clearing out of Australia. A five-day notification lead time is required to get an exit appointment at the Customs jetty.

When I arrived in November, I removed the dodger because there were many zipper slides that had corroded to the point where I could no longer move them. I had to cut some zippers loose to get the dodger off the frame. The bimini and connector panel had already been removed and stowed below long before, after they were damaged in heavy winds sailing south through the Atlantic. I didn't have either in place since leaving the ad hoc anchorage behind a tall cliff near the east entrance to the Strait of Magellan. I took all three pieces—dodger, bimini, and connector panel—to The Canopy Man, recommended as the best canvas guy in Darwin. I told him I'd be back in April to pick up everything, so he had plenty of time to do the repair work. I picked them up on April 22 and installed them on the boat, a multihour effort because the canvas must be stretched tight across the frame. It takes some pulling and cursing to get it all connected. Everything went back together OK except for two forward window panels on the dodger that each had one zipper reversed. I immediately took them back to Nick, the Canopy Man, to have the zippers flipped. There was some urgency to get the fixed panels back since I had made an appointment with the ABF to clear out at 1100 on Wednesday, May 1. An Australian holiday had closed Nick's shop for a few days, but I did manage to get the fixed panels back in time for my scheduled departure.

I made a major change to my route while I was home. After watching the weather along my original planned route, going north to India, for months while at home and seeing nothing good, I decided to change my landing in Asia from India to Indonesia, specifically the island Lombok, just east of Bali where I had landed my plane during my 2011 around-the-world flight. Lombok has some good anchorages and a marina. My only purpose in going to India was to claim I'd sailed to Asia. After spending some time researching it, I couldn't find any authority that argued Indonesia was not considered part of Asia even though it is an island country and not attached to what we consider to be the mainland of Asia. The change in my landing destination would keep me in the southeast trade winds, making the most of my Indian Ocean crossing downwind. It would also considerably shorten the length of my overall around-the-world route.

One thing I forgot to do while at home was make a boat stamp. Many countries, like Indonesia, are obsessed with stamping paperwork of all kinds. Documents are "official" when they have been stamped and signed, stamped by them and stamped by me with my boat stamp. If I had jumped on it when I arrived in Darwin, I could have had one made there, but I didn't think about it until a few days before my departure while reading some Indonesian clearing-in instructions. It was too late to get one made by my May 1 departure date, but I did find a DIY rubber stamp kit at Officeworks, the local version of Staples. DIY (do it yourself) in this case meant using tweezers to pluck individual tiny rubber letters and numbers from a tray and place them in the grooves in the stamp. It was sort of like old-fashioned typesetting. After losing a few letters to ham-handed tweezer work, I finally had assembled three rows of basic information the stamp should include. It looked like crap but I thought it would suffice. No choice at that point.

After spending time making that stamp, it turned out I really didn't need it in Indonesia after all.

Preparing for the Centennial

In chapter 16, I mentioned that I had a phone conversation with a retired US Air Force general named Frank Goodell, the co-chairman of the First World Flight Centennial. He invited me to participate in the Centennial, scheduled for September 2024, commemorating the 100-year anniversary of the first flight around the world in 1924 by a group of four US Army planes with two-man crews. They departed from Seattle and returned there. Only two of the planes were able to complete the entire flight, but it was still a remarkable achievement years ahead of Lindbergh's flight across the Atlantic in 1927. It took incredible logistical efforts involving several naval ships for refueling and resupply (the planes were equipped with floats to land on water) and diplomatic efforts with several remote developing countries where aviation was still a very rare thing.

He asked for my help in selecting pilots, with their planes, who had also flown around the world to participate in the Centennial. There is a website called Earthrounders.com that is primarily a list of pilots who have flown light aircraft around the world. As one myself, I know this group pretty well and was able to line up six other pilots for the event who were willing to fly their planes to Seattle and have them on display at the Museum of Flight during the Centennial. Some of them were world record holders for fastest circumnavigations in their class of aircraft. All of us would participate in a flyby of Magnuson Park, the departure and arrival location in Seattle for the original 1924 flight.

When I had committed to my long ocean voyage, I expected I wouldn't be flying my plane for two years or more. I decided to have it configured for long-term storage, or "pickled" in the parlance of the aviation world. That meant the engine oil was drained and replaced by special conservative oil. Desiccant spark plugs replaced the regular spark plugs, all in an effort to keep moisture from getting into the engine and causing corrosion. Any other access points to the engine were plugged. To fly the aircraft for the Centennial, all of this needed to be undone so the engine would run again. While I was home from Darwin in April, I got my mechanics to complete this process because I knew I wouldn't have time to do it while I was home for two weeks in September for the Centennial.

Besides the plane being pickled, I had also let my pilot currency lapse because I was sailing. To remain current and be legal to fly solo, every two years a pilot must complete a flight review, which usually consists of one hour on the ground and one hour flying with a certified flight instructor (CFI). The flight review is not a pass/fail test but basically a confirmation that a pilot is still sufficiently skilled and knowledgeable enough to fly safely. I completed the flight review with a CFI friend of mine on April 7.

Finally, once I could fly solo again, I had to take the plane to an avionics shop to have the transponder recertified. That test confirms the transponder accurately reports the plane's altitude to air traffic control. I completed this step at the avionics shop at the nearby Tacoma Narrows Airport.

Because participating in the Centennial came up unexpectedly while I was in Vava'u, all this work to get the plane and me flying again was also unexpected but had to be done before I could participate in the Centennial. While regularly flying, I was used to the routine of keeping myself and the plane current and ready to fly. By stepping out of that routine for a couple of years, I was reminded of all the work involved with staying in flying condition.

En Route to Lombok

With help from a friend in the Cullen Bay Marina, I made my way outward through the locks to the Customs jetty to clear out of Australia on May 1, 2024. The agents showed at the scheduled time. The process went pretty quickly because there were no biosecurity issues with provisions or other matters of that sort to address. They gave me two sheets of paper with details for arriving at Christmas Island and Cocos (Keeling) Islands, both Australian possessions in the Indian Ocean where cruisers often go after leaving Darwin. They knew I was headed for Lombok but thought I might stop at these two places as well.

The passage to Lombok from Darwin is not complicated, only about 960 nm. For the next seven days I had weak to moderate winds from the southeast that made for reasonable broad reach and downwind sailing. On May 8 I turned to the north to go through the Lombok Strait, where I encountered very strong currents and rough water, largely from a wind-against-current situation. As the water smoothed out a bit, the countercurrent increased and my SOG was reduced to just 2 knots. Running the engine, I clawed my way north through the strait until I got to wider water on the north side and the countercurrent diminished.

Fishing boats in Medana Bay

My initial destination was Marina Del Ray, which had a long dock where I could stern tie. I had contacted them ahead of time to book space. I also thought that Immigration and Customs were available at Marina Del Ray and I could clear in to Indonesia there. This turned out to be a misunderstanding. They used to have that capability but lost it. I spent one night tied to their pontoon, not exactly legal since I hadn't cleared in to the country yet, and then left early the next morning for Medana Bay Marina, where I was sure I could clear in to Indonesia.

The short voyage to Medana Bay started out smoothly, but when I was about 20 nm away my engine developed a major leak in the exhaust elbow of the seawater cooling system. On marine engines, seawater is pumped through the engine to cool it and then combined with the engine exhaust gases in an exhaust elbow. The combination is then sent overboard.

I first noticed an unusual dribble of water on the cabin floor. Opening hatches to the bilge, I was shocked to find the bilge full of water. I immediately turned on the bilge pumps which successfully started drawing down the water level. Investigating further, I found a substantial jet of water coming from the underside of the exhaust elbow. The only way to stop it was to shut down the engine, which I did for a while because there was enough wind to sail. That wind eventually disappeared, so I had no choice but to motor again if I wanted to make Medana Bay by nightfall. Of course, the leak returned, but now the main bilge pump had failed, so it was a race to see if the secondary

Phywave in Medana Bay

bilge pump could hold down the water level until I reached the marina. It did, barely, with a little help from me and a bucket scooping water out of the bilge and dumping it down the sink. I finally arrived in Medana Bay on May 10.

Fixing the Engine

Once at the marina with the engine stopped, I had time to assess the situation. I found that the exhaust elbow had completely rusted through in one place and was spraying the cooling water directly into the bilge. I was hoping that the rusted hole in the exhaust elbow could be welded closed with a patch of some sort but it's made of cast iron, which can be tricky to weld, especially when I'm in a place where there are usually only semiskilled bush welders. Doing some research, I found that such welds in cast iron rarely last, especially under pressure in a saltwater environment.

The right solution was to replace the elbow with a new one, but shipping boat parts into a place like Indonesia is a nightmare, sometimes taking months, even if you're willing to pay the 40% duty and taxes that a boat in transit shouldn't have to pay. I was not waiting months for anything. Tracking down and ordering the parts I needed in Sydney, Australia, I jumped on the fast ferry to Bali, caught a red-eye flight from the Denpasar airport to Sydney and spent the next day picking up the new parts along with spare bilge pumps and a few other things. I flew back to Denpasar with the parts in my carry-on bag

Rusted hole in exhaust elbow

and skated through Customs with no problems. Returning to Lombok and Medana Bay on the fast ferry, I was back where I started with the parts to replace the leaking elbow. At that point I hoped to get it installed quickly and get going again by the end of the week.

What was surprising about this problem was that the engine was only two years old, with about 1,250 hours. A failure like this should never have happened with such a relatively young engine. I was worried there was an undiscovered collateral problem that led to this failure. After I pulled the elbow off, I didn't notice any additional problems that might have led to the leak.

The failed exhaust elbow replacement went well, but a new problem arose when I tried to start the engine—it wouldn't start. Having seawater sprayed on the starter for several hours from the exhaust elbow leak likely caused some other problems. I pulled the starter off and bench tested it on the galley countertop. The motor did spin but the solenoid was not kicking the starter gear into place to engage the flywheel; it was possibly rusted stuck. I was thinking I might need a new starter, but I decided to try to fix the one I had. By "exercising" the solenoid (turning it on and off multiple times) and liberally lubricating it with T-9 lubricant, which is better than WD-40, I was able to get the starter gear to reliably kick into place. With the starter solenoid operating smoothly, I reinstalled the starter.

However, as is sometimes the case, that was not the only problem. To minimize electrical leakage currents, my engine is equipped with a grounding relay that only connects the start battery negative to the engine block when the start switch at the helm is pressed. If that relay doesn't close, the start battery negative won't be connected to the engine block and there won't be any battery voltage across the starter to make it run. After a few tests I concluded the relay had failed. I got around that by using my battery jumper cables to bypass the relay and connect the battery negative directly to the engine block for startup. With that in place I was able to start the engine. Once the engine was running, I could remove the jumper cable; in effect, I was replicating the action of the relay.

While I was doing all this, I also wired a manual switch across the terminals of the starter so if the Volvo Penta MDI control box should fail for startup (they have a reputation for failing on boat engines), I

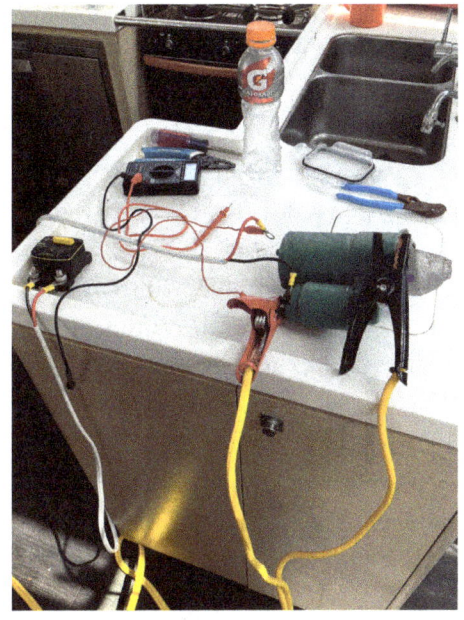

Bench testing the starter

could still directly start the engine with that manual starter switch and the jumper across the grounding relay.

I was not particularly happy with having to use a jumper cable to start the engine, so I decided to try to find a replacement for the failed grounding relay. The part number of that relay was not in the Volvo Penta parts catalog so I sent the Volvo parts supplier in Perth, Australia, a photo and they came up with a relay with the same size, shape and connection terminals as the failed one. They made no promises it would work but I was willing to try it. Once again, I got on the fast ferry to Bali to catch a flight to Australia, this time to Perth, a shorter flight than the one to Sydney. I took advantage of the trip to also buy a new starter, in case the one I repaired failed again, and some additional tools. I spent one night in Perth and then flew back to Bali. After returning to Medana Bay I installed the new grounding relay in place of the failed one and, amazingly, the engine started perfectly! The jumper cable was no longer needed and the engine was back to its normal configuration. I hoped it would last.

Getting the engine operational again was only one result of this episode. There were also the lessons learned, particularly that I was underequipped in terms of spare engine parts for this voyage. Recognizing that lesson, and acting on it while in Perth, I had picked up a few more spare parts and tools

I'd wished I'd had, like a set of metric ratchet wrenches. Getting the starter in and out of its tight space was a pain because there was very little room to move a standard wrench to tighten the bolts.

The engine repair reminded me of when I was in my 20s and used to work on my own cars before they became computers on wheels. I could continue my voyage a little better equipped with spares and a little more knowledgeable about my engine.

In addition to issues with *Phywave*'s main engine, I also had a problem starting the Yamaha 6-hp outboard motor for my dinghy. I gave it to some bush mechanics at Medana Bay to work on. I also replaced the gasoline I used with it in case old fuel corrupted with water was the source of the problem. The mechanics got it running again but I didn't have a lot of confidence in their work. That turned out to be justified when I had problems with it again at my next stop.

Rice paddies

Lombok Diversions

While in Medana Bay considering the best course for fixing my engine, I was immersed in a new book by Paul Theroux titled *Burma Sahib*. Well-known for his many novels like *The Mosquito Coast* and engaging nonfiction travel books like *Dark Star Safari*, Theroux turned to historical fiction this time to describe the life of young Eton graduate Eric Blair who, in real life and for reasons never clear to himself, signed up to be a British policeman in Burma in the early 1920s. The book describes the imagined twists and turns of maturing Blair's life as he navigates the brutal, racist, exploitative hegemony of the British Raj and deals with the society and bureaucrats that ran it, their sparsely furnished minds hypocritically justifying the coercive control of the Indian subcontinent. Several years later Eric Blair became famous for his jarring, yet no longer very far-fetched, projection of humanity's dystopian future under his pen name George Orwell.

On one of the first days at Medana Bay I decided to walk into a town a few kilometers east with another sailor also there for repairs and maintenance: Barry Perrins, whose Adventures of an Old Seadog is a YouTube sailing video sensation with more than 120,000 subscribers. He was on a mooring buoy with his boat *White Shadow* when I arrived but later had his boat hauled and put on land so he could repair rust spots on the steel hull. Just as we started down the road, Peter (an Englishman who settled there long ago and was the owner of Medana Bay Marina) drove by and offered us a lift. That "lift" turned into a three-hour tour of the north side of Lombok, past rice paddies, Hindu temples, Muslim mosques and the verdant countryside surrounding its active volcano, Mt. Rinjani, at 3,786 meters high the second highest point in Indonesia. It last erupted in 2016.

Muslim girls interviewing me

One day I shared a vehicle and driver with a few other sailors on a trip south to Mataram, the main city on Lombok, in search of tools, parts, provisions, liquor, etc. It was a bustling place with an upscale shopping mall hosting the usual selection of American restaurants (KFC, Pizza Hut, Burger King, Starbucks) and boutique clothes shops, international brands you'd likely find in big malls all over the world. It was a good break from the routine of the Medana Bay Marina, which had become very familiar after being there two weeks.

On a second trip with Barry to buy provisions, we were sitting outside a small market in Senggigi when a delightful group of Muslim high school girls came by and asked to interview us, mainly to practice their English, I think. I was happy to oblige. It was great to see their enthusiasm and positive energy. Contact between Muslim women and a strange man would not have been allowed in many Muslim countries.

Leaving Lombok

Barring any new issues, I planned to complete exit formalities to leave Indonesia on Monday, June 3, and head back south through the Lombok Strait at first light the next day. Once through the strait I would turn west across the Indian Ocean toward the Cocos (Keeling) Islands, one of the few places in the world where parentheses are an official part of the name.

I had spent nearly a month in Medana Bay, mostly devoted to fixing the engine, but it was also a rare occasion to spend significant time with other cruisers. There was one restaurant/bar, the Sailfish Cafe, at Medana Bay where we would routinely gather in the evening for beer, dinner and conversation.

It was interesting to learn different people's perspectives on why they were cruising the world. I didn't meet anybody like me who was on a real mission with a specific goal. Many had houses somewhere but dedicated several months a year to cruising. They would leave their boat somewhere on land for several months, usually during hurricane or tropical storm seasons, then return for several months of cruising with no grand destinations in mind, just slowly moving from one port or anchorage to another where they might spend several weeks. When the season was over, they put the boat on land again and went home. It was a recurring cycle that could last for years.

There was a large catamaran at Medana Bay called *Cerebral Seabatical*. Gerard was the owner and captain. He would also stop for extended periods, but primarily to interview young people to join him as crew. With another experienced captain helping him, he would teach the young crew the fundamentals of sailing, diving and various water sports as they cruised among the islands of French Polynesia and Indonesia. I thought he was committed to this routine, so I was surprised when I got a message from him from Cape Town. He clearly had decided to complete a circumnavigation instead of just meandering among the islands of the South Pacific and Southeast Asia. Recently checking the location of his boat, I saw he was sailing in the Bahamas.

Sunset in Medana Bay

Then there are people like Barry Perrins who make the boat their home. They don't have a residence on land where they can return for a break. For me, that would be the hardest approach to cruising. I take comfort in knowing I have a solid, reliable place to call home, one that doesn't move around on the water, that's roomy and, in my case, that I designed myself and perfectly suits my needs. I also like having a real street address for mail, although that may seem archaic in a world connected by the internet where the only seemingly meaningful address is a URL.

The cruising world is a versatile world where people can choose what fits their ambitions and desires.

As I boarded *Phywave* to pull away from the rickety little dock at Medana Bay, I noticed one of the settee cushions in the salon had a hole torn in it, or should I say chewed. Rats can be a problem in some marinas. I had noticed a few rat droppings on my deck before but none inside. A rat on a boat is a serious problem. It can cause enormous damage by chewing through critical wires and other components. I had cleared out of the country the day before, so I really couldn't leave the marina grounds to buy rat traps or anything else to combat the problem. I sent the marina manager a message on WhatsApp telling him I thought there was a rat on my boat. He brought me rat poison blocks and sticky cardboard, like super flypaper, that was supposed to catch a rat or mouse if it tried to walk across it. I deployed the poison and cardboard in the bilge where I noticed a few more rat droppings. With that, I left the marina. I never caught a rat with the cardboard and I can't say I noticed the poison blocks being chewed on. I also never caught the smell of a dead rat or noticed any damage in the boat like chewed wires. It's possible the rat was on the boat for a while, chewing on the settee cushion, then went back to shore before I left Medana Bay. I was worried about it all the way to Cocos (Keeling) but never saw any further evidence of a rat on board. However it was resolved, it didn't affect my voyage.

20

Cocos (Keeling) Islands

I arrived at south atoll of the Cocos (Keeling) Islands on June 13, exactly nine days after leaving Medana Bay on Lombok, a reasonably quick trip across 1,200 nm.

The route from Medana Bay to the Indian Ocean took me back through the Lombok Strait again, southbound this time. Unlike before, there were several big cargo ships and tankers going through the strait, so I was glad to be negotiating this waterway during daylight. Once through the strait, with the sun setting, I turned southwest on a course of 260–265 degrees directly to Cocos.

I decided long before I left Lombok that I wouldn't stop at Christmas Island. There really wasn't anything I wanted to see there, and the offshore anchorage for yachts was in a bay that is not well-protected from the ocean waves and winds. Consequently, it was reported by other cruisers to be a very rolly anchorage. Besides, I wanted to spend more time in the atoll at Cocos (Keeling). I had missed anchoring in atolls in the Tuamotus, so given my planned route, Cocos (Keeling) would be my last opportunity to anchor in the turquoise waters of an atoll.

Sailing to Cocos (Keeling) I had good following winds, with sails set for broad reach or downwind sailing the entire way. The winds finally became unreliable on June 12 as I neared Cocos. I had the engine on for a few hours but was able to keep sailing. To arrive during daylight hours in the morning, I deliberately slowed down during the last day.

Cocos (Keeling) is an Australian territory. Following instructions on the Cocos arrival document I had been given by the ABF as I left Darwin, I called Cocos ABF on VHF channel 20 when I was still outside the 12-mile territorial limit. When they answered I discovered there was a problem. I should have given them 96 hours' advance notice of my arrival as I did for the Australian mainland. That was definitely not on the Cocos arrival document I was given in Darwin. The 96 hours' notice was explicitly spelled out on the arrival document for Christmas Island, so I had reason to believe that Cocos was different and didn't require this notice.

The formal clearing-in process is streamlined at Cocos because the Australian officials come to each boat after they're notified on channel 20 that the boat is anchored. Because I had failed to give them the required

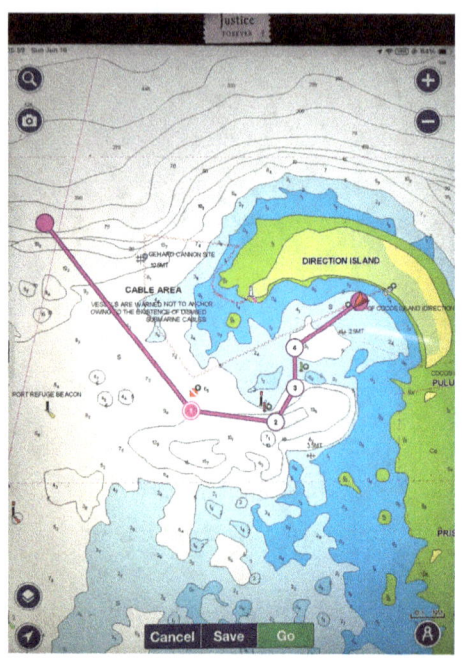

Route among the coral from the ocean to the Direction Island anchorage

96 hours' advance notice, when they arrived at my boat, they said I had committed a "serious offense." I could be fined several thousand dollars. I showed them the arrival document I had been given by ABF in Darwin. They agreed the document was unclear about the advance notice. To resolve this, in effect they gave me a warning, a seriously written letter they must have printed before they left their office to come to my boat. The letter said if it happened again, I would be subject to a fine. OK, but I'll never come back to Australia in a boat so I didn't care. Once they left my boat, I threw the letter away. Just like their "biosecurity" forcing me to discard most of my food in Cairns, the Australians had once again proved themselves to be hostile to private yachts.

The weather was nice the day I arrived but soon turned cloudy, windy and rainy. The barrier reef protects the anchorage from the ocean waves like the lagoon inside any atoll, but with only a string of low-lying islands (motus)

My dinghy on the beach

around the perimeter, some with palm trees, it offers essentially no shelter from the southeast trade winds or storm fronts that blow across the Indian Ocean. During the eight days I spent anchored at the Direction Island anchorage in Cocos (Keeling), a strong wind was blowing and the rain was falling for five of them.

To avoid coral heads (bommies) in the lagoon, there is a specific route to follow from the open ocean in the north to the yacht anchorage just off Direction Island. There are also coral heads in the anchorage area but it is mostly sand, so it wasn't hard to find a place to drop my anchor. I tried a couple of spots I wasn't happy with for various reasons, but finally found a good spot in 3 meters of water. I let out 27 meters of chain because I knew from other cruiser blogs that strong trade winds can really blow through the anchorage.

Although the Immigration clearing-in process was easy because they came to my boat, there was still a hassle paying the AU$10/day or AU$50/week anchoring fee. It must be paid at the shire office on Home Island, about 1.4 nm away from the anchorage at Direction Island. You can't officially clear out of Cocos without a receipt showing the fee has been paid. A distance of 1.4 nm can be a pretty long ride in a dinghy across shallow waters with numerous coral heads in the relentless 20 knot winds that blow there. There is a great, fairly new inter-island ferry (air-conditioned!), but it only connects Direction Island with Home Island on Thursdays and Saturdays and the shire office is closed on Saturdays, along with almost everything else on Home Island except the grocery store Shamrocks. I planned to take the Thursday ferry to Home Island to pay my fees and be on my way to Réunion Island the next morning. Given the poor weather, I would have left sooner except for having to pay the anchoring fee and get an official outbound clearance. Not having an official outbound clearance from the last port can sometimes be a problem when trying to clear in at the next port.

Direction Island itself is uninhabited, but with a white sand beach and park facilities like shelters, BBQ grills, toilets, and a historical trail with interpretive displays, it's a popular day trip getaway for the local Aussie population who live on West Island. West Island also has a few small hotels and the airport, the main way tourists and supplies get to Cocos (Keeling). I really can't see a big tourist appeal to this place when there are so many other places to go if you want a white sand beach holiday on an atoll. There really isn't much in the way of tourist infrastructure either—hotels, restaurants and the like. Maybe its remote location and rarity is the appeal for the few tourists who do go there.

Phywave **anchored at Direction Island**

Hermit crab

I walked the trail around the perimeter of Direction Island where I found the usual collection of sea debris washed up—flip-flops, plastic bottles and baskets, broken pieces of wood, bits of clothes, etc., pretty much anything that can float and that people would freely throw away. That was mixed with coconuts, fallen palm fronds and tree trunks. By contrast, the part of the island with the picnic facilities was cleaned up and free of this kind of debris because it is actively used as a beach getaway for residents of Cocos (Keeling). I suppose the fallen coconuts were good to eat; other cruisers had done that, but I don't really like coconut, so I didn't try to do anything with them. I probably shouldn't have been sitting under a tree with hanging coconuts. Someone once told me more people are killed each year by coconuts falling on their heads than by shark attacks. It would have been really ironic to have sailed that far only to be clunked on the head by a coconut.

Home Island itself had one small grocery store, Shamrocks, and one café for hot food. If you count the grill outside the entrance to the grocery store where cheeseburgers and a few other things were available, there were two places to get hot food. Other than that, and a small hardware store, there wasn't much on Home Island. A few abandoned restaurant attempts looked permanently closed. There was a layover of several hours between when the ferry arrived from Direction Island and when it returned. After some shopping at the store, I wandered along almost every road on the island, from the beach area at the northwest end to an old mansion at the southeast end that was apparently a bed-and-breakfast place of some kind. That place was dead, no one around and nothing happening inside. Later someone told me you can book it (it's shown as a hotel on Google Maps) and someone will come to let you in and show you to a room. It was so desolate-looking, though, it would be weird to stay there with no one around. I supposed it may be used more often as an event space.

The southeast end also had a sailing club of some sort, with small sailing dinghies stacked up outside a small building. The water there was also very shallow for a long way out from the shore. I saw a fisherman who had waded 200 meters off the shore and was only knee-deep in the water. He was throwing his net out and dragging it back in again, over and over, hoping it had caught some fish.

When I arrived at Direction Island I was the only boat there, which surprised me because I knew it was a popular stop for yachts to break up the long passage across the Indian Ocean. After a few days, an Australian guy named Dave showed up in a wooden ketch he had restored, *Arcana Celeste*. A few days after that a Swedish family I had met at Medana Bay arrived, so the

Direction Island beach with *Phywave*

anchorage became a little livelier. Dave was sailing the same route as I was, so we would cross paths again at several places down the line.

One of the positive things I accomplished while at Direction Island was successfully submitting all the required advance paperwork for my arrival at Réunion Island. Starlink was really handy for that kind of communication. The officials there responded that the documents I submitted were OK and they would have a berth for me at Marina Darse Titan when I arrived. It's great to get confirmation of arrival details rather than just having to rely on the expectation there'll be a place to put my boat. I remember arriving in Tangiers where they had told me by email that I had a berth reserved. When I arrived, I had to wait around most of the day for them to find a place for me. I pulled into that berth late at night.

I thought that it would be a refreshing break to get back to a well-developed place like Réunion with a population of over 800,000 and fresh croissants! I was already creating a list of things I needed to get in Réunion before moving on. I expected maybe two weeks there or longer depending on when a suitable weather window opened for making the difficult passage around the southern end of Madagascar to Richards Bay in South Africa.

Leaving Cocos (Keeling) Atoll

I usually like to leave an anchorage first thing in the morning to make the most of daylight to get my passage started. However, the morning of my scheduled departure was a beautiful, wind-free morning. Up to that point I hadn't tried to launch my drone because of the high winds. I really wanted an elevated panoramic video of the anchorage and Cocos (Keeling) Atoll, so I grabbed the drone case, jumped in the dinghy, struggled to start the outboard and went ashore. Launching the drone from a stable location like the beach is much better than from the boat because the boat is constantly moving around and the rigging threatens to interfere with bringing the drone back in to land. I launched the drone from the beach, maneuvered it out over the water and got some great 360-degree panoramic videos with the drone at about 50 meters above the water. I also flew the drone around to get still photos of the other boats in the anchorage, which I sent to them by email before I left.

As I motored back to *Phywave* in the dinghy, I was really pleased with the drone photography I got. The turquoise waters, submerged coral heads, white sand beaches and palm trees are the iconic images of sailing Pacific

Cocos (Keeling) ferry

South Sea islands that I had missed when I cruised through French Polynesia. Though I was in the Indian Ocean, the images were basically the same. It would hardly be acceptable to return from a voyage around the world without photos like that.

I left the anchorage at about 1500 local time, waving to the people on the other boats as I was motoring out along the route, avoiding coral, to the open ocean. Saying goodbye among cruisers is not the casual thing it would be on land. Everyone knows, and accepts, the dangers that sailing the oceans presents. It may be the last time you ever see that boat, the fate of its crew in the hands of the wind and waves and storms.

Once out of the lagoon and north of Pulau Luar Island I turned west again, enjoying fast sailing on a broad reach riding the southeast trade winds toward Réunion Island.

Reflecting on my time at Cocos (Keeling), I realized it was one of the most remote places I'd stopped so far on my solo voyage to seven continents, at least in terms of being far from other populated places. Deception Island in Antarctica is another candidate, but there were cruise ships coming and going nearly every day during the week I was there so it didn't feel so remote or unpopulated.

21

Réunion Island

"Ah oui, les espions, on trouve partout." It's 2 a.m. I'm standing in the deep shadows in an alley off Rue Sadi Carnot, my hat pulled low across my face, a Gauloises hanging from my lips, staring at my phone. My contact is late, not like her. There's a full moon somewhere above a solid overcast sky that's threatened to rain all day. Walking here I could feel the cool breeze blowing in from the nearby harbor, carrying the salty smell of the ocean. The intense green and red lights marking the harbor entrance reflected off the walls of the buildings lining the street at the water's edge. As I walked, I would sometimes quickly duck into a doorway alcove to check for a tail. I saw nothing; if they were back there, they're good. We set the meeting at a spot behind a defunct Chinese restaurant with a broken-down bamboo fence in front of its forlorn entrance. As I waited, the scratching of a restless rat in an empty cardboard box was the only thing disturbing the quiet night. No kung pao chicken tonight, pal.

Everyone knows the next moment, when the world seems to hold its breath, the clock fails to tick forward, a beating heart pauses, and your brain involuntarily skids down a slope of anticipation. Far down the alley, the sound of a scuffle, a panicked shout, and the crack of a gunshot shatters the night . . .

* * *

An important stop for ships on trade routes to Asia until the Suez Canal opened in 1870, Réunion was a spy novel of an island that collected more than its share of misfits, miscreants, Foreign Legion rejects and con artists, a place Rick and Louis might have headed for instead of Brazzaville. Now it's a popular French holiday-home location with direct flights from Paris. With my arrival by sailboat on July 10, I was the latest miscreant to sully its shores.

My passage there from Cocos (Keeling) was pretty fast, a total elapsed time of about 18 days, but it could have been faster. I originally notified Réunion officials I would arrive on July 12 but soon realized I would arrive earlier but was not sure when. I finally told them July 10. I stooged around, sailing slow the last couple of days so I would arrive at the harbor entrance during daylight on that day. I also slowed down during the passage when the winds were running 25–35 knots and confused 4-meter seas were hitting the boat broadside.

Map of Réunion Island

When a big wave slammed into the side of the boat, it was like being hit by a truck. Other waves broke over the deck, briefly inundating it, the seawater cascading down the opposite side. The boat would roll into the deep wave troughs to the point where the edge of the deck was in the water. That roll would also turn the heading of the boat in the direction of the trough, forcing the autopilot to throw the rudder hard over to correct the course. This often resulted in an alarm when the rudder was all the way over against its limits. I usually try to trim the sails so the boat was reasonably balanced, not inclined to turn one way or the other, with a bit of weather helm left in. The autopilot doesn't have to work so hard when the boat is balanced, saving electrical power. In these very rolling conditions such balancing efforts are futile. The best I could do was reduce sail to slow down so the ride wasn't so rough, like driving slow instead of fast over a rutted road is a bit more comfortable. Otherwise, I stayed below deck in the cabin, getting rattled around like a marble in a jar.

View from Piton Maïdo

Entrance to the Darse Titan marina is a narrow 90-degree turn. As I approached this turn, I saw a huge mast coming toward the entrance from inside. I stopped and backed away as a large catamaran full of tourists came through. During my time in Titan, I got to know this boat because it was moored on a jetty nearby. It would take tourists out for a few hours then return. I don't know if it ever actually put up the sails or just cruised around offshore for a while.

The clearing-in process at Réunion was incredibly efficient. Angelique, the marina manager, had prepared all the entry documents and handed them to me as I arrived after helping with the mooring lines at my berth. Fifteen minutes later the Immigration and Customs people showed up. They didn't need to come aboard, had no need to confiscate my eggs, meat or anything else like the morons in Australia. They stood on the dock, I handed them my passport and prepared entry documents, they stamped everything, bid me a pleasant stay and left. It took minutes! I've been stuck at red lights that took longer. This was amazing compared to other places I've been where I had to take a car to multiple offices all over town to clear in and clear out.

The entry stamp in my passport is important. Réunion is an overseas department of France and, like other Schengen countries, France limits a stay to 90 days in a 180-day window for nonresidents of the Schengen Area. The 90 days started when I arrived on July 10. I needed to return home to the US in September to participate in the First World Flight Centennial. Initially I thought I would take the boat across to Richards Bay in South Africa in August and leave it there while I returned home. However, the best month weather-wise to make the tricky passage to Richards Bay is October. I also have security concerns about leaving the boat in Richards Bay where onboard thefts have been a problem in the past. The marina in Réunion is very secure. I was thinking I'd leave the boat there while I returned to the US in September, then come back again to Réunion in October to make the passage to Richards Bay. From there I'd make short hops along the South Africa coast to Cape Town where I'd be positioned to make the homestretch run northwest across the Atlantic to the Caribbean and the US. The days I spent traveling back to the US in September would not count against the 90-day limit, so looking at the numbers, this plan would work out all right.

I rented a car for a few weeks to explore that amazing volcanic island and to facilitate buying things I needed and picking up things I ordered.

Buying Things

Unlike the last two places I stopped, Réunion is directly connected to the global world of commerce. It was straightforward to order things from Amazon, for example. They would automatically add any required customs duty to the purchase price. The one hitch was that the shipping address I was given didn't work, so I had to drive to Saint-Denis from the marina in Le Port to pick up packages.

In particular, I ordered a replacement for my Icom IC-7300 ham radio, which I had been using as a general purpose SSB radio. I had modified it so it would transmit on marine band frequencies but only used it that way a few times to talk to a cruiser net that was operating on the US East Coast. I used it for ham radio contact several times. I also used it as a shortwave receiver, listening for English-speaking stations wherever I went. I got to know the schedule and frequencies for BBC World Service. Before I had Starlink, this was a primary source for up-to-date news. I first learned of the death of Queen Elizabeth II on the BBC while crossing the Atlantic.

View into Cirque de Mafate

Somewhere along the line the touch screen on my 7300 had failed. It would turn on but I had no control. Maybe it was just the continuous salt environment that caused the failure since this radio wasn't really designed to be used on a boat. I suspected it was a connection to the circuit board on the front panel but there was no feasible way for me to fix it. Even though I now rarely used it, I still wanted it working. I ordered the replacement from a ham radio shop in the US that could do the modification so it could operate on all frequencies. In the case of this shipment I had to pay the duty and pick it up at the DHL office at the airport in Saint-Denis.

The variety of shops in Réunion was extensive. There was a large DIY store called Leroy Merlin, somewhat equivalent to Home Depot in the US, with tools and hardware. There was a huge mall called Cap Sacré-Coeur with a Carrefour supermarket where I could buy provisions and home goods. Carrefour is a very well-known name with stores found throughout France, even in Papeete. There were also several restaurants in the mall. I found myself going there often because it was only a few minutes' drive from the Titan marina where my boat was docked.

Farther away in Saint-Denis, I was glad to find an authorized repair shop for TAG Heuer watches. I had broken the bracelet and clasp on my watch while crossing from Cocos (Keeling). Even though keeping track of time on the boat while crossing the ocean is pretty irrelevant, as I mentioned before, I still liked having the watch on my wrist. It told me when it was four in the afternoon and time to pour a finger of whiskey and relax in the cockpit, watching the rhythmic rolling of the waves.

Of course, to get to these places it was essential to have the rental car. There was no taxi service or Uber in Le Port or elsewhere on the island. Without the car I would have had to walk or figure out how to use the buses.

Touring

I spent a few weeks making a number of excursions into the interior of Réunion Island, where its spectacular volcanic history is found. I've included a map of Réunion which shows the three calderas (cirques) near the island center—Cirque de Mafate, Cirque de Cilaos and Cirque de Salazie, all dormant. At the conjunction of these cirques is Piton des Neiges, at 3,071 meters the highest point in the Indian Ocean. In the southeast corner of the island is Piton de la Fournaise, the only active volcano on Réunion, which last erupted in April 2021.

To access these places, you have to drive up incredible winding, narrow mountain roads built all over this island, some with one-way tunnels blasted from solid rock. You must look for oncoming headlights before entering. The French certainly excel at building roads like this—they're found all over France as well.

I first took a day trip from the boat to a point on the rim of Cirque de Mafate, an overlook called Piton Maïdo. It has a captivating view into the cirque, where several small villages are perched on flat spots. As expected, the road up to the rim was very winding, with cars having to take the switchbacks slowly to avoid cars coming the other way. There were also buses using this road which made the drive even more challenging.

A few days later I went farther afield, planning a trip with two overnight stops. The first was at Hôtel Les Géraniums in the village of La Plaine des Cafres. On the way there I first drove farther southeast to Cascade de Grand Galet, a waterfall I had seen promoted in travel brochures for Réunion Island. Parking was haphazard on the narrow roads and the waterfall wasn't particularly spectacular compared to others I have seen. After staying the night in La Plaine des Cafres, I drove to Pas de Bellecombe, a viewpoint on the edge of the caldera surrounding Piton de la Fournaise. I had my hiking poles with me and struggled down the very steep trail along the caldera wall to its floor, where there is a cinder cone nearby. I stopped at the cinder cone but hearty hikers continue on to climb to the summit of Piton de la Fournaise. Climbing back up was actually easier because I didn't have to plunge down the steep steps of the trail with my old, creaky knees.

Cascade de Grand Galet

Back in the car, I drove from Pas de Bellecombe to the northeast coast of Réunion then back inland again through Salazie. From there the road led up the mountain to the Sarana Hotel. It's a high-end hotel and a great break from the boat. The restaurant was also first class; I enjoyed an excellent dinner with red wine. After breakfast there the next morning, I continued up the mountain to the end of the road. From there, I took a short hike up to Col des Boeufs, which had a great view into Cirque de Mafate from the east, opposite Piton Maïdo. After hiking back to the car, I started down the winding road to the coast and the coastal road back to Le Port.

Solidified lava flow

On the way down the hill I picked up two young Swiss women who had been hiking in the calderas for a few days. I dropped them off in Salazie where they could catch a bus. After I parked at the marina, I discovered one of them had left an expensive camera in the back seat. I didn't know their names or have any contact information for them. That night I speculated on how I might get the camera back to them. I didn't need to make much effort to accomplish that. I had told them I was sailing around the world and my boat was currently in the marina. The following day they contacted Angelique, the marina manager, asking for an "Americain" staying on a boat in the marina. Angelique emailed me and put me in touch with them. They came to the marina that morning to pick up the camera.

Cinder cones in the caldera around Piton de la Fournaise

My final excursion was to the village of Cilaos, situated in the middle of the Cirque de Cilaos. This was the most challenging of the narrow mountain roads; in places the road and tunnels were only one lane. There weren't any lights controlling traffic in the tunnels. Showing up at an entrance, it was a matter of looking for headlights coming the other way. If no headlights were in sight, you could then proceed into the tunnel, essentially seizing it so cars coming the other direction would have to wait at the far entrance. Usually, I was following another driver who had to make that "go, no-go" headlight decision, but a few times I was in the lead.

I stayed overnight at Hotel des Neiges in Cilaos and had another great dinner at Restaurant L'Isabelle nearby. In the morning, I wandered around the few streets with shops and restaurants, and drove to a nearby viewpoint that overlooked the village. Taking a side road that connected to the road back down the hill, I saw full parking lots at trailheads for trails leading up and out from Cilaos to the adjacent cirques and to the summit of Piton des Neiges.

Piton des Neiges

After visiting Cilaos, I felt like I had seen the highlights of Réunion on these excursions. I would hate to have gone to such a remote island and not made the most of my time there. It's very unlikely I would ever be coming back.

Maintenance

With *Phywave* tied up in Darse Titan marina, I took the opportunity to service the main halyard winches which get the most use from routinely raising and lowering the mainsail. They had become

Servicing the winches

noisy, especially under heavy load, so I thought the solution was to clean them. The process requires the winch to be completely disassembled and all the individual parts cleaned with a degreaser. Once that's done, the parts need to be lightly lubricated again and the winch reassembled. Not having done this before, I followed a YouTube video on how to do it—very helpful. After cleaning and lubricating, I got them back together without a problem. I didn't notice that they moved any more freely or were less noisy than before. Oh well, at least I now know how the servicing process works.

The marina had washing machines but not dryers, so on a sunny day I washed clothes and hung them out to dry along the lifelines and other lines I had strung up on the boat.

Leaving Réunion

The 1,400-nm passage from Réunion Island to Richards Bay in South Africa follows a route around the southern tip of Madagascar (Mada for short). Strong storms with gale-force winds spinning out of the South Atlantic Ocean and Antarctica periodically cross the route. The best time to make this passage is in October, as I mentioned, when these gales become less frequent during the austral spring and before tropical storm season begins later in November.

That led to a dilemma for me. I was comfortable in the marina at Réunion Island. When I arrived, I told them I'd like to stay until October which they seemed OK with then. Meanwhile, I'd been watching the weather forecasts daily, as I always do when flying or sailing. I spotted a weather window I thought could work, which would have me leaving Réunion on August 8. Considering that option against staying until October, I went to the marina office to confirm I could stay until October. To my surprise they told me I had to be out by September 30 because the marina was fully booked with sailing rallies that would start arriving October 1.

This is the problem with the big sailing rallies I discussed in an earlier chapter. As described there, rallies are potentially large organized groups of boats sailing to the same destinations, like across the Atlantic or even around the world. Because of the large number of boats arriving at the same time, they usually consume all of a marina's resources like berth space. That's the reason I could not stay past September 30. It was annoying and frustrating but there was nothing I could do about it. I imagine the marina had a contract with the rally organizers they had to fulfill. It's good recurring business for the marina because these rallies return to the same places year after year.

Laundry day on *Phywave*

Now that I would be kicked out of the marina by September 30, I had to adjust my schedule. I had to be in Seattle to participate in the First World Flight Centennial from September 26 to September 29. There's no way I could be back in Réunion to leave on September 30. Moreover, I hate to be forced to leave into weather circumstances that were not my choice and could be terrible. To participate in the Centennial, I planned to return to the US in mid-September. If I waited in Réunion until later in August, there would be no way to know if I'd find a better weather setup than the August 8 setup I had already identified.

Considering all these factors, I decided to leave Réunion on August 8. I paid my marina bill the day before and cleared out with Immigration that same day. On the morning of August 8, I left the marina and drove over to the fuel dock to top up my diesel tank. Dave, the Australian sailor I met in Cocos (Keeling), had arrived in Réunion several days after me. We had met a few times for a beer, so when it came time for me to leave, he offered to help with mooring my lines at the fuel dock. Fueling completed, I sailed out through the harbor entrance to begin the next ocean crossing of my solo voyage to seven continents.

22

Crossing to Richards Bay

As I left the harbor entrance of Réunion Island on August 8 and turned southwest, I saw clusters of boats in the distance and wondered what was going on. I soon found out. As I approached them, I was treated to the sight of a pretty amazing concentration of humpback whales actively playing off the point of land at Saint-Gilles-les-Bains. It was a parting treat as I left Réunion.

Refueling from jerry cans during calm seas

On August 9 I was 24 hours and 130 nm into my passage to Richards Bay in South Africa. I was relying on a forecast weather window that suggested a smooth and relatively uneventful passage around the southern end of Madagascar. You can never trust long-range forecasts 10 days out to hold, especially in that part of the world. In this case it was important that it held at least until I could get around ("weather" in sailor lingo) the southern tip of Madagascar (Mada). Once I passed that I could retreat north up the Mozambique (Moz) channel if necessary to wait out bad weather, either by heaving-to or heading for two well-known weather anchorages, at Baie de Saint-Augustin on the west coast of Mada or the north side of Ilha da Inhaca just outside Maputo in Mozambique. Generally, if a yacht is taking shelter from bad weather and nobody on board goes ashore, it's permissible to anchor in a country's waters without going through the often-arduous process of formally clearing in to the country. I was hoping I didn't have to test that theory.

The weather forecast had a pair of successive high-pressure systems along the route to Richards Bay. In the Southern Hemisphere, high-pressure systems spin counterclockwise, meaning the winds along the northern edge of these systems were blowing east to west, exactly what I wanted. This is the weather setup that primarily motivated me to leave Réunion when I did.

Approaching Cape St. Lucia

For the first few days heading southwest to the tip of Mada the weather worked out pretty well, but as I got to the point where I needed to turn in a more westerly direction toward South Africa, these systems began to fall apart and I encountered strong countercurrents.

One of the high-pressure systems in the string I was watching was forecast to unexpectedly intensify, with 40-knot winds and 5-meter seas. I rounded the tip of Mada and turned more northwest on a course toward Ilha da Inhaca. I was downloading the forecasts every 12 hours, as soon as the latest update became available. I finally noticed the forecast pattern start to break up a bit. Although the high seas were still in the forecast, the time period between wave crests was extending, meaning they would be rolling waves rather than breaking waves—much easier to deal with in a small boat. A

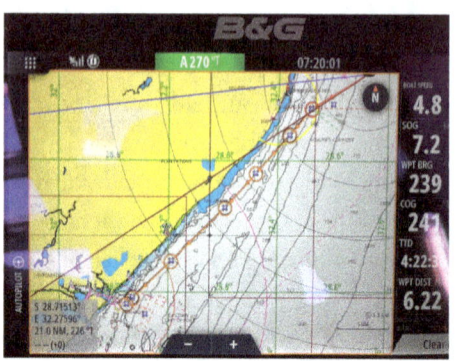

Close-in approach course from Cape St. Lucia to Richards Bay

relatively light wind corridor emerged from east to west that would make for easier sailing. I seized on the corridor and turned due west to a waypoint I set as a decision point on whether to continue to Richards Bay or retreat to the Ilha da Inhaca anchorage. The corridor held, so when I reached the decision waypoint I turned for Cape St. Lucia on the South African coast. From there I could follow the coast south to Richards Bay.

I was still wary of my heading because I started to encounter the strong southwest-setting Agulhas Current about 75 nm offshore. The wind also died, so I was now motoring and crabbing into the current so I could arrive at Cape St. Lucia as planned. Once there, I turned south along a course about 5 nm from shore. That route basically took me on the inland side of the Agulhas Current and out of the fastest part of the stream. This approach worked out well. Arriving in Richards Bay and turning west into the harbor along the well-marked channel was easy, no drama.

After a 12-day passage from Réunion Island through some rapidly changing weather conditions and unexpected countercurrents, I arrived in Richards Bay, South Africa, at 1300Z on August 20. I was very glad to have completed that passage without having to contend with any southwest gales which were, in effect, blocked for a while by the high-pressure systems. That changed the night I arrived when a southwest gale blew in over Richards Bay. Fortunately, *Phywave* was securely tied to the reception jetty so it had no impact on me as it quickly blew through and moved on.

I had already landed on the continent of Africa at Tangiers. For that reason, this was not a big moment that arriving at a new continent would be nor an addition to my tally of continents. However, getting across from Réunion around the tip of Madagascar to Richards Bay is regarded by many as the trickiest passage on this route around the world. Others who go north of Mada, then to Nosy Be, and then straight south down the Mozambique Channel usually have no easier a time of it. Several boats that arrived in Richards Bay after me, which had chosen that route, were pinned down at emergency anchorages for several days along the Mozambique Channel.

Richards Bay

When arriving in South Africa at Richards Bay boats must first tie to the concrete wall of the reception jetty for Immigration clearing-in procedures. After the Immigration agent came by and cleared me in to South Africa it was still a great pleasure to walk down the jetty and have dinner at a restaurant, Dros, even though I had left Réunion only 12 days before.

There were strong crosswinds in the small harbor by the jetty the day I arrived. Unfortunately, as I approached the jetty a big gust slammed *Phywave* into the wall and scratched and dented the aluminum hull a bit. I hoped I could get that cosmetic damage repaired or at least smoothed out while I was in Richards Bay. It was very poor boat handling on my part, the most serious such mistake I made on this voyage. I should have had all my fenders on the side of the boat that would contact the jetty wall.

Phywave **tied to reception Q jetty in Richards Bay**

The Customs building is a few miles away from the reception jetty, so a taxi ride was required the next day to get there. The taxi driver all the foreign boats coming into Richards Bay and Zululand Yacht Club use is named Eric. I ended up getting several rides with him for various reasons, including the ride to the Customs building for clearing-in procedures that morning. I moved *Phywave* across to a berth in the Zululand that afternoon. The club seems more like a local social club, not just a yacht club for boaters.

From Richards Bay, the plan to get around the coast of South Africa to Cape Town in the spaces between periodic southwest gales is well established. Wait for a weather window three or more days long and incrementally move the boat to the next port along the coast. Typical stops are Durban, East London, Port Elizabeth, Mossel Bay, Knysna, and others. How long the weather window lasts determines how far along the coast you can go before stopping at a port to wait for the next weather window. Maybe some stops can be skipped. I would be considering that process in more detail when I embarked on this passage in October after returning from my break in the US.

I'd mentioned to Eric, the taxi driver, and a few other South African people I'd met that this was not my first time in South Africa. They were a bit astonished when I told them I hitchhiked from Nairobi to Cape Town and back again in 1975. Apartheid was still in place in South Africa, and Rhodesia hadn't yet become Zimbabwe though it was under enormous economic and political pressure with international monetary sanctions in place. I had many stories from those days that came up as I hung out in the yacht club bar during my stay in Richards Bay.

Haul Out

Just before leaving Darwin in May, with the boat still in the marina, I had a diver attempt to clean growth off the hull so I'd have a more efficient sail across the Indian Ocean. He was only partly successful. He said freshwater rains and hot temperatures in Darwin during the months *Phywave* was there had stimulated a lot of growth on hulls, especially small barnacles which he wasn't able to remove on my boat.

Wanting to get the Indian Ocean crossing done when the winds were favorable, I didn't have time, or a place, to get the boat hauled out of the water and the hull properly cleaned before arriving in Richards Bay. The facilities for

Phywave **on the travel lift at Richards Bay**

doing this at Réunion were fully booked for months, so I made arrangements ahead of time to get this done when I arrived.

September 5 was the day. I came to realize the facilities they have there, although very commonly used by cruisers sailing this route, were pretty primitive compared to others I've seen and used. First, the travel lift itself is pretty small and has a low crossbar. The slope of the bottom of the haul-out ramp is such that you have to go into the lift bow first. As a result of these two factors, the forestays on boats have to be loosened, disconnected at the deck end and pulled to the side. Their tension holding the mast is provided by running rigging—in my case, the spinnaker and genoa halyards. Getting enough slack on the forestay to disconnect it at the deck end required loosening the backstays and the shrouds. The backstays had been dropped entirely before when loading the boat on the transport ship that brought it to the US. I also dropped them to get the boat on the travel lift in Puerto Montt. I'd never loosened the shrouds or taken off the forestay before. These are all fundamental things that hold the mast upright. For any sailor, loosening these supporting steel cables is an uncomfortable thing to do. In this case there was no choice if I wanted to get the boat hauled out of the water in Richards Bay.

***Phywave* on wooden stick supports ready for antifouling paint**

After the boat was out of the water and positioned where it would sit while work on the hull was completed, it needed to be supported upright above the ground. Every other boatyard I know uses heavy telescoping metal support jacks designed for this purpose. At Richards Bay they cut wooden posts to support the boat. One end of the post is seated in the ground while the other end, with a flat piece of wood attached, is propped against the hull. I'm fortunate with *Phywave* because it's capable of sitting upright on its own when the centerboard is retracted. In fact, it's possible to beach it. Fixed keel boats can't do this and need to sit higher in the air. Of course, if *Phywave* sat flat on the ground there would be no room to clean the hull and renew the antifouling paint. That work began on September 9. I was hopeful it could be completed so the boat could go back in the water by September 13, a few days before I was scheduled to fly home. Unfortunately, that didn't happen.

Overall, the process to haul a boat out of the water and get it supported on land so the travel lift is cleared to handle another boat takes several hours. Considering that there are 2-meter tides in Richards Bay, and they need high tide to haul or launch boats, realistically they can only handle one boat a day. Scheduling the lift is the reason *Phywave* didn't go back in the water before I left on my trip home.

I'd be flying to the US on September 16, arriving the 17th, to participate as a pilot in the First World Flight Centennial at the end of September. I'd return to Richards Bay the first week of October to resume my voyage.

Back Home to Fly

As the Centennial date got closer and I was still sitting around my boat in Richards Bay, I volunteered for a few things that added to the already-busy two weeks I planned to be at home. The first was a dinner presentation at the Rainier Club in downtown Seattle, a venerable club in a classic brick building that's been there for more than 100 years. The club hosted the First World Flight pilots at dinner upon their return in 1924. I usually talk to pilot groups about my flying where a lot of technical details are appropriate. This was a much more diverse group of about 100 people in a banquet room. Appropriately, for the presentation to this group I put together a highlight reel of the most interesting moments from my four major international flights, including some of the cool videos I've posted on my YouTube channel and linked to on my website. It was an engaging group and dinner was great; I was glad I accepted their speaking invitation.

For the Centennial, I helped the organizers line up a group of small planes and pilots who, like me, had flown around the world and were recognized on the Earthrounders website. The plan was to have the planes on display at Seattle's Museum of Flight beginning September 26. On September 28 we would participate in a flyby of Magnuson Park in Seattle, the departure and return point for the original flight in 1924. It was an ambitious plan and the flyby really didn't come off very well, according to the spectators in the park.

My plane in Yellowknife, Canada, en route to my solo transpolar flight over the North Pole

As pilots, though, we had fun getting together to display our planes and do some flying.

The evening before the flyby I hosted a BBQ dinner party for Earthrounders pilots and their guests at my house on Bainbridge Island, not just those pilots participating in the Centennial but also any Earthrounders who happened to be in town for the event. It was a lively group of 20 or so. The broiled steelhead, grilled steaks and salads were perfect.

While home I discovered something that surprised me—I started to like flying again. After achieving the goals I had for international flying by 2019, I have to say I was a little burned out on flying. Flying to local airports for lunch, just to fly somewhere, really had little appeal and didn't require any imagination. Climbing into the plane for the Centennial, flying felt fresh again; maybe a 2+ year hiatus from flying is what I needed for a renewed perspective. There is a simplicity and elegance to airplanes and flying, especially compared to sailing around in a cruising sailboat like mine. My boat is filled with many systems to support living on it, the deck cluttered with standing and running rigging, the navigational systems more complex in some ways than those on my plane, the dinghy and outboard motor a separate little boat with its own issues. It's a lot of stuff that needs maintenance, sometimes doesn't work and sometimes breaks. Not simple, not elegant.

I reflected on the great, far-flung solo adventures I'd had in my plane N788W, from flying over the North Pole to landing in Antarctica. I looked forward to flying my plane again when my circumnavigation and voyage to seven continents was completed.

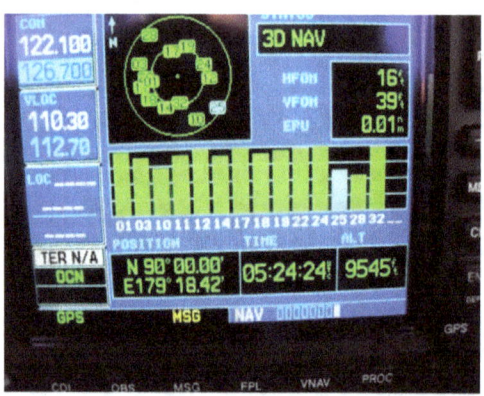

The GPS in my plane over the North Pole
(90 degrees north latitude)

To get home for the Centennial events, I had to endure 30 hours of flights and layovers en route from Richards Bay to Seattle. And my departure was delayed a day. I had planned to have at least two weeks at home but that got reduced to about 12 days. Then, of course, it was another 30-hour trip from Seattle back to Richards

Bay. It was an exhausting interlude from sailing but at least I got to fly my plane for a few hours.

Flying over the arctic sea ice en route to the North Pole

Leaving Richards Bay

As I mentioned, there is a well-known strategy for sailing along the coast of South Africa from Richards Bay to Cape Town. Even while I was still at home before returning to Richards Bay, I started watching the weather patterns along the coast knowing I might have to immediately jump on a suitable weather window when I returned because another might not come along for several days.

I arrived back in Richards Bay on October 4 and was happy to see the marine service company I hired to clean the hull and renew the antifouling paint had moved *Phywave* back to the marina and put all the standing rigging back in place. They had also put the genoa sail back on and filled the fuel tank with diesel. I only needed to buy new perishable provisions and I would be ready to go.

It appeared a weather window to move south along the coast would be forming at the beginning of the following week. As always, it was important to have wind blowing in the same direction that the Agulhas Current was flowing, that is, southwest. The wind was forecast to turn so it would be coming out of the northeast, but it would be strong, gale force, 30–35 knots or greater for much of the time. I hesitated going then with such strong winds, but when I talked to some local sailors about it, they said, "That's the weather window!" OK! I set my sights on moving down to East London, about 340 nm away. The weather window would only last about 60 hours. I needed to take advantage of the strong wind and favorable current to hustle on down there.

I made plans to depart on October 8, which entailed clearing out of Richards Bay the day before. Once again, I enlisted the help of Eric the taxi driver to take me over to the port where I first cleared Immigration, then to Customs for more stamped paperwork, and finally to the harbor authority to get their exit clearance. This was all very unusual since I was not leaving South Africa but simply continuing to another port in South Africa. At the time, this exit process was unique to Richards Bay; I wouldn't need to do this as I left any of the other South African ports I visited. This issue was getting a lot of attention from the Ocean Sailing Association of Southern Africa (OSASA) in the hope of simplifying the administrative chores cruisers had to complete for sailing along the South African coast. By the time this book is published, it may have changed.

23

South Africa

After arriving at Richards Bay, I visited several places in South Africa, primarily waterfront towns with harbors and marinas as I incrementally made my way along the coast in *Phywave* to Cape Town.

iMfolozi Game Reserve

While the boatyard crew was working on cleaning and putting new antifouling paint on my boat in Richards Bay, I took a break from boating and drove up to the town of St. Lucia for a couple of nights. While I was there I took a tour of the iMfolozi Game Reserve which I had booked a few days before.

iMfolozi Game Reserve, part of Hluhluwe-iMfolozi Park, is apparently the oldest game reserve in Africa. In an open vehicle with a few other people and a guide, I saw a variety of wildlife, including four of Africa's Big Five (elephant, water buffalo, leopard, lion and rhinoceros). We missed out on a leopard, but we did see a cheetah. I toured the major game parks in Kenya and Tanzania when I first visited Africa in 1975. My brother and I, along with some other Peace Corps volunteers from their posts in Zaire where my brother was also stationed, rented a VW van painted with zebra stripes and drove around ourselves, no guide, through the major game parks of Serengeti, Tsavo, Amboseli, Lake Manyara and Ngorongoro Crater. We also stopped at the famous Leakey archaeological digs at Olduvai Gorge. We saw a lot more

Touring East Africa game parks in 1975 with Mt. Kilimanjaro in the background

animals then, before African safaris became big business. We got much closer to the animals, maybe a little too close, when a hippo climbed out of the mud and charged the van. Good times!

East London

Returning to my boat in Richards Bay, I was anxious to get moving again. In a comfortable marina like the Zululand Yacht Club, it's easy to get stagnant and let the days drift by. I was determined to break that, so while I was still at home I started looking for a suitable weather window to continue, as I mentioned. I started sailing again on October 8 headed to East London, 350 nm southwest along South Africa's Wild Coast, a name I now understand. For the first few hours the wind was sublime but rapidly built to 30-40 knots (gale force) with commensurate rough wave action.

To further complicate things, I would be sailing in the famous Agulhas Current that runs southwest along the coast at speeds that can reach nearly 5 knots. That's quite high for an ocean (not tidal) current. As I mentioned earlier in this book, it is a seriously bad idea to sail in such a current when the wind is blowing in the opposite direction. Standing waves are created by the conflicting forces. Rogue waves along this coast can reach 30 meters in height, resulting in

A fraction of the genoa set in strong downwind to East London

many ships being sunk or seriously damaged over the years. The 60-hour weather window I had chosen was long enough for me to easily make it to East London when the greater speed from the strong winds and the contribution from the current were taken into account. After 60 hours the wind would change direction and blow against the current so I had to safely be in East London before then. It wasn't difficult; with the strong wind aft, I could set only a fraction of a headsail and still clip along at 6+ knots. The speed boost from the current added another 2 to 3 knots to my SOG. In the end I deliberately slowed down, as I have before, so I would arrive in East London during daylight hours.

After that quick run down from Richards Bay, I was tied fore and aft to mooring buoys, aligned with the river, at the Buffalo River Yacht Club. Tying the bow and stern to moorings keeps the boat from swinging around with the changing direction of the tidal flow in the river.

The people at the yacht club were great. As I arrived, they found a mooring spot for me and hitched *Phywave* to the muddy mooring lines, which needed to be pulled up out of the water. A few hours later a guy came by in a dinghy and asked whether I needed fuel. I had four empty jerry cans I hadn't filled in Richards Bay so I said yes. He took the cans away, filled them, and brought them back to the boat with a young woman from the club who had a credit card machine so I could pay. I've been in a lot of marinas and anchorages but I've never experienced this kind of concierge service. Truly brilliant.

The balance of my voyage around to Cape Town was planned to proceed in a similar fashion—wait for a weather window to move on to the next place along the coast—Port Elizabeth, Knysna or Mossel Bay, Simonstown, and maybe Hout Bay. I would clear out of South Africa at Cape Town and begin

Buffalo River Yacht Club with bow and stern moorings

the homestretch of my voyage back across the Atlantic for the third time headed for North America, which would be my seventh, and last, continent.

Overall, East London is not an attractive town. The yacht club and moorings are in a remote place nearly under a bridge with no restaurants, shops or anything appealing within easy walking distance. The yacht club itself had a bar, but with no food and limited opening hours. Uber worked well in East London, so that was the most efficient way to get around without a rental car. I decided to rent a car to explore East London a bit, but mainly so I could drive to a Yamaha shop to get my outboard motor fixed.

Fixing the Outboard Motor

Of course, since *Phywave* was tied to a mooring I needed to get the dinghy off the foredeck, put it in the water, then drag it around to the stern where I could pull the outboard motor out of its locker and mount it on the transom of the dinghy. As I've mentioned in previous chapters, it's a 6-hp Yamaha outboard and weighs about 60 pounds. When I pulled the cord to start it, I could feel it had no compression and, not surprisingly, it wouldn't start. I had last used it at Cocos (Keeling) where starting it and keeping it idling had been problematic. I would need it to work at future anchorages, so I had to find a place to get it repaired. I did an online search for a Yamaha dealer in East London and fortunately found one.

The Yamaha dealer was TKY Power Products located about eight miles northeast of East London. I called them and asked if someone could come down to the yacht club to fix my outboard. They said it wouldn't be possible until the following Monday morning, October 14. I had rented a car from Budget at the East London airport, using Uber to get out there, so I decided to take the outboard motor to TKY rather than having them come to me at the marina. It was a good decision. I got to their shop as they opened on Monday. Their outboard motor expert had just arrived. He quickly took the motor apart and discovered there was rust in the cylinder, which kept the valves from moving, resulting in no compression. He tapped the valves with a hammer to break them loose then thoroughly lubricated them to keep them moving freely. He said it was not a repair he could have done at the marina.

Approaching the narrow entrance to Knysna (center)

Once he got it running, he adjusted the idle and did more lubricating. He said the rust was likely due to water in the gasoline. This surprised me because I had replaced the gasoline at Lombok specifically to eliminate this problem. Given the bush operation at Medana Bay, it certainly was possible I got bad gas there. He also said these motors really need to run at least once a month to keep them lubricated and get them up to temperature to dry out any moisture. I certainly hadn't been running it that often. I watched what he did, as he did it, and got a bit more educated on outboard motors.

Once he completed his work, I loaded the motor into the trunk of the rental car and drove it to the marina. I was lucky to find a Yamaha dealer with such a knowledgeable guy who could fix it.

Knysna

Ignore the K—it's pronounced "nyz-na." I said it wrong several times before someone corrected me. It was another quick 330-nm passage along the South African coast where, again, the suitable weather window for a passage consisted of gale-force winds blowing in the right direction. Rough but quick. However, it was not quite quick enough to get me to Knysna before dark on Wednesday after leaving East London early Tuesday morning, October 10. Knysna has a well-known tricky entrance between the Knysna Heads to the estuary that shouldn't be attempted at night or with the wrong tide, especially by someone like me who's never done it.

Because I didn't make it as far as Knysna before dark, I had to lay up at an anchorage in Plettenberg Bay, along the Robberg Peninsula, about 22 nm east of Knysna. I was initially indecisive about anchoring there, thinking I could lie ahull or heave-to and wait until daylight to enter Knysna. I sailed slow for some hours with that strategy in mind but finally decided the anchorage would be better, especially if the wind kicked up overnight, which it did. With that decision made, I motored through calm winds to the anchorage, arriving at 11 p.m. It had been a long time since I anchored in the dark in a strange place. The e-charts on my chartplotter provided horizontal guidance, and with the depth finder I was looking for a depth less than 8 meters. Once found, I slowed the boat to zero knots, dropped the anchor, and put out about 40 meters of chain for a 5:1 scope. With that done, I went to bed and actually got five hours of solid sleep.

Leaving for Knysna early the next day I knew I would be bashing into 15-to-20 knot headwinds and waves all the way. There was no choice but to motor fast enough to hit the best time to pass through the narrow Knysna entrance, around 1200 local time. Mike Jacobs of the Knysna Yacht Club (KYC) was available via WhatsApp and radio to help newcomers get safely through. I was following a large catamaran, Nesi, which passed through several minutes before me. I didn't see the entrance until Nesi had already passed through, so its particular route wasn't any help to me. I had gotten to know the crew of Nesi in East London. The passage through the headlands was actually marked on my e-chart and turned out to be straightforward, except for crabbing into the 20-knot westerly crosswind. It's a little unnerving to steer the boat so the COG track is through the passage but the bow is pointed at the rocks.

In the narrow headlands at Knysna

KYC, where I arrived on October 17, was a very welcoming place. They let me stay tied to the reception dock instead of putting me out on a swing mooring where I would need to use the dinghy to get to shore. KYC has a great restaurant and bar a few meters from where I was tied up. From what I could tell, Knysna is something of a resort, second-home tourist town. There is a small shopping complex with many restaurants and a few hotels 50 meters from the yacht club. Charter boats take people out on the water for sailing excursions from the small marina there. It was the most comfortable stop I've made in Phywave since Darwin.

Even though Knysna was a pleasant place, it was always onward with my mission. A

Phywave **tied up in Knysna**

good weather window was opening Monday, October 21, that would get me to Hout Bay, just 12 miles south of Cape Town. I planned to jump on that to complete my passage along the coast of South Africa.

Container ship in the sunset on the way to Hout Bay

Hout Bay

About 12 miles south of Cape Town by road and a much easier place to find a berth for my boat compared to the two crowded marinas in Cape Town, the marina at Hout Bay Yacht Club is a great alternative. Arriving there still represented a complete transit of the coast of South Africa from Richards Bay and put me decidedly on the Atlantic Ocean side of Cape Agulhas, the southernmost point in Africa.

Leaving Knysna through the narrow neck at high slack tide was a few minutes of challenging boat handling. The wind was blowing into the narrow passage, creating short-period 4-meter swells, some of them breaking, that I had to drive through. The boat would ride up on the face of a swell, the bow then crashing down on the backside, sometimes getting buried in the face of the next wave. It took full concentration, increased engine power and a solid grip on the wheel to keep the boat perpendicular to the waves as I powered through to clear them. Getting caught sideways in a broach would have been a disaster in that narrow, rocky place. I was surprised the water was so active. When I arrived a few days before, I had flat water passing between the heads into the Knysna estuary.

After sailing south for several miles, I turned west and had good wind pushing me toward a waypoint I had set well south of Cape Agulhas. I probably gave the cape a wider berth than necessary, making the passage to Hout

Bay longer than it needed to be, but in strange areas like that, staying farther out to sea in deeper water was the more conservative approach. I'm sure local sailors could navigate a shorter route much closer to the cape. The downside of being farther away was that I didn't get any photographs of the cape as I rounded it in *Phywave*.

After the cape, I had high winds and a quick nighttime passage toward Hout Bay, turning north around the Cape of Good Hope at daybreak. The winds dropped to almost nothing so I could no longer sail, instead motoring the rest of the way into Hout Bay.

The entire coastal transit took three two-day passages spread over 15 days with stops in East London (five nights) and Knysna (four nights). True to its reputation, the weather along the coast was volatile and violent. On each of the three passages I had to contend with gale-force winds, fortunately at my stern, and large, very choppy and confused seas that made getting any sleep difficult. That was partly due to sailing in the shallow coastal waters where the typical depths are only 50–150 meters. In the open ocean, with water depths of thousands of meters, the swells and flow of the wind waves take on a much more regular and rhythmic characteristic.

Busy fishermen's pier at Hout Bay

I was damn glad to be in Hout Bay, which is about 12 nm of Cape Town, and in a pretty nice marina. In a week I would move *Phywave* 70 nm north to Saldanha Bay and skip taking *Phywave* to Cape Town proper. Just before my arrival, Saldanha Bay had been added as a port of entry where it was now possible to clear in and out of South Africa. Before this change, Cape Town was the only port of entry on that side of South Africa. I would be one of the first boats taking advantage of that change. From there I would be looking at my homestretch passage across the Atlantic to North America via St. Helena and the Caribbean.

One thing I wanted to accomplish while there was undertaking some simple repairs to my mainsail. One of the batten sleeves needed to be resewn and I needed to replace the broken top batten. Unlike my previous stops in South Africa, Cape Town has capable sailmakers who could easily accomplish these tasks. I contacted Ullman Sails on Friday and they sent a team Monday morning to collect the sail from my boat and take it back to their shop. They came with a long sail bag and four guys so the sail could be rolled up with the battens still in place and taken away, especially easy with a furling boom. This was very efficient, avoiding having to take the sail down, remove the battens and flake the sail into a square bundle for transport. They brought it back Thursday afternoon with the repairs made and fitted it back on the boom, with my direction. It was expensive to have the sail collected and delivered from their shop in Cape Town but the convenience was well worth it.

Western Cape

I kept my boat at the Hout Bay Yacht Club marina a total of 10 days, partly to fix a few things but also to have some time to explore this southwestern part of South Africa.

I had a rental car while in Hout Bay I had picked up at the Cape Town airport, using Uber to get there. I drove east to visit friends Alex and Ronel Ponot and their three kids, who now live in Stilbaai on the coast. I first met them in Oregon, where they owned a motel in Pacific City and then a horse ranch near Salem. A few years ago, they sold it all and moved to the Périgord region of France, even transporting several horses there. They had a horse ranch in Périgord as well, but Alex, who is French, said the French bureaucracy was so stifling he couldn't make a business of it so they decided to move again, to South Africa, but without the horses this time. Ronel is originally from

Old farm ruins near Stilbaai

Pretoria. They have a beach house in Stilbaai and a large ranch outside of town where I stayed with them for the night. I had a good time seeing a slice of South African life visitors don't normally see.

After Stilbaai I drove down to Cape Agulhas, where I spent the night in a great B&B near the lighthouse on the cape. Of course, they also have a prominent marker there, and a precise line, declaring it the point separating the Indian and Atlantic Oceans, all a pretty artificial construct. The oceans don't know their names or where one begins and the other ends.

On the drive to Stilbaai and back I was amazed by the vast farm fields, orchards and vineyards on both sides of the N2 highway. The soil and climate must certainly be conducive to agriculture, no doubt a key reason Europeans were drawn to settle here centuries ago.

Before returning to my boat in Hout Bay I spent the afternoon in the Victoria & Alfred (V&A) section of Cape Town, an area of old industrial wharfs and warehouses that have been repurposed and expanded to house many restaurants and shops. With broad walkways and plazas along the water, it reminded me a little of Fisherman's Wharf in San Francisco. There is also a

Marker at Cape Agulhas

nice marina there where I could have put the boat instead of Hout Bay. If you want your boat in Cape Town, this is a better place to go than the larger marina at the Royal Cape Yacht Club (RCYC). I had lunch at RCYC one day when I was in town buying spare parts. The club and marina are situated in a very industrial part of the port. Walking out the front door you are confronted with railroad tracks and long lines of trucks waiting to unload their containers onto ships. Unlike at the V&A marina, there are no restaurants or shops anywhere nearby. You would definitely need a rental car if you put your boat at the RCYC marina and you wanted to see anything beyond the marina.

V&A marina in Cape Town

The busy port at Saldanha Bay

Saldanha Bay

I chose to stop at Saldanha Bay, about 60 nm north of Cape Town, mainly to clear out of South Africa. The process at Saldanha Bay was reported to be much more streamlined than clearing out at Cape Town, the alternative. That turned out to be the case.

I was able to book a berth at the small marina at Yachtport SA in Saldanha Bay. They primarily do maintenance on boats, especially hull maintenance on large boats, because they have the only 100-ton travel lift in South Africa.

Of course, I didn't need the travel lift service, having just had the hull cleaned and repainted in Richards Bay. *Phywave* was much faster in the water after that work, by at least a knot or more. It pays to have a clean hull.

But given the technicians on-site at Yachtport SA, I had them do a few maintenance tasks, like changing the oil in *Phywave*'s Volvo Penta D2-50 engine. I also had them clean one side of my dual Racor diesel fuel filter and replace the 10-micron filter cartridge. I furnished the filters and oil which I already had on board. I have done these things myself in the past but took the lazy way this time and had them do it. This is very common maintenance work on a boat but they seemed inexperienced with it, especially the Racor filter change. I wish I had done it myself. All this was in preparation for the long Atlantic crossing ahead of me, and I wanted to do whatever I could to avoid any problems along the way. I wouldn't have any serious help

Rounding the lighthouse headed north to Namibia

with engine problems, or a place to get filters or parts, until I reached the Caribbean.

I also took the opportunity to add to my provisions. With a rental car I visited the Checkers supermarkets in two large malls that are within a 20-minute drive from Yachtport.

While in Saldanha Bay I decided to change my route once again. Since arriving in South Africa people had been telling me how great Namibia is, that I really should stop there. In particular, a cruiser I met in Hout Bay who was from Namibia gave me some specific information on where to go and what to see. I vacillated for several days over whether to make the extra stop. This voyage was beginning to wear on me; I was eager to wrap it up by returning to North America. However, I realized I would probably never pass this way again, so if I ever wanted to see Namibia, this was the time. Secondarily, I didn't want to arrive in the Caribbean too soon, like during the Christmas and New Year's holidays, when the place would no doubt be jammed with boats and people. Some additional delay, like a stop in Namibia, would help in that regard.

With those two factors in mind, I decided to head for Namibia to be followed by St. Helena Island on my original itinerary. I left Yachtport SA on Friday, November 8, at 1200Z, headed north to Walvis Bay, Namibia, with very favorable winds forecast along the route.

24

Namibia

"Namibia—Land of Sand." It's probably not the tagline the Namibian public relations people want to see, but it's accurate based on the week I spent there and the parts of the country I saw. There are other places I didn't see in the north with big game animals, but I do know that Namibia promotes the Namib Desert and its huge sand dunes as its primary attraction.

The 685-nm passage north from Saldanha Bay to Walvis Bay went by quickly, less than five days en route with strong following winds well offshore most of the way. The winds finally died nearing Walvis Bay so I motored part of the last day. Walvis Bay is a large bay with several cargo ships anchored inside waiting their turn to load or unload at the port. There were also ships coming and going through the entrance to the bay that I had to contact on VHF radio to coordinate movements.

The Walvis Bay Yacht Club is very accommodating and helpful to visiting yachts. I contacted them ahead of time asking if there would be room for me to tie alongside their jetty. It was no problem, with a dockhand available to assist with my lines. The yacht club secretary, for a modest fee, drove me to the Immigration and Customs offices to clear in to Namibia. Following that, I treated myself to lunch at the yacht club restaurant with a cheeseburger and a celebration mojito.

Unfortunately, my iPhone with my AT&T unlimited data plan would not connect to the local cellular networks. Apparently, AT&T had never

A ketch that sunk in Walvis Bay near the marina

The wreck of the *Zeila*

bothered to make reciprocal roaming agreements with Namibia. In every country I had visited on this voyage thus far, and in the many countries I had visited in my plane, my cellphone had always connected to the local networks for both voice and data. It was never an issue. The grandfathered AT&T plan I had was expensive, but the convenience of being able to use my phone without having to hunt around for local SIM cards, as many cruisers did, more than made up for the additional expense. As an example, the yacht club gave me the name of a woman who would do laundry. The only way I could contact her was using Starlink on my boat and setting my phone in airplane mode so calls would come over Starlink's Wi-Fi network. It meant I had to be at the boat to call her. If I found working Wi-Fi somewhere else, I could use the same approach. As I traveled throughout Namibia the lack of wireless communication never changed. Even as accustomed to using my phone as I had become, it really didn't matter much that I didn't have the instant communication I was used to. I was able to get my laundry done, picked up from and delivered to the boat. I was also able to arrange the rental of a 4×4 pickup truck to drive the rough roads of Namibia.

Namibia Inland

With my boat tied to the concrete yacht jetty at Walvis Bay, I headed out in the 4×4 Ranger pickup I rented, first north to Swakopmund and the Skeleton Coast. Leaving Walvis Bay, the scenery quickly turned to pure desert on both sides of the road, which ran parallel to the ocean a couple of hundred meters inland. There's really nothing to see except sand along this road until arriving in Swakopmund.

Swakopmund is regarded by locals as probably the most attractive town in Namibia. Situated right on the water, it's a pleasant, walkable place with many restaurants, shops and hotels, unlike Walvis Bay, which is a heavy-duty industrial port town.

I drove north from Swakopmund along what is known as the Skeleton Coast because of the many ships wrecked there over the centuries, and because of the many dead whales that have washed ashore, their bleached bones sometimes scavenged in the past by local tribes to build huts. Essentially all the shipwrecks have been so degraded over time that there's nothing left to see. One recent, very visible wreck, the *Zeila*, not far north of Swakopmund, had actually been sold for scrap and was in the process of being towed from Walvis Bay when the towline broke. It drifted to its current location aground, not because of a navigation error or a storm. No crew were lost. It's a pretty bland, inauspicious shipwreck story as shipwreck stories go.

I had lunch at De Duine, a hotel-restaurant in the small seaside town of Henties Bay. The view from there was pure ocean, and given where I was, no other land was out there until South America. From what I had read about other shipwrecks, there was no point in driving further north along the Skeleton Coast; it would just be more desert for many miles. I turned around and headed back to Swakopmund, where I had booked a room in the Atlantic Garden Boutique Hotel for the night.

Moon Valley

The small hotel was in a great location; I could walk a few blocks down to the waterfront and to a cluster of restaurants around the expensive Strand Hotel. I had dinner there, and the next morning returned to take photos of the small harbor and beach created by a man-made breakwater. I also spent the morning wandering around Swakopmund looking at its primary claim to fame—the Bavarian style of many of the buildings. Namibia was a German territory for a long time before gaining independence. That legacy still lingers here, and especially further inland at the capital, Windhoek. The shops held little of interest for me, but I did find a great outdoor restaurant, the Ankerplatz Restaurant, on Sam Nujoma Avenue, where I had springbok pie for lunch.

Departing Swakopmund, I drove over rough gravel roads into the Moon Valley and spent the night at the Goanikontes Oasis, a cluster of bungalows and camping sites among the trees along the river at the bottom of the parched Moon Valley. Not an impressive place to stay but the restaurant and bar were OK.

Sossusvlei

Next, I moved on to the showstopper in Namibia—the big red sand dunes around Sossusvlei. It's about a 300-km drive from Walvis Bay over a road that is only partly paved, the rest being gravel, sometimes very rough washboard gravel, that rattles the bones and the vehicle. I was glad I was driving a 4×4 pickup.

From driving many miles on these rough roads through this landscape I had the impression I could have been in many deserts I have known, like driving around Nevada or Arizona. Though I was far away in Namibia, it wasn't very different. The Moon Valley had exposed rock formations along a river that distinguished it from the flat desert around it but otherwise was not particularly noteworthy. Nevertheless, it is definitely promoted as a tourist attraction in Namibia. I eventually came to realize Namibia is being over-promoted in some ways.

I stayed two nights in the Sossusvlei Lodge, certainly the nicest accommodation among many available accommodations of varying quality near the big sand dunes. I thought I would need a full day to see the place but a half day was enough. The park gate opens at 6 a.m., so everyone was lined up to enter then and see the dunes before it got too hot. I drove in with the rest, stopped at a few viewpoints for photos, then got to Dune 45. Yes, the dunes are named or numbered. This is a very popular dune to climb so I made the effort. I was slow with younger, stronger people passing me going up and then going

View from the top of Dune 45

down. There really isn't any convenient opportunity to exercise on the boat, so my cardio fitness and basic muscle strength had deteriorated since I started this voyage. I persevered and made it to the top after about 40 minutes of climbing.

Big Daddy dune, the tallest in Namibia

After Dune 45 the road leads farther into the valley. For the last 6 km over sand, it's advisable to take a 4×4 shuttle car with an experienced sand driver. The objective is Deadvlei, a large, ancient flat pan where water dried up eons ago leaving stark dead trees. It's found at the end of the road after a 1.5-km walk over relatively flat sand. This is also the starting point to climb Big Daddy, the largest dune in the park and one of the largest in the world at over 325 meters tall. After the struggle to climb the smaller Dune 45, there'd be no Big Daddy for me.

And that's it. There's a smaller version of Deadvlei called Hidden Vlei if you want to see it. There is also Sesriem Canyon, a 30-meter-deep narrow, rocky canyon that runs for about 2 km. Because of shade throughout the day, sometimes water will pool there, attracting animals. None were there when I stopped. Anyway, if you're not climbing Big Daddy you can see it all before lunch and before the afternoon heat. Overall, I was disappointed with the place. There are certainly the advertised huge red sand dunes, but they're far away from the road, so you don't get the sense of them looming over you.

Deadvlei

The restaurant at the lodge had an inviting outdoor dining space illuminated by the desert sunset and, later, by a canopy of stars made more prominent by the lack of any lights from surrounding buildings. The buffet tables offered a variety of dishes, but the real attractions were the grills offering cooked African meats that would be difficult to find anywhere else, like oryx, springbok and ostrich. I can't say the taste of these meats was memorable but to say I've eaten them is.

The lodge was largely filled with tour groups, not individual travelers, that had arrived in caravans of 4×4s from Windhoek or Walvis Bay. They filled the long outdoor tables that were available at the restaurant.

The one experience I regret missing at Sossusvlei was a hot air balloon ride. It's something that must be booked well in advance. If I'd known how spread out the dunes were, I would have definitely done it. The majesty of the extensive red dunes I think could only be really appreciated from above in the slow, drifting quiet of a balloon. An airplane would have been too noisy and too fast.

From Sossusvlei I drove back to Walvis Bay along the same poor gravel road. I spent my last morning there, before departure on November 21, on a half-day tour south to Sandwich Harbour. That tour is basically a lot of driving on white sand dunes that run down to the sea. I had been on a dune-driving tour before in Dubai during my 2011 flight around the world.

One of the driving tricks is letting air out of the tires so they have greater contact with the sand and achieve more traction that way. I went on the Sandwich Harbour tour mainly to satisfy myself that I had seen it all in terms of what Namibia promotes as its top attractions.

Sunset dinner at Sossusvlei Lodge

According to a few local tour guides I met along the way, "land of sand" tourism suffers from the poor roads and limited infrastructure. Tour operators from Europe and elsewhere don't want to send people there and subject them to the bad roads and sparse accommodations.

I'm glad I saw it for myself, though. If you're in the neighborhood, as I was, it's worth a visit, but I don't think Namibia is spectacular enough to warrant a special trip just to see it.

Walvis Bay is a cruise ship destination. While there I saw two large cruise ships come and go, staying only a day tied up near where the yacht jetty is located. I encountered several of their passengers coming through the security gate to join excursions that were leaving from the harbor. Local Namibians selling mostly tourist trinkets—wood carvings, colorful cloth, metal objects—were clustered around the security gate where deboarding tourists would first see them. If a cruise ship wasn't there, neither were these vendors. The yachting crowd wasn't big enough for them to spend the time sitting there all day in the hope someone would buy something.

It was a scene I had experienced all over Africa when I hitchhiked from Nairobi to Cape Town in 1975, during a more recent visit to Senegal in 1984, in Zanzibar and East Africa in 2016, and again on this voyage. When there were sufficiently large crowds to justify the effort, the vendors would show up. It seemed like a hard way to make a money, and depressing for that reason.

Sandwich Harbour

Like many others, it was an enduring image of Africa as I prepared to sail away from Namibia westward across the Atlantic and ultimately to my home continent, leaving Africa in my wake.

25

Across the Atlantic Again

I've spent almost my entire adult life living on the West Coast, very near the Pacific Ocean, and yet I felt like the Atlantic Ocean was my home ocean since I'd sailed across it twice and was starting to cross it for the third time. It seemed familiar to me in a way only an ocean sailor can understand.

I was on the homestretch of my voyage, headed from Namibia to St. Helena Island, then onward to Antigua and South Florida, the finish line for my solo voyage to seven continents that I could visualize over the horizon to the northwest. I expected to arrive there in early February. From St. Helena I'd have about 5,200 nm left to sail, shorter than my passage from Puerto Montt to the Marquesas.

Until that point I kept thinking, generally, "I have a long way to go" without really putting a distance or time frame on it. Buying provisions was affected: I needed a lot of food on board because "I have a long way to go." I still had many cans of tuna, salmon and vegetables I bought in Chile 18 months before. I needed to start eating more tuna and draw down those reserves instead of buying new things because the remaining days of my voyage were certainly numbered.

I was reminded of these things the morning I sailed across the Greenwich meridian, zero degrees longitude, into the Western Hemisphere, definitely my home hemisphere, after spending more than a year on the east side. I was incrementally getting closer to US time zones, so I wouldn't have to get up in the middle of the night to watch football games with Starlink as I did sailing across the Pacific and Indian Oceans. I expected that the winds and currents would be mostly favorable for the remaining legs of my voyage, although I'd learned never to take these things for granted or the mythology of the sea might rise up to smite me. You are well-served by humility when sailing the world's oceans.

The Australian guy, Dave, that I first met in Cocos (Keeling) left Walvis Bay bound for St. Helena about the same time I did but I soon passed him, as he chose a slightly different course and his wooden ketch is not as fast as *Phywave*. They say anytime there are two boats going to the same place, it's a race. Well, not really, but it's always interesting to compare sailing strategies. I expected I'd see him again in St. Helena.

St. Helena from my anchorage with Jacob's Ladder on the right

St. Helena Island

I arrived in St. Helena on November 30 and anchored in James Bay in about 17 meters of water, the deepest anchorage so far on this voyage. I put out 70 meters of chain hoping that would be enough. The forecast didn't show any storms coming during the few days I would be there.

They used to have a popular field of mooring buoys for visiting yachts, but they shut it down in January 2024, because it urgently needed repairs. They told me it really needed to be entirely replaced, but they don't have the money to do it. The anchorage was not great, pretty rolly. Fortunately, they have a little harbor ferryboat that will pick people up from their anchored yachts and take them to shore, £2.50 return, which is a bargain. And it saved me from having to use my dinghy. When the swells are running in the harbor, though, stepping off the jetty onto the ferryboat can be a little treacherous, especially if the tide is out and the boat is well below the level of the jetty. As I left for the last time, a set of big swells came in and the ferryboat had to back well away from the jetty and nearby rocks to remain safe and undamaged. Once the big swells had passed through, the pilot once again pulled up to the jetty to pick me up. With my creaky knees I wasn't going to jump for it, but he had fixed a strong vertical pole on the stern of the boat that I could grab to stabilize myself as I stepped down to the slippery deck. Climbing back aboard *Phywave* from the ferry was easy in comparison.

Harbor ferryboat in James Bay

St. Helena Island is best known as the second exile location of Napoleon Bonaparte, the first exile being on the island of Elba in the Mediterranean, which may be best known for the famous palindrome "Able was I ere I saw Elba." I landed my plane on Elba while touring Europe in 2018. Napoleon died on St. Helena in 1821 and was buried there. Through some diplomatic maneuvering and a rapprochement between England and France, in 1840 the French persuaded the English to let them dig up Napoleon's tomb and take his remains back to France. They were reinterred at Les Invalides in Paris where they remain today.

Never inhabited before Europeans arrived, St. Helena was supposedly discovered in 1502 by some Portuguese guy with too many syllables in his name, though some dispute that he was the discoverer. Even so, it was in use early on by ships making the journey from Asia back to Europe as a stop for fresh water, timber for repairs and provisions once it was populated

Sandy Bay on St. Helena Island

with animals. In this way it was similar to Réunion Island, both formed by seamount volcanoes. Réunion is much bigger, with a population of over 800,000; St. Helena's population is only about 4,500. Of course, Réunion is totally French-fried; St. Helena is tout à fait British. British pounds are used there although there is also St. Helena money in circulation that is at parity with the pound sterling. It's hard to understand why they'd go to the trouble and expense of having their own currency which is useless anywhere else. They also have local credit cards that are more widely accepted than foreign credit cards like Visa.

Like in Namibia, my AT&T cellphone wouldn't connect to the local cellular network, but I didn't bother to get a SIM card; I really didn't need to call anyone. I couldn't remember the last place I was where the phone numbers were only five digits and the license plates were four digits.

I visited all the Napoleon-related locations, of course, and I took a tour of the island to get a feel for the place during the four days I was there. It was mildly interesting. Tourists do

Napolean's original grave on St. Helena Island

come on the weekly flights from Johannesburg to visit these places and also swim with whale sharks. Cruise ships stop for a day about once a month.

I moved most of my fenders to the starboard side of *Phywave* where the ferry came alongside to pick me up and drop me off. After spending two nights ashore, with my boat unattended and rolling around in the swells, I lost a fender overboard. No doubt I had done a sloppy, casual job of tying it on. It's now somewhere adrift in the Atlantic Ocean or maybe has washed ashore on St. Helena. Buying a matching replacement was added to my list of things to do when I got to Florida.

I did manage to have conversations with a few locals in bars. One guy, a retired fisherman, claimed to have been born on St. Helena and spent most of his life there except for a stint in South Africa. He was slurring his words so I figured he'd already had a lot to drink or maybe he was just talking in cursive. He told me that sometimes the swells and chop in the harbor get so bad the little ferry can't operate. That's great, I thought, I need to ride it at least once more to get back to *Phywave*. Not wanting to dwell on bad boat stories, we changed the subject and he started talking about his family. "My mother started walking 10 miles a day when she turned 65. Now she's 93 and we have no idea where she is." Yup.

It was time to say goodbye to St. Helena, climb back on *Phywave* and start sailing northwest. As I watched the island recede over the horizon, I felt sentimental and a bit sad that this voyage was coming to an end even though there were still several thousand miles left to sail. From the early planning in

Phywave at anchor in James Bay at St. Helena Island

2020, to setting off to the Azores in 2022, until that point, it felt like I didn't savor all the moments enough, that they quickly slipped by. In writing this book, I hope I can recapture their fleeting intensity and the enduring impact on how I've experienced the world.

In chapter 20, I mentioned that Cocos (Keeling) was the most remote place I'd been on my voyage to that point. It certainly was the least populated remote place. In terms of farthest distance from other populated places, St. Helena Island now takes the prize (Ascension Island is closest), though it has a much greater population and more buildings and infrastructure than Cocos (Keeling).

While anchored in these remote places I was reminded of what I wrote in the epilogue of my 2015 book, *Flying 7 Continents Solo*:

> There is always the appeal of a faraway place, the rarely-visited, remote, little-known mystery circumstance. I was recently in Barrow, Alaska, where a small community college had been built catering to "outlying" villages. Outlying? I thought Barrow was outlying. The lines of civilization, of human activity, get increasingly stretched, ultimately broken, moving beyond the last signpost, the end of the road, the hesitant smile, the final conversation. Further. Past the last trail, the disappearing footprints, the lonely, windy mountaintop where recognition is a memory. Further still. Beyond process and reason, merging here and there, blurring yesterday and tomorrow, until finally arriving at a last thin space between the shadow and the silence.

Sailing away from St. Helena Island headed to Antigua

The Long Passage to Antigua

From St. Helena my destination was Antigua in the Caribbean Sea, almost 3,900 nm to the northwest. Riding the eastern and northeastern side of the high-pressure system that dominates the weather in the South Atlantic Ocean, I would enjoy broad reach and downwind sailing angles until near the equator, where the ITCZ weather would stir things up. There were also some supporting ocean currents flowing in my direction.

Four days out from St. Helena Island I experienced a serious autopilot failure. While sailing along the west coast of South America, I started to get random occurrences of the autopilot disengaging itself. I had to jump to the nav station and quickly re-engage it, but in the several seconds it took to do that, the boat had no helm control and would sail far off course with the sails wildly flapping in the wind and the boat sometimes tacking or jibing. Once I had the autopilot re-engaged, I had to sometimes struggle to get the boat back on course, especially if the sails had gone from a port to a starboard tack or vice versa. Sometimes I would have to go on deck to get the boat re-established on the correct course. This happened infrequently and for no apparent reason. When I queried Allures about the problem, they said it was probably due to a "microfailure" in the power supplied to the autopilot control computer, which comes via the Scheiber network. "Microfailure" is another word for a glitch in the power supply. They said to use the bypass fuse in the Scheiber power module to prevent this. I put in the fuse and for a while it seemed to solve the problem, but then some days later it happened again. I tried switching to the other autopilot computer but it eventually did the same thing. I just decided to live with it.

However, the problem I encountered four days out of St. Helena was much worse. The autopilot would disengage with an error message that said "No rudder response." When the autopilot commands the rudder to move, a small sensor arm on the rudder feeds its position back to the autopilot computer. If the computer doesn't get a response, it means the rudder hasn't moved as commanded. With no autopilot, I would have to steer manually. To investigate this new problem, I dropped the sails and let the boat drift in the bumpy seas while I went below to examine the rudder sensor.

My boat has two rudders and two helms; each is connected to its own rudder. For redundancy, it has two autopilot computers; each is connected to a drive unit that is connected to one rudder. The drive unit turns the signal from the autopilot computer into the "muscle" to move the rudder. On each drive unit there is a rudder position sensor arm that feeds the rudder position back to the corresponding computer. To keep the rudders synchronized and pointing in the same direction, there is a heavy metal bar that connects the two. Obviously, only one autopilot computer can be on at a time; otherwise, the two drive units would "argue" about where to position the rudders.

When I got the "no rudder response" alarm, I assumed a rudder position sensor arm had disconnected somehow, but when I checked them, both were in place. Then I decided the link between the drive unit and computer had failed, so I switched to the other autopilot. That didn't solve the problem, so I went to the more extreme solution of disconnecting the metal bar that connected the rudders, assuming I would then have to continue with the emergency rudder setup in which the failed rudder is locked amidships and the boat is steered with only one rudder. Before disconnecting that connecting bar, I went to the helms and locked down each one because I didn't want the rudders moving around due to wave action and potentially getting my fingers jammed in the drive unit control arms. After doing this, I manually tried moving the control arm of each drive unit and found they were both moving OK, so I reconnected the metal bar and unlocked the helms. I re-engaged the autopilot and it seemed to be working OK, so I started sailing again. However, I realized when I got to Antigua that this episode was the harbinger of a serious problem I had to deal with there.

Other than the autopilot problem, the first two weeks out from St. Helena were easy, relaxing sailing. On my original route plan I had included a stop at Ascension Island. Some weeks before, in Namibia, I decided to eliminate it. Although a UK territory, Ascension is mostly a military base populated with US and UK personnel. Getting a visa to visit was an involved process. I started that process, which led to a few questions from the base administration that I answered. I never did get final confirmation that I could visit. The anchorage at Ascension is also fairly open and rolly. Unlike St. Helena, there is no local ferryboat with an experienced captain to pick up cruisers from their boats and take them ashore. You are on your own to launch your dinghy to come ashore. If high swells are running in the harbor, getting to and from shore in your dinghy can be dangerous to the point that it can't be done. Cruisers have been known to anchor at Ascension Island and never go ashore because during the time they were there the conditions were never safe to take their dinghy in. It's an interesting place, but given the problems associated with visiting there, I decided to skip it.

The Equator—Where Is It?

On December 17 at 2241Z I crossed the equator going northbound at 32.0758 degrees west longitude. I've crossed the equator twice on this circumnavigation, once southbound more than two years earlier and northbound this time. You'd think there'd be a big dashed line like you see on globes and world maps but nope, nada!

Of course, nobody precisely knows where the equator is because zero degrees latitude (the equator) is a made-up thing. That will come as some disappointment to people who build stone monuments with bronze plaques that say "Dude, you're standing on the equator." I passed a sign by the gravel road in Namibia that said "Tropic of Capricorn" like they knew where it was. Trust me, Henry Miller's book is way more interesting.

An approaching rain squall

As I mentioned in chapter 12 on Antarctica, over the years increasingly refined mathematical models have evolved to represent the earth's surface. The current model is an oblate spheroid designated as WGS84. It was preceded by WGS60, WGS72, and others. Of course, every time the earth model is changed the location of the equator in relation to physical points on the earth also changes. That's why the real location of the equator isn't a physically fixed place on the earth but simply an imaginary line derived from the model of the earth's surface currently in use.

North of the Equator

The first half of the passage home, south of the equator, was sublime, with solid following winds and sunny skies. When I crossed the equator into the ITCZ, the weather became cloudy with occasional rain squalls, one of which accelerated the wind from 15 knots to 40 knots and changed its direction by 40 degrees, all in less than two minutes. Fortunately, that one occurred during the daytime and I saw it coming, confirmed its location and approach speed on radar, and was able to reduce sails in preparation for it hitting me. If a squall came at night when I was trying to sleep it would usually be a big surprise, causing me to quickly scramble out of my bunk and get on deck to reduce the sails.

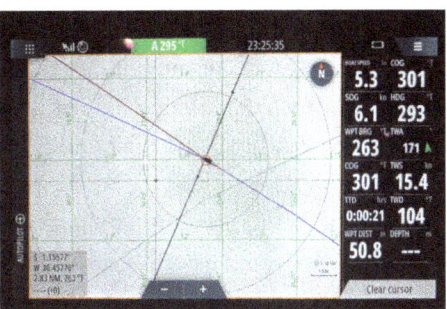

Crossing my southbound track from more than two years before

North of the equator there are also strong, circulating currents that slowed my progress. I struggled to figure them out. The weather forecast showed a large area of very little wind along my direct route (about 300 degrees true) from St. Helena to Antigua. I had to divert west to sail around the worst of this no-wind zone. Still, I had single-digit wind speeds for a few days and was lucky to get 4 knots of boat speed. When trying to get past a crossing current of 2 knots with a slow boat speed it results in a lot of crabbing, sometimes up to 30 degrees. It's miserable sailing. I finally ran the engine for six hours to get out of the last of the strong cross currents. The wind eventually picked up and I had a reasonably fast remaining week into Antigua, although the 2-meter waves were right on the beam of the boat, causing a lot of rolling and an uncomfortable ride.

As I came within range of, and sailed past, other Caribbean islands, I was counting down the miles until I reached Antigua. The Caribbean is renowned as a cruiser's paradise, with many island countries to visit and often steady

15-to-20 knot winds. Whether a cruiser is interested in staying in comfortable marinas in bustling towns with nightlife or anchoring in quiet, remote lagoons inside coral atolls, it can all be found among the islands in the Caribbean Sea.

For me, though, my driving motivation was to cross the finish line of my seven continents voyage. I had been to the Caribbean on several occasions in the past in my plane and via commercial flights, so I already had sampled the island beach experience. I'd learned to scuba dive in Antigua in 1993 followed by visits to Saint Kitts and Nevis. I first flew to the Bahamas in my old plane, an Archer II, in 2004. I stopped in Turks and Caicos and Grenada in my plane in 2013 on my way to South America and Antarctica.

Still, there was no deadline for me to finish my voyage—I'd finish when I finished. Would it be so bad to spend a month cruising among Caribbean islands? Though I was some miles to the east, I could have easily turned west to Barbados, Martinique, and Saint Lucia, working my way north along the Windward Islands to Antigua. Why didn't I? Because there was nothing to be found there that was new to me. Sitting in a harbor at anchor, or in a peaceful lagoon, held no surprises, no novelty, no progress toward any goal, and would be boring for those reasons. Though many cruisers routinely make an annual sojourn to the Caribbean to spend months among the islands, it really didn't hold any appeal for me. I continued sailing north to Antigua, still occasionally questioning my decision to skip island-hopping in the Caribbean.

26

The Caribbean

Conch fritters, stormy cocktails and a great reggae band at the Sea Dream restaurant made for a pretty good first night in Jolly Harbour after a nearly 4,000-nm, 30-day passage from St. Helena Island in the South Atlantic to Antigua.

As I motored into Jolly Harbour on January 3, I disengaged the autopilot and was shocked to discover my manual steering range at the helm was greatly reduced to about ±10 degrees from the normal range of ±35 degrees. I was barely able to steer the boat to dock by the Immigration and Customs office where I could tie it up for entry formalities. Once I had completed that process, which took less than an hour, I was faced with getting my boat into my reserved berth at the marina, typically requiring a lot of tight turns, full rudder steering range and the bow thrusters. I called the marina dockmaster on the VHF radio and explained my problem. With his help and the help of a dockhand, we finally got *Phywave* past the tight turns into my berth.

I couldn't continue on from Antigua with this steering problem. Once *Phywave* was tied up in my berth, I started taking things apart. As I explained in chapter 25, my boat has two rudders, two helms (one connected to each rudder), two autopilot computers (one as a backup) and two autopilot drive units that convert the signals from the autopilot computer into the power needed to actually move the rudder. There is a heavy metal bar that connects the rudders to always keep them in sync. After disconnecting all the mechanical components, it was clear the port side drive unit had failed. The control arm from the drive unit to the rudder would only move over a very limited range compared to the drive unit on the starboard side. Once I disconnected the port drive unit from the rest of the steering system I had my full range of steering back. It was unlikely I could fix the drive unit in Antigua, so I decided to find a replacement. Sourcing it, getting it to Antigua and installing it would be a challenge.

Approaching Antigua, first land in 30 days

I thought my stop in Antigua would be a relaxing holiday, but it seemed an offshore sailboat is a demanding taskmaster never relenting on what's required to keep it going.

While contemplating how best to fix the autopilot, I took time to explore the area around the Jolly Harbour Marina. There were several restaurants there, including a Mexican restaurant; I hadn't had Mexican food in a very long time. There was a place to get laundry done and I took advantage of that. Epicurean Fine Foods and Pharmacy was just a block away from the marina. The first time I walked in I was surprised to see an extensive selection of products you'd normally find in a supermarket in the US. The marina caters to the large number of American cruisers, as I learned when several stopped by my boat to say hello and ask about my voyage. The supermarket would naturally bring in the items that these customers wanted.

There is a large marine chandlery two blocks from the marina, where I bought additional filter elements for the Racor primary fuel filters and oil filters for the Volvo Penta D2-50 engine on *Phywave*. The chandlery was an important supporting business for the large boatyard at Jolly Harbour where a lot of maintenance work and boat construction was going on.

Phywave in Jolly Harbour Marina, Antigua

My berth at the Jolly Harbour Marina was right at the head of dock B. Consequently, all the cruisers who had boats farther out along dock B would walk by my boat, resulting in a lot of people stopping by to chat, especially after I strung up the colorful courtesy flags for all the countries and other places I had visited on my voyage. With all the yellow jerry cans strapped to my deck, they also recognized me as a long-haul ocean sailor, not just a seasonal Caribbean cruiser. I learned that many of these Americans left their boats on the hard in the boatyard during the hurricane season but would return during the winter, put their boats back in the marina and stay on them for several months. I asked them if they actually sailed anywhere. Usually, they would take short trips to some nearby islands, just a day's sail away, but rarely any overnight passages. Most of the time they stayed on their boats in the marina, in effect, waterfront condos in Antigua, though I imagine a lot less expensive than a condo on land. It's not something I'd want to do. As I've alluded to before, I really don't like the tropics. For me, the heat and humidity are stifling. Without air-conditioning on my boat, it would be uncomfortable to stay there for months at a time.

It was helpful to talk to these other American cruisers. I had a long list of maintenance and repair tasks I needed to get done once I reached Fort Lauderdale. Though I had flown through Fort Lauderdale in my plane several times, I knew nothing about the marine side of things there. One cruiser I met was from Fort Lauderdale. He gave me the name of a very experienced boat guy living there whom I contacted by email, explaining the kind of work I needed done. He sent me a detailed list, with phone numbers and his reviews, of the marine contractors he would recommend for the work I had in mind. I made good use of one of them once I got there.

Quick Trip to Miami

From the experience of other cruisers, successfully shipping things into Antigua was almost impossible. They charge high customs duties compared to other nearby islands; that is, if what you ordered gets through at all. As a test, I ordered some simple, relatively inexpensive things from Amazon before I arrived with a promised delivery date of January 3, the day I was to arrive. I then got a message saying delivery was delayed five days. Well, the package never arrived, and I have little doubt it was actually stolen somewhere along the line, probably in Antigua. Someone suggested the trick is to pay a freight forwarder to keep an eye out for the shipment. Even paying him a nominal fee of US$50 or US$100 represented another expense. It all seemed unreliable and untrustworthy. Incidentally, Amazon was quick to refund what I had paid for the shipped items that had gotten "lost."

Given that experience, I concluded it would be foolish to try to ship a replacement autopilot drive unit to Antigua, if I could find one in the US. With an internet search I actually found one at a place I knew well: Fisheries Supply in Seattle, a chandlery where I had shopped many times. Since I was unwilling to ship it to Antigua, I decided instead to ship it to a UPS store in Miami. I would make the relatively short flight from Antigua to pick it up. While I was there, I would pick up a few other things I wanted, like what I ordered on Amazon that never arrived.

I hopped on a flight from Antigua to Miami, rented a car and stayed in a hotel near the airport for a couple of nights. The UPS store where I chose to receive the autopilot drive unit from Seattle was also close by. The drive unit was pretty heavy, over 28 pounds, so I bought a small, cheap rollaboard suitcase to carry it back to Antigua. As it was a carry-on suitcase, I hoped it wouldn't be checked by Customs in Antigua. The drive unit arrived on time at the UPS store. After unpacking it from its cardboard box at my hotel, I repacked it in the suitcase along with the few other things I bought in Miami. This certainly reminded me of when I had done the same thing on Lombok by flying to Australia (twice) to buy parts for the engine on my boat. Those Australian trips definitely took longer.

Arriving back in Antigua, I breezed through Immigration and Customs with no questions asked, took a taxi back to the marina and contemplated how I would install the new unit. After considering the problem for a while, I decided not to install it. Removing the failed unit and installing the new one would have been a fair amount of work in a tight space in an aft compartment of my boat. While contemplating how to install the drive unit and communicating with Allures about it, I realized I could make the starboard side autopilot completely independent of the port side autopilot. The starboard autopilot could successfully steer the boat on its own. There was also a favorable weather window opening on January 15 for sailing north that I wanted to hit, which didn't leave me time to install the new drive unit. I'd wait to replace the failed unit until I got to Florida. It meant I would now be sailing with only one working autopilot, but most boats only have one autopilot anyway. Having a backup autopilot was a luxury I wanted when I ordered *Phywave* back in 2020. It turned out I needed it.

Of course, since I had figured out how to make the starboard autopilot independently steer *Phywave*, my trip to Miami hadn't been necessary. I could have waited to order the new drive unit and had it shipped to Fort Lauderdale when I arrived there. It was a wasted trip that could have been avoided if I'd done a little more research in the first place on how the autopilot works.

Leaving Antigua

I left Jolly Harbour on January 15 at 1050Z, just at dawn in a light rain that, as I found out later, turned into a downpour. I sailed northwest, passing Saint Kitts and Nevis on my port side and later Saint Martin and Anguilla on my starboard side. From that point I turned more northerly to reach the open sea to the east of the Leeward Islands, leaving the British Virgin Islands to port. I heard a lot of radio traffic from boats coming and going into these islands, and even US Coast Guard radio announcements from Puerto Rico.

Past the British Virgin Islands I was happy to once again be in open seas without the persistent risk of encountering other boats. My intermediate destination was a special waypoint in the ocean north of Mayaguana Island.

72.9875 Degrees West Longitude

It was a seemingly insignificant longitude to everyone except me. Crossing it that day, January 20, 2025, at 0928Z, marked the completion of my solo circumnavigation. I'd now sailed around the world solo, crossing all the meridians and the equator.

Some may wonder why that didn't happen when I crossed the longitude of Tangiers, my farthest excursion east in 2022. As I mentioned, I took a break at home after successfully sailing to Antarctica and back. During the break I had a crew from Puerto Williams in Chile deliver *Phywave* through the difficult channels of Patagonia to Puerto Montt. When I returned to Chile, I resumed my solo voyage from the Club Náutico Reloncaví marina in Puerto Montt. The longitude of that marina is 72.9875 degrees west longitude, so technically it marks the beginning of my solo circumnavigation. I've now completed the circumnavigation by crossing that same longitude again. Even though I didn't return to my starting point, it's still considered a circumnavigation because I crossed all the meridians.

I wanted to stop someplace in the extensive island nation of the Bahamas, partly because it's a famous cruiser destination for yachts coming from the US

Ridiculous Coco Cay

but also because I had already paid US$300 for a cruising permit and wanted to get some use from it. I picked out some intermediate destinations that were ports of entry in case the weather turned bad. One was Clarence Town on Long Island, but the weather remained favorable so it wasn't necessary to make use of any of them.

My original Bahamas destination was Rock Sound on the southern end of the island of Eleuthera, another easy port of entry. It offered a large bay with good anchor holding reported by other cruisers and a reasonable degree of protection from a storm that was looming a few days out. I sailed north into Exuma Sound with that in mind for my next stop.

Great Harbour Cay

Ultimately, though, I decided to skip Rock Sound, mostly driven by my desire to finish my voyage at Fort Lauderdale as soon as possible. Every alternative I considered was weighed against the question of how quickly I could finish. I knew I would have to shelter somewhere to wait out the forecast high wind system, but instead of Rock Sound I decided to push on to the Berry Islands where Great Harbour Cay is located. To do this most easily, I turned north and sailed between Eleuthera and Little San Salvador Island, then north on the east side of Eleuthera. Finally, I turned northwest, then west, on a direct course for the Berry Islands. As I made this passage, I watched the winds rotate around from following winds, then winds on my beam, then on my bow, and finally back again behind me, closely following the forecast. I knew when I would have to motor and when I could start sailing again. I also slowed a bit to arrive at Great Harbour Cay in daylight.

I made my way around Little Stirrup Cay, as it's labeled on the charts, but which had apparently been renamed Coco Cay by its owner, Royal Caribbean, which uses it as a private island so passengers could have some beach time off the ship. This was more than beach time, though; what I saw there was a garish amusement park with multiple slides, what appeared to be a rollercoaster, and arcades. A huge sign announcing "Coco Cay" was visible from miles away. Why would people join a cruise when a destination consisted of something they could find ashore? The cruise industry has gone completely around the bend with its massive ships carrying thousands of passengers jammed into relatively tight spaces so they feel like crowded cities. I don't get it, but it isn't the first time I felt disconnected from the desires and motivations of modern society.

Beach along the harbor on the east side of Great Harbour Cay

Cutting across the shallow 2-to-3 meter depths, I headed for the very narrow man-made cut that leads to the inner harbor at Great Harbour Cay and the marina where, after multiple attempts by email, I finally managed to book a berth to ride out the impending high winds. Other boats that had been anchored on the west side of the island were moving through the cut to anchor in the inner harbor or take a berth in the marina, as I was, to shelter against those strong north winds.

It turned out to be a good stop. There was a lively crowd of cruisers in the marina who had more or less taken up residence on their boats, sometimes for a few months like the guy on a powerboat in the berth next to me. I arrived on Thursday, January 23, and was met by the Immigration and Customs people who had come from the airport at the request of the marina personnel to clear me in to the Bahamas. Because I had already filed the paperwork and paid for the cruising permit, the process was quick and easy.

Ruins of a failed golf resort

Beautiful sunset for Great Harbour Cay marina

On Friday I managed to get laundry done and also pay for dinner at the weekly Friday night party they have under the big gazebo at the marina. Several of the cruisers were accomplished musicians who set up a sound system and provided live music for the gathering. I met other cruisers who were very interested in my story of sailing solo to seven continents. Like the people I met in Antigua, these people were not really offshore cruisers who crossed oceans but mostly escapees from winter weather along the East Coast, the sailing version of snowbirds. They were nice folks, though, and it was a pleasant change to engage in real conversations about a variety of things.

I also took advantage of being ashore to walk around a bit, first to the village, where there are a few shops and restaurants. I had lunch at a small restaurant/bar, the Breakaway, with a very limited menu, mainly whatever they decided to cook that day. I bought wine and a bottle of whiskey at 700 Wines and Spirits, the only liquor store on the island.

I also walked up the road that leads to the other side of the island and the large harbor there with a broad arc of a beach. This would be a good place to anchor in a west wind. I only noticed two boats anchored in the distance on the far side of the harbor. On the way back I stopped at the ruins of a failed golf resort, the project of an American gangster from decades before who hoped to make Great Harbour Cay competition for Nassau. Apparently, it never opened, the clubhouse never finished, with remnants of some of the

Exiting the narrow cut leading to Great Harbour Cay's inner harbor

fairways and greens still visible from the road. The whole place was a little spooky.

My real purpose in being at the cay was to wait out the strong northerly winds that would have made crossing the Gulf Stream current to Fort Lauderdale treacherous. Those winds weaken as forecast, and it was time to move on. I left Great Harbour Cay marina the morning of January 27 with one more stop in mind before arriving in Fort Lauderdale.

27

Florida—Voyage Completed!

My departure from Great Harbour Cay was a matter of timing; I wanted to cross the Gulf Stream when the wind from the north had diminished and shifted to the west and southwest so it wouldn't be blowing against the current. I'd been watching the forecast carefully, and to arrive in the Gulf Stream at the right time I needed to spend another day somewhere. I decided to spend that day anchored off North Bimini Island.

Though I had never been there, I had no real interest in going ashore on Bimini Island. However, for me it was a historic place, one favored by Hemingway in his deep-sea fishing adventures, and the setting for the first third of his novel *Islands in the Stream*. Based on how it was described there, I imagined the relatively quaint island place it must have been then, a handful of ramshackle beach bars and hotels with hurricane-battered island homes scattered along its shores.

I could only guess what the place had become, catering to the very nearby Florida boating crowd who can easily make it over and back for a weekend. An island crawling with drunken Floridian boaters did not appeal to me at all. I noticed cruise ships also stopped there, dropping their passengers on the dock so they can wander around for a day among the shops that, no doubt, sell a variety of the usual inauthentic tourist junk manufactured in the Far East.

I anchored off the northeast side of North Bimini where several anchorage locations with good holding were shown on the charts in 2 to 3 meters of water. I had come overnight from Great Harbour Cay, arriving at Bimini in the morning with enough light to find a patch of sand instead of coral where I could drop my anchor. I would be there all day and night watching the unbusy side of Bimini, far from the crowds on the west side. Only a few fishing skiffs and runabouts were visible, some of those people coming ashore to walk the white sand beach and pick up shells. No other boats were anchored along this side of Bimini overnight; I had the place to myself.

As I left Great Harbour Cay and came directly west across to Bimini it occurred to me that I was in about the last place on this voyage where I could look around and not see any land. Though I knew I was still in busy waters with other boats nearby, it was a moment of reflection I would have on how far I had come and the rare experiences I had along the way.

Fort Lauderdale

I pulled up the anchor at Bimini on January 29 at 1110Z and headed around the north end of the North Shoal and south of a small island marked as an obstruction on the charts. The depths along this route were also 2–3 meters. Crossing into deeper water to the west, I had a straight shot across the Gulf Stream current to Fort Lauderdale.

The Gulf Stream flows straight north along the Florida coast at speeds typically around 3 knots, so it's necessary to crab south against the current.

Passing under the SE 17th Street Bridge

Boaters I met in Antigua who live in South Florida and have a lot of experience crossing the current told me to point the boat at Miami, south of Fort Lauderdale, if I wanted to end up in Fort Lauderdale. By pointing the boat at Fort Lauderdale, you will end up north in West Palm Beach. I guess that was a simple way for them to remember to crab across the current.

The thing that surprised me on this crossing was the wind. Following the forecast, I had planned carefully to avoid north wind opposing the current. However, as I got past Bimini the winds were 10–12 knots from the northwest. That lasted most of the way across to Florida. These winds were relatively light and didn't create any rough standing-wave conditions by blowing against the current, but there was a consistent chop. The winds were blowing right on the bow, so it was impossible to efficiently sail into them unless I wanted a long trip tacking back and forth across to Florida. I wanted to get to the marina in Fort Lauderdale that afternoon; motoring was the only way to ensure that would happen.

Overall, it was an uneventful crossing and seemed very lame as the finale to my grand solo voyage. There were many fast powerboats passing me going both directions, the number increasing as I got closer to the entrance of the harbor at Fort Lauderdale, known as Port Everglades. The port is a major departure point for huge cruise ships following itineraries across the Caribbean, so I was wary of them transiting the relatively narrow entrance to the port. It was a Wednesday and typically the cruise ships arrange their departures and arrivals around the weekend. The well-marked entrance to the port is about 180 meters wide and well-dredged, but big powerboats going too fast in the entrance channel can still create a significant wake that rolls around boats like mine.

CBP arrival approval

To get to the Bahia Mar Yachting Center where I had booked a berth, I knew I would have to pass under the SE 17th Street Bridge going north. This is a high bridge that also opens. Most boats, even large megayachts, can pass underneath without having the bridge open but not sailboats with tall masts. Not having dealt with bridges on this voyage, except the low pedestrian bridge in Lagos and the swing bridge in Mar del Plata, I had never really thought much about the height of my mast with a VHF radio antenna at the top. I had detailed drawings from Allures with the boat's dimensions, but without the antenna. Based on those drawings, I was a little uncertain whether I could get under the bridge with it closed. It's a bad idea to be uncertain about clearance when passing under a bridge.

Phywave at Bahia Mar marina

The bridge operator monitors VHF channel 9, and if contacted and requested, willingly opens the bridge for sailboats on the hour and half hour. I started monitoring channel 9 and watching the clock as I started into the port entrance. As I got farther along, I heard another boat call the bridge to open at the next time slot, which turned out to be 3 p.m. I accelerated to get behind them and take advantage of that opening to accommodate both of us. It worked out pretty well. I only had to stop, idle and drift around for about 10 minutes before the bridge was fully opened and we could easily pass under it. Another event added to my sailing repertoire.

From the bridge I wound my way north and east along a well-marked channel that was full of boats going both ways; the most intense boat traffic I had contended with on this voyage. The channel was lined with large waterfront mansions, each with its own boat dock. I suppose it's a lifestyle many people aspire to but not me.

Finally turning toward the north basin of the huge marina at Bahia Mar, I called them on VHF channel 16 and asked for a dock guy to come down to my assigned slip, H824, and take my dock lines. On the final turn onto the fairway for my slip I had to come to an abrupt stop. There was a large construction barge maneuvering back toward me, blocking the way to my slip. I saw the dock guy standing by my slip with a perplexed look on his face. We had no idea what the barge was trying to do or where it was going. I finally backed off a good distance, almost out of the marina, because I thought the barge might be trying to get out. That wasn't the case, but it was in the way. Finally, the marina called me and temporarily assigned me to a different, nearby slip that wasn't blocked. The dock guy moved over to that one, took my lines and got *Phywave* tied up. I was officially back in North America and could count it as the seventh continent I had sailed to solo.

Celebration mojito

After shutting down the engine and electronics, I had one final task to complete. Clearing in to the United States, at least for me as a US citizen on a US flagged boat, had become almost trivial. Customs and Border Protection (CBP) had developed an app for cellphones to complete the process. After registering myself (name, passport number, cellphone number) and my boat name on the app and completing an arrival notification, it was only necessary for me to contact them when, and from where, I actually arrived, in this case, the Bahia Mar marina in Fort Lauderdale. After posting my arrival, I got a phone call five minutes later from a CBP agent to confirm my arrival. The only question he asked was whether there were any other people on board. After I answered "No," he said "Welcome to the United States" and ended the call. A few minutes later I got an email confirming my entrance into the US. It was, by far, the easiest clearance into a country I experienced on the entire voyage.

I climbed off the boat and headed for the bar for a celebration mojito. No one was there to greet me in Fort Lauderdale, but nobody really knew exactly when I would arrive. As before, there was no one to join me for a celebration drink. The next morning I strung up all the courtesy flags from countries I had visited the way, making *Phywave* a more colorful sight. However, I was near the end of the dock, where few boats were moored and nobody was staying on board. No one stopped by to ask about the flags or where I had been.

It was an anticlimactic arrival, not the champagne-spraying celebration one might imagine. Mostly, I felt relieved I would not have to focus most of my time and energy on the boat and completing the voyage, that I could now start to move on to other things. That was liberating.

Repairing and Relaxing

With its huge boating community, Fort Lauderdale is home to many companies that support every facet of the boating industry. Upon arrival I contacted a number of companies to repair and upgrade *Phywave*. The replacement autopilot drive unit I had from Antigua need to be put in place, a difficult job I got a local marine contractor to handle. I found a company that could duplicate the teak inset for my cockpit table that had swelled up and broken when I tried to remove it in Puerto Montt.

High on my list was replacing my 9.5 foot AB RIB dinghy with a shorter one of the same model. The shorter one would fit under the stern arch so I would no longer need to carry the dinghy on the foredeck. Even though I was concerned about it swinging around on the arch, I was convinced I could find suitable ratchet straps that would hold it solidly in place, even in rough seas. I was able to do exactly that. I was very pleased with the new dinghy arrangement and glad to have the foredeck uncluttered with the dinghy. Finding a buyer for the old one was a challenge but by mentioning it to everyone I met, I found a buyer who would take it off my hands for a reasonable price.

I also found a shop that could make inside covers for the many salon windows on *Phywave*. This had been an issue for me from the first marinas I stayed in. The position of the long side windows is such that anyone walking by could easily see into the salon, limiting privacy. The large windows also caused the salon to get beastly hot in the sunshine of the tropics. The company I found fabricated window coverings that easily snap in place and solved these problems.

One of the things I wanted to do was visit my long-time friend Becky whom I first met in Quincy, Illinois, in the early 1980s. She's married and has lived in Fort Lauderdale for many years. We have stayed in touch over the decades; she is one of the people I have known the longest outside of my family. I stopped by her home for a morning of conversation with her and her husband. I've lost track of many people over the years. Long-time friends seem like an enduring touchstone marking life's transitions.

Final Sailing Route

Appendix A has a spreadsheet showing the navigation route I actually sailed with landings on seven continents and many places in between. The spreadsheet also shows distances and dates for the ocean passages. The map here shows the final sailing route. Overall, the voyage took longer than I anticipated, with some lengthy breaks at home waiting for weather conditions to improve, or for other reasons, before I could resume my voyage.

A Unique Accomplishment

With my arrival in Fort Lauderdale on January 29, 2025, my North American landing, I had completed a solo voyage to seven continents and become the first person to both fly and sail solo to all the continents. There aren't any official records, and I don't know what solo sailors have done over the years in terms of sailing to all the continents since Joshua Slocum first sailed solo around the world in 1898. Of course, he didn't go to Antarctica. There is no way to know whether any other solo sailors have sailed to all the continents. However, I do know the few other solo pilots who have landed on all the continents. None of them are offshore sailors. For that reason, primarily, I'm confident in my claim that I'm the first person to do both.

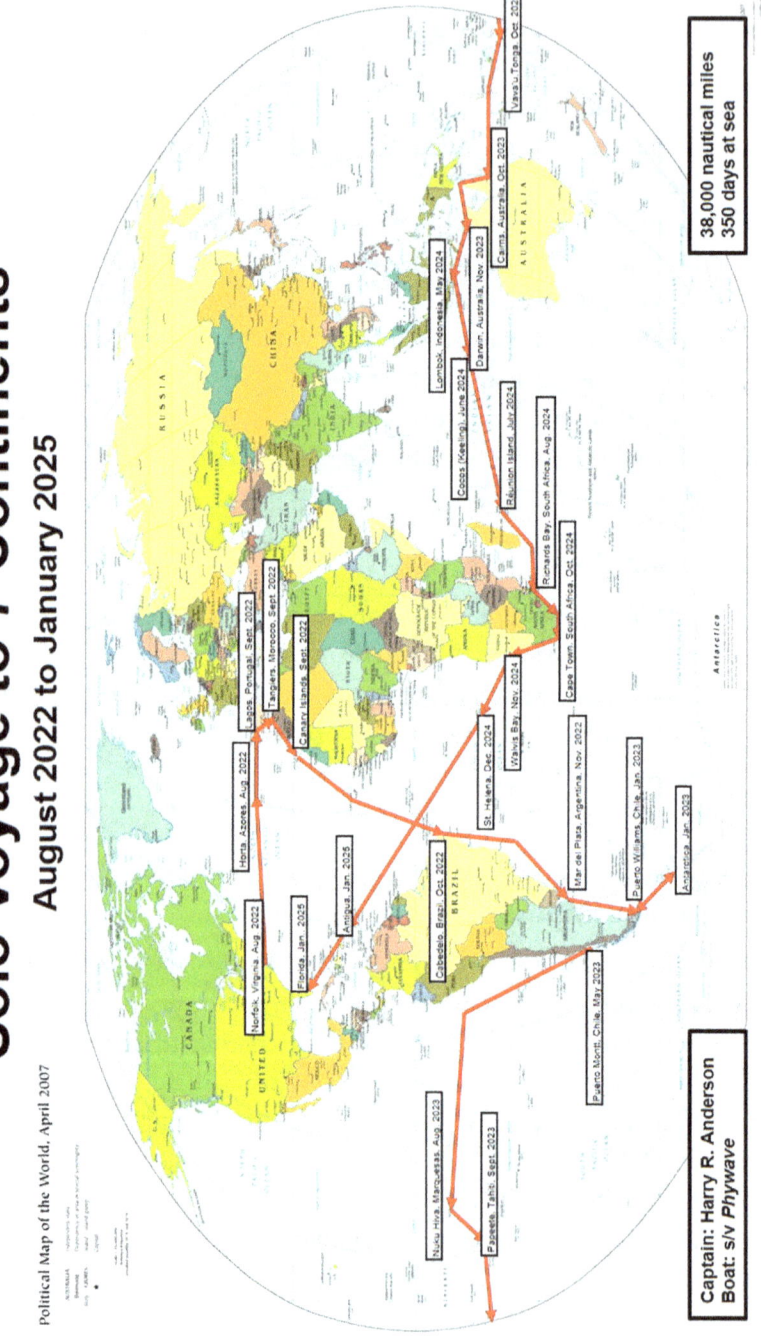

Epilogue

The many cruisers I met during this voyage had a variety of reasons for being out on the ocean. I didn't meet anyone who had a singular driving objective like mine other than sailing around the world eventually. The route they chose, and how long they would spend at stops along the way, was always flexible. Cruisers are adept at sharing information about wonderful places they have been and also difficulties they have encountered. Though it wasn't a location I visited on this voyage, as an example, the Maldives was one of those places where some cruisers had great experiences while others complained vociferously about hassles with local officials and high fees. There are many chat groups on WhatsApp and other platforms where such information is shared, information that can inspire route changes for those taking a leisurely approach to sailing around the world.

Cruisers who make their boat their only home are a special breed, but not uncommon. The small, simple space of a boat mirrors the tiny house movement becoming popular in some places. At least a tiny house is on land with room to walk and wander instead of being surrounded by water.

Then there are cruisers who spend several months on their boat followed by several months at home. They may focus on cruising in a particular area, like French Polynesia, the Caribbean or the Mediterranean, but with no underlying ambition to sail somewhere else or around the world.

I was glad that, for me, this voyage was a mission with a clearly defined and significant goal. Otherwise, I don't think I would have taken the time and put in the effort to do it. Just hanging out on a boat, wherever it might be, is not very interesting to me. Undeniably, this voyage was a better way to spend my time than being at home following an ordinary daily routine. The best moments of the voyage certainly were those alone at sea, feeling the independence and self-sufficiency of solo sailing, unbothered by the inevitable constraints that come with modern life in a populated place.

As I write this in my home on Bainbridge Island, overlooking Eagle Harbor, I watch a sailboat leave the harbor headed somewhere around Puget Sound, or maybe farther away. For some reason it struck me then that ocean sailing was a long-term effort to be gone, to be anywhere else, that anywhere else perhaps undefined, unknown, imaginary. The enduring allure of the sea uniquely offers an escape to a place where the horizons are uncluttered by land and buildings, inherently a less complex place, its fundamental simplicity and clarity framed by wind, water and sky. Is the sea itself that elusive destination?

This voyage has been a brilliant addition to my life's experiences. As the years go by, I don't want my thoughts filled with would have, could have, should have. I'd rather think I made the most of my time here on earth.

My Dad's Sextant

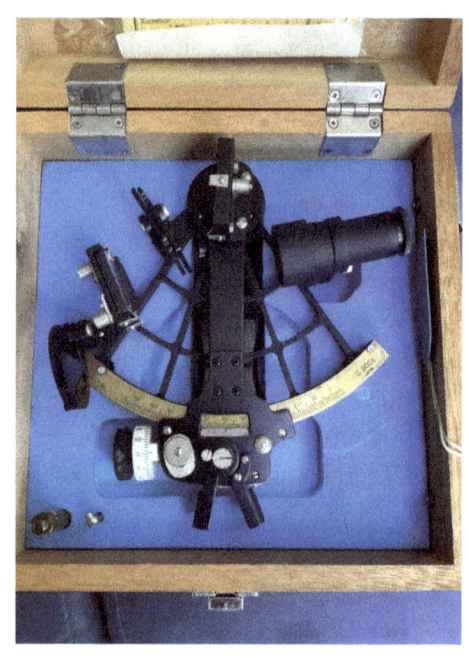

My dad's sextant

My dad was a radioman in the navy in World War II, flying on patrol bombers searching for German submarines off the coast of Brazil and later over the English Channel. He flew out of an airfield at the small English village of Dunkeswell, a place I flew to myself in my around-the-world flight in 2011. He had become a ham radio operator as a teenager in the 1930s, so being a radioman in the navy was a natural fit. Morse code to him was a second language and part of the soundtrack of my childhood.

He had a long career in broadcast engineering, ultimately becoming VP of Engineering at KCET, the PBS television station in Los Angeles. He retired early to pursue a long-held dream to sail the world's oceans with my mom. As a retirement gift the PBS executives gave him a sextant.

My parents bought a suitable sailboat, moved on board and started sailing along the California coast in preparation for bigger things. In 1980 they started sailing south along the Baja Peninsula. They were a thousand miles into their voyage when my mom discovered a lump in her neck. They suspended their voyage and flew back to San Diego to have it evaluated. It was cancer. My mom put up a valiant fight, still living on the boat, which was brought back to San Diego by a delivery skipper, but she passed away in 1986.

My dad sold the boat, eventually got remarried, and bought a house in Vista, California. His sextant was prominently displayed on a wall in the house. When my dad passed away in 2005 the sextant was handed on to me.

I've carried my dad's sextant with me everywhere I've sailed for the past two and a half years, across the world's oceans, to seven continents, several countries and dozens of harbors and anchorages around the globe. In this small way they were along with me, sailing the world as they once dreamed of doing. I think they would have liked that.

Recognition

I had become the first person in history to both fly and sail solo to all seven continents, but completion of my voyage did not result in the victory celebration and recognition I might have expected. Though friends and family members sent notes of congratulations after I arrived in Fort Lauderdale, there wasn't any press coverage despite several news agencies, including local newspapers and TV stations, being notified of my arrival. No one was interested in my achievement. I put together a press release along with representative photos from my flights and voyage and sent them to a few journalists I know. None responded.

I posted about it on the Ocean Cruising Club Facebook page, where many liked the post and offered favorable comments and congratulations. As oceangoing sailors themselves, they could understand and appreciate the magnitude of what I had accomplished.

My local Bainbridge Island hometown newspaper ran a short follow-up article that connected to the longer article they published after I successfully returned from Antarctica. That was the only newspaper story reporting the completion of my voyage.

Overall, I was disappointed in the lack of interest in what I had done. I guess I really don't know what news people are interested in these days, reinforcing the underlying feeling I had during the voyage that I'm out of sync with the what makes the world tick.

Wasington State House Resolution

One unexpected bright spot came by way of the efforts of Frank Goodell, the retired US Air Force general who had organized the First World Flight Centennial and whom I had closely worked with arranging for Earthrounders pilots to display their aircraft at the Centennial. He has a good relationship with Representative Tom Dent, a longtime member of the Washington State House of Representatives and a pilot. He encouraged Tom to put forward a House resolution recognizing and honoring my flying and sailing achievements as an inspiration to others to pursue their own adventures. With 25 cosponsors, the resolution was adopted on April 7, 2025. A copy of the resolution is included here. Despite the limited press coverage I otherwise received, it was a great honor to be recognized by this resolution.

House Resolution No. 2025-4645

HOUSE OF REPRESENTATIVES

RESOLUTION

HOUSE RESOLUTION NO. 2025-4645, by Representatives Dent, Dufault, Walen, Orcutt, Burnett, Ryu, Klicker, Salahuddin, Bernbaum, Ley, Schmick, Bronoske, Zahn, Duerr, Fosse, Waters, Donaghy, Morgan, Parshley, Stonier, Steele, Callan, Stuebe, Nance, and Dye

WHEREAS, On January 29, 2025, Harry R. Anderson of Bainbridge Island, Washington, became the first person in history to both fly and sail solo to all seven continents; and

WHEREAS, Harry has flown solo in his small, single-engine airplane, a Lancair Columbia 300, tail number N788W, around the world twice, once eastbound in 2011 and once westbound in 2019. Harry has been awarded Circumnavigator Diplomas from the Federation Aeronautique Internationale (FAI) in Switzerland for those flights; and

WHEREAS, On January 31, 2014, Harry landed his aircraft in Antarctica, becoming only the fifth person to fly solo to all seven continents; and

WHEREAS, On July 16, 2018, Harry flew solo in his aircraft over the North Pole from Resolute, Canada, to Longyearbyen in the Svalbard Islands, Norway. A transpolar flight of 10.5 hours covering more than 1,600 nautical miles; and

WHEREAS, On January 29, 2025, Harry arrived back in the United States of America, completing his solo voyage to all seven continents and a circumnavigation of the earth. He spent 350 days at sea, traveling over 38,000 nautical miles on his 43-foot sailboat, an Allures 40.9 named *Phywave*; and

WHEREAS, Harry's courageous solo flying and sailing achievements can serve as an inspiration to other adventurers in the State of Washington and around the World;

NOW, THEREFORE, BE IT RESOLVED, That the Washington State House of Representatives recognize and honor the flying and sailing achievements of Harry R. Anderson; and

BE IT FURTHER RESOLVED, That copies of this resolution be transmitted by the Chief Clerk of the House of Representatives to Harry R. Anderson.

I hereby certify this to be a true and correct copy of Resolution 4645 adopted by the House of Representatives
April 7, 2025

Bernard Dean, Chief Clerk

Glossary

aft: Toward the back (stern) of the boat.

AIS: An automatic identification system that uses a VHF radio to broadcast a boat's position, course and speed and receives that same information from other nearby boats. It uses the information to automatically calculate the possibility of a collision and warn a boat if there is the possibility of a close encounter.

apparent wind: The wind direction and speed on the boat that is the vector subtraction of the boat speed and heading from the true wind speed and direction.

backstay: Steel cables (stays) that support the mast from the back.

bail: A U-shaped rod or strap used to attach a block to a mast or boom.

batten: Narrow, thin, flat flexible fiberglass slats that slide into horizontal sleeves on a sail to hold its shape in the wind.

beam: The side of the boat or its width.

bimini: A large canvas awning covering the helm on the boat, mainly for protection from the sun.

block: A pulley on a boat.

boom: A horizontal pole that is attached to the mast. It holds the bottom of the mainsail.

boom brake: A pulley-like device hanging from the boom with a line wrapped around it that is designed to control the movement of the boom, in particular, to keep if from swinging violently across the boat during a jibe.

bow: The front of the boat.

bridle: Heavy lines attached from the anchor chain to boat cleats to remove the strain on the windlass as the boat pulls on the anchor.

centerboard: A retractable board or fin that provides the function of a keel but can be raised to allow a boat to navigate in shallow water.

chart: A map used in boating and aviation.

chartplotter: A primary navigation instrument with a moving map display showing the boat's position on electronic nautical charts. It can also control the autopilot and follow routes defined by waypoints programmed into the chartplotter.

cleats: Fittings on the deck or elsewhere used to secure lines.

clew: The lower back corner of a sail.

cockpit: The outside recessed area lower than the deck where the crew can sit while controlling the boat.

COG: The course over ground as measured by successive GPS positions.

deck: The top surface of the boat.

dodger: The canvas or hard enclosure with windows at the front of the cockpit to deflect waves that may splash over the boat.

e-chart: Electronic navigation chart used in a chartplotter or mobile device.

EPIRB: A waterproof, floating emergency beacon that transmits the latitude and longitude of a boat's position to satellites. That information is shared worldwide by rescue services in assisting a boat in distress.

flake: To fold a sail in an accordion formation.

forefoot: The lower part of a boat's bow where it meets the keel.

forestay: Steel cables (stays) that support the mast from the front.

forward: Toward the front of the boat.

furler: A device for winding the sail around a forestay or other stay. A furling line is used to wind up (furl) the sail.

GBR: The Great Barrier Reef.

genoa: A large headsail hoisted and wrapped around a furler on the forestay.

GMT: Greenwich mean time; this is a synonym for UTC.

gooseneck: A device that attaches the boom to the mast allowing the boom to pivot horizontally and vertically.

GPS: The Global Positioning System is a satellite system broadcasting signals that are converted to latitude and longitude in a GPS receiver.

halyards: Lines (ropes) used to raise the sails.

headsail: A sail located in front of a mast.

heaving-to: Pointing the boat 45 degrees off the wind with a small sail set so it will drift more a less in place. It is a good technique to deal with storm conditions or to stop the boat at sea.

helm: The wheel or tiller used to control the rudder and steer the boat.

holding: A term used to describe how well an anchor holds in the sea bottom at an anchorage area.

hull: The body of the boat, which provides buoyancy and supports all other components.

IAATO: International Association of Antarctica Tour Operators.

IEE: An Initial Environmental Evaluation prepared for the EPA.

ITCZ: The intertropical convergence zone is a band of unsettled weather around the equator where the weather systems of the Northern and Southern Hemispheres meet.

jacklines: Strong lines running along the deck of the boat from bow to stern. Sailors clip a tether attached to their life vest to the jacklines to avoid becoming detached from the boat if they fall overboard.

jib/headsail: A smaller sail located in front of the mast.

jibing: Turning the stern of the boat through the wind to change direction.

keel: A large, heavy fin on the bottom of the boat that provides stability and prevents the boat from sliding sideways through the water.

knots: The measure of boat speed equaling nautical miles per hour.

leech: The rear edge of a sail.

leeward: The direction opposite to windward.

lifelines: A pair of steel cables that run the length of each side of the boat and serve as a railing to prevent a sailor from falling overboard.

lines: The nautical term for the ropes used on a boat.

luff tape: A rope sewn into the leading edge of a sail (luff) that fits inside a track to guide and control a hoisted sail.

mainsail: The large, primary sail attached to the mast and boom.

mast: A vertical pole that supports the sails.

nm: Abbreviation for nautical miles.

NSF: The US National Science Foundation.

OCC: The Ocean Cruising Club.

offshore: A general term used to describe sailing far from land as opposed to sailing along the coast or on inland waters.

outhaul: A line that controls the shape of the sail's foot (bottom edge).

PLB: A personal locator beacon.

point of sail: The relationship between the wind direction and a boat's direction of travel.

port: The left side of the boat when facing toward the bow.

pulpit: The chrome bars at the bow of the boat that serves as a railing.

pushpit: The chrome bars around the stern of a boat that serves as a railing.

reach: Three of the points of sail where the wind is coming across the side of the boat. A close reach is sailing with the wind coming from forward of the beam but not close to the bow. A beam reach is sailing with the wind coming on the beam (side) of the boat. A broad reach has the wind coming from aft of the beam but not so far aft as to have the wind directly on the stern.

reef the sail: To pull down and tie off, or wind up, part of the sail.

reeve: To pass a rope through a hole or around something to fasten it.

RIB: A rigid inflatable boat.

rig: The arrangement of masts, sails and supporting rigging that propels the vessel. This refers to standing rigging (the fixed rigging that supports the mast) and running rigging (the adjustable rigging used to control the sails).

roach: The curving section of a sail.

rudder: A control surface at the rear of the sailboat controlled by the helm (a steering wheel or tiller) and used to steer it.

sail loft: A workshop where sails are made or repaired.

sheets: Lines (ropes) that control the shape of the sail.

shore line: A line to shore used to anchor a boat.

shrouds: Cables attached to the side of the mast that support it laterally.

SOG: Speed over ground as measured by successive GPS positions.

SSB radio: Shortwave radio used for communication over long distances.

starboard: The right side of the boat when facing toward the bow.

staysail: A secondary, supplemental sail.

stern: The back of the boat.

tacking: Turning the bow of the boat through the wind to change direction.

thru-hull: A fitting permanently installed in the hull for outlets from sinks or engine exhaust and for inlets for cooling seawater for the engine or water for the watermaker.

travel lift: A large steel frame on wheels with heavy straps that are used to lift a boat out of the water and move it to a place on land.

UTC: Coordinated universal time; this is a synonym for GMT.

vang: A pole or lines to control the vertical angle of the boom.

VHF radio: Very high frequency radio used to communicate over short distances between ships or from a ship to shore.

winch: A machine used to adjust sail tension and control lines.

windlass: The winch on the boat that raises and lowers the anchor.

windward: The direction from which the wind is blowing.

whisker pole: A pole used to wing out a headsail to catch more wind when sailing downwind.

Appendix A – Route Details

Final Sailing Route

Port	Distance to next Port (nm)	Total Distance (nm)	Date of Arrival	Date of Departure	Nights in Port	Nights Enroute to next Port	Notes on Route (Route #'s from Cornell book)
Baltimore, MD, (final outfitting in Annapolis and Rock Hall) USA	138	0		6/1/2022	59	2	
Norfolk, VA	2,404	138	8/1/2022	8/2/2022	1	21	Route AN144. best time May
Horta, Azores	984	2,542	8/23/2022	9/1/2022	9	10	Route AN133A, Best time May to September
Lagos, Portugal	38	3,526	9/11/2022	10/1/2022	20	0	Land in Europe, continent #1. Fly to Switzerland to visit friend.
Faro Island, Portugal	125	3,564	10/1/2022	10/3/2022	2	1	Overnight anchorage enroute to Tangiers
Tangiers, Morocco	590	3,689	10/4/2022	10/8/2022	4	5	Land in Africa, continent #2.
Marina de Rubicon, Lanzarote Island, Canary Islands	2,615	4,279	10/13/2022	10/21/2022	8	24	Route AT11A. Best time September to February
Cabedelo, Brazil	2,340	6,894	11/14/2022	11/22/2022	8	21	Route AS23. Best time September to February
Mar del Plata, Argentina	1,198	9,234	12/13/2022	12/20/2022	7	18	Route AS24. Best time December to April.
Bahia Aguirre (Puerto Espanol), Argentina	55	10,432	1/7/2023	1/8/2023	1	0	stop to break up transit to Puerto Williams along Beagle Channel
Bahia Relegada	12	10,487	1/8/2023	1/9/2023	1	0	stop to break up transit to Puerto Williams along Beagle Channel
Puerto Williams, Chile	40	10,499	1/9/2023	1/17/2023	8	0	Route AS36A. Best time January, February.

Final Sailing Route

Port	Distance to next Port (nm)	Total Distance (nm)	Date of Arrival	Date of Departure	Nights in Port	Nights Enroute to next Port	Notes on Route (Route #'s from Cornell book)
Isla Lennox, Chile	549	10,539	1/17/2023	1/19/2023	2	5	Route AS36A. Best time January, February. Cruise past Cape Horn (Isla Hornos)
Deception Island, Antarctica	700	11,088	1/24/2023	1/30/2023	6	8	Anchor in Stancomb Cove in NW corner
Isla Picton, Chile	27	11,788	2/7/2023	2/10/2023	3	0	Best time January, February
Puerto Williams, Chile	1,193	11,815	2/10/2023	4/15/2023	64	26	Best time January, February, March (see other worksheet)
Puerto Montt, Chile	5,400	13,008	5/11/2023	7/6/2023	56	45	route PS15A. Best time November to March. Haul boat for maintenance. Fly home
Nuku-Hiva, Marquesas	770	18,408	8/20/2023	8/27/2023	7	7	Route PS22. Best time May to September
Papeete, Tahiti	1,475	19,178	9/3/2023	9/15/2023	12	15	Route PS32. Best time June to October
Vava'u, Tonga	2,500	20,653	9/30/2023	10/6/2023	6	21	Route PS41. Best time June to October
Cairns, Australia	1,250	23,153	10/27/2023	10/30/2023	3	11	Route PS53/PS77D. Best time June to October
Darwin, Australia	963	24,403	11/10/2023	5/11/2024	173	9	Route IT19A. Best time April
Lombok, Indonesia	1,155	25,366	5/10/2024	6/4/2024	25	9	Route IS21B. Best time June
Cocos (Keeling) Atoll	2,475	26,521	6/13/2024	6/21/2024	8	19	Route IS34. Best time June, October
La Reunion	1,395	28,996	7/10/2024	8/8/2024	29	12	Route IS43A. Best time June, October
Richards Bay, South Africa	340	30,391	8/20/2024	10/8/2024	49	2	Route IS62. Best time January to March

ROUTE DETAILS | 295

Final Sailing Route

Port	Distance to next Port (nm)	Total Distance (nm)	Date of Arrival	Date of Departure	Nights in Port	Nights Enroute to next Port	Notes on Route (Route #'s from Cornell book)
East London, South Africa	330	30,731	10/10/2024	10/15/2024	5	2	Route IS62. Best time January to March
Knysna, South Africa	275	31,061	10/17/2024	10/21/2024	4	2	Route IS62. Best time January to March
Hout Bay, South Africa	75	31,336	10/23/2024	11/2/2024	10	0	Route AT25C. Best time January to April
Saldanha, South Africa	685	31,411	11/2/2024	11/8/2024	6	5	Route AT25C. Best time January to April
Walvis Bay, Namibia	1,232	32,096	11/13/2024	11/21/2024	8	9	Route AT25C. Best time January to April
St. Helena Island	3,868	33,328	11/30/2024	12/4/2024	4	30	Route AT25C. Best time January to April
Jolly Harbour, Antigua	1,107	37,196	1/3/2025	1/15/2025	12	8	
Great Harbour Cay, Bahamas	76	38,303	1/23/2025	1/27/2025	4	1	
Bimini, Bahamas	52	38,379	1/28/2025	1/29/2025	1	0	
Fort Lauderdale, Florida		38,431	1/29/2025	1/29/2025			
Totals	38,431					348	total days underway or at sea.

Appendix B – Boat Gear

Equipment Group	Description/Type	Quantity
Life raft	Winslow 4-person aviation life raft from the plane.	1
Diving	Mantus Mini Scuba system with spare tank	1
	Spectrum Full Face mask with clear lens	1
	Orcatorch D550 dive light. 1000 lumens	1
	Promate Blunt Tip Titanium dive knife	1
	Weight belt with 20 pounds of weights	1
Flares	Orion flare gun, 4 12 Ga. red flare shells	1
	Solas Flare kit - 3 red parachute, 3 red handheld, 2 orange smoke, 1 dye marker, case. g From Landfall Navigation	1
Docking/ Anchoring	Unimer U-Cleat dock line snubbers. 12-16 mm line	10
	SS wire rope slings. 13' x 3/8" T304SS, Thimble and thimble. Custom order from US Cargo Control	5
	Nylon Webbing Sling, 1" x 14' from US Cargo Control	5
	Shoreline reels, Large size RH, from Fisheries Supply	4
	poly line for shore ties. 600 foot reel of 1/2' CWC blue steel poly line.	3
	AVID Power 20V cordless tire inflator	1
	Tuff End Inflatable Boat Fenders / Buoys, 12" Orange	3
	C. Sherman Johnson Grab-N-Go mooring hook	2
	Black Diamond Hot forge locking carabiners from REI	8
	Neon cable ties to mark anchor chain. Package of 100, assorted colors.	1
	Cape Hatteras 14" Dock line chafe guard.	6
	Perimeter Industries removal chafe guards	6
	Chafe-Pro 3/8"-7/8" chafe guards	4
	GM 8301 15" prusik loop	4
	Eversprout 5-13 foot telescoping boat hook	2
	Beckson HM-8 fixed length 8 ft boat hook	1

Equipment Group	Description/Type	Quantity
	Mantus M2 65 lb anchor	1
	Mantus medium anchor bridle with 3/8" chain hook	1
	Jordan Series Drogue, Amsteel, 132 cones on 289 ft rode, 2 bridle legs 32 feet long, from Ace Sails	1
	3/8" galvanized chain, 15 feet, Home Depot, anchor weight for JSD.	1
	Galerider Drogue, 36" with 2150 feet of 3/4" rode	1
Diesel fuel handling	Mr. Funnel AF15CB fuel filter	2
	Milwaukee 2771-20 M18 Li-battery transfer pump with fittings for plastic tubing	1
	Milwaukee transfer pump impeller kit , # 49-16-2771	2
	10 ft braided plastic tubing 1/2" ID, 3/4" OD	2
	Terrapump battery pump to transfer fuel from jerry cans	2
	replacement EZ-Pour replacement spouts	3
	5 gallon Midwest yellow plastic jerry cans. Modified with flame mitigation insert removed.	10
	treated 2"x6" x 8' treated fir with holes drilled for straps to hold jerry cans. Homemade	2
	Redpoint 1" x 60" webbing straps from REI for fuel cans	20
	ATL 200 liter FuelLocker fuel bladder with short filler neck	1
	Biobor JF diesel biocide, 16 oz bottle	3
	3M HP-156 oil absorbent pads, 17" x 19", pack of 100	1
Propane	Viking 22# fiberglass composite propane cylinders	2
	ACME to All Europe Refill Adapters Set (includes shipping from the UK)	1
	ACME 1 3/4" to 1/4" FNPT adapter	2
	POL to 1/4" flare adapter	2
Tarp, hold downs	Everbilt 12'x16' hevy duty tarp. Home Depot	1
	Rubber straps (bungees), assorted lengths, 10 pack	1
	Bungee cords, flat, assorted in a plastic jar	2

Equipment Group	Description/Type	Quantity
	Stainless steel Rachet straps, 1", set of 4 for holding dinghy on foredeck	1
Shackles, blocks	1/2" long D shackles Marine Grade US Stainless Inc.	2
	3/8" long D shackles Marine Grade US Stainless Inc.	2
	1/4" long D shackles Marine Grade US Stainless Inc.	2
	Jacklines, kit of 2	1
	Ronstan RF6730 snatch block	2
	18 mm sling, 47", 5000 lb test, Metolious	2
	Soft shackle, Marlow 7mm x 350 mm	4
	Misc. blocks, 72 mm & several other sizes	various
Lubricants	Harken BK4513 winch grease	4
	McLube One Drop	4
	Sailkote, 8 oz spray can	5
	MareLube Valve and Equipment Lubrication	4
	Boeshield T-9 12 oz can Corrosion Sheild Lubricant	2
	WD-40, small can	1
	BoatLife Silicone rubber, tube	1
	T-9 spray lubricant, can	2
Miscellaneous	Virkon S disinfectant, 50 tablet bottle, for Antarctica	2
	Blue Performance Lee Cloth (BunkNet)	2
Miscellaneous	Dual cup holders, Brocroft	2
	ATN Mastclimber (bosun's chair and ascenders)	1
	Palmer Safety Harness for mast climbing	1
	Petzl Ascenders, left hand and right hand	2
	Leaktite 5 gallon plastic buckets from Home Depot	3

Appendix C – Tools

Tool Group	Description/Type	Quantity
Cordless power tools	Milwaukee 2648-20 orbital sander with 21 sanding discs	1
	Milwaukee 2780-20 grinder with assorted grinding wheels	1
	Milwaukee 2719-20 Hackzall with assorted blades	1
	Milwaukee 2801-22CT 1/2" drill with charger and two M18 batteries	1
Drill bits	Bosch 14 piece M42 cobalt drill bit set	2
	Milwaukee screwdriver bit set	1
	Neiko Nut driver set, SAE 1/4" to 9/16"	1
	Neiko Nut driver set, Metric 8 to 14 mm	1
Soldering gun	Weller 200/240 Watt with solder and shrink tubing	1
Hand tools	Phillips screwdriver set	1
	Slot head screwdriver set	1
	Metric nut driver set	1
	Craftsmans metric box wrench set in a roll	1
	Craftsmans SAE box wrench set in a roll	1
	17 piece 1/4" drive metric socket set	1
	20 piece SAE/metric 3/8" drive socket set	1
	Allen wrench set, English sizes	1
	Metric Hex key set, 13 sizes	1
	Torx wrench set	1
	Knipex 95 62 190 wire rope cutter	1
	Large crescent wrench	1
	Small crescent wrench	1
	Large channel lock pliers	1
	Small channel lock pliers	1
	putty knives	2

Tool Group	Description/Type	Quantity
	small multimeter	2
	AstroAI DM6000AR multimeter	1
	Misc. files, flat, rattail, triangular	1
	1 foot level	1
	small wire brush	1
	Stanley 8 m/26 ft metric/English tape measure	1
	Dewalt 100 ft tape measure	1
	Milwaukee 6" diagonal pliers (wire cutters)	1
	Commercial 8" Long nose pliers	1
	Needle nose pliers	1
	Stanley utility knife	2
	Large vice grip pliers	1
	Small vice grip pliers	1
	Tin snips	1
	Wire stripping tool	1
	hacksaw with extra blades	1
	Tekton torque wrench, 3/8" drive, 10-80 ft-lb	1
	Campbell swagging tool 1/16"-3/16"	1
	NOCO GB40 lithium battery pack for starting engine	1
	Clamp-on DC ammeter	1
	Ram-Pro inlne spark tester for outboard engine	1
	BK Remote starter switch	1
	Klein ratcheting crimper	1
Miscellaneous	leather gloves	1
	Klein 50' fish tape	1
	Davis SS riggers tool	1
	Assorted chisels with sharpens stone and guide	1
	jumper cables	1
	WorkPro 16 piece Plastic clamp set	1

Tool Group	Description/Type	Quantity
	Duct tape roll	3
Miscellaneous	Estwing Pro Rubber mallet	1
	Safety glasses	3
	Plumbers tape, roll	3

Appendix D – Spares

Group	Description/Type	Quantity
Volvo-Penta D2-50F Engine	fuel filter, part # 861477	2
	Oil filter, part # 3840525	2
	Impeller kit, part # 21951346	2
	Inlet silencer (air filter) part # 3809924	1
	Belt, part #3584086	2
	115 Amp alternator, part #874502	1
Stainless steel hose clamps	ABA SS hose clamps # 52	4
	ABA SS hose clamps # 40	4
	ABA SS hose clamps # 32	4
	ABA SS hose clamps # 20	4
	ABA SS hose clamps # 12	4
	ABA SS hose clamps # 8	4
Leak Repair	Marine Sealant (tube)	1
	X-treme Silicone Rubber Self Fusing Tape, 1"x36'	2
	Eternabond RoofSeal 2"x50', 35 mil	2
	Boatlife Life Seal Cartridge	2
	PC-Products PC-11 Epoxy Adhesive Past, 2 part Marine	2
	Aqua Plumb 01040 Plumbers Putty	2
	Caulking gun	1
Basic Parts	multi-section plastic box of assorted wire nuts	1
	multi-section plastic box of assorted wire connectors	1
Basic Parts	multi-section box of screws, grommets, eyebolts, etc.	1
	100 8" fluorescent cable ties	1
	assortment of SS wire rope clamps, various sizes	1
	10 count 14" cable ties	1

Group	Description/Type	Quantity
	SS Phillips Pan head machine screws kit, assorted 8-32, 10-32, 1/4-20	1
	SS hex head bolts kit, assorted 1/4-20,5/16-18,3/8-16	1
	SS sealing washer kit, sizes #6 thru 1/2"	1
	SS Nylon lock nut kit, sizes #4 thru 1/2"	1
	SS #10x1" sheet metal screws, pack of 100	1
	SS #8x2" Deck screws, pack of 50	1
	SS Phillips Pan head sheet metal screws, assorted #6, #8, #10	1
	zinc clad copper 1/8" sleeves, package of 25	1
	copper 1/8" stops, package of 50	1
	SS 1/8" thimbles, package of 50	1
	SS 1/8" wire rope, 150 feet	1
Northern Lights Genset	Spare parts kit HE M673L2, Part# 38-08015	1
Antennas	Shakespeare 4 ft Centennial spare VHF antenna	1
	Rail mount for Shakespeare antenna	1
	Spare VHF radio	1
Running rigging	spare main sheet	1
	spare genoa sheet	1
	spare main halyard	1

Appendix E – Electronics

Group	Description/Type	Quantity
Instruments	Vexilar LPS-1 Portable depth sounder	1
	Holdpeak HP-866B Portable wind meter	1
	GOGOGO laser rangefinder	1
iPad	8th generation iPad 10.2" 128 GB with GPS	2
	DTTO iPad case	2
	5th generation iPad (backup)	1
iPhone	iPhone SE, 128 GB and 32 GB	2
Calculators	Texas Instruments TI-35X	1
	HP 20S	1
Card reader	Navionics Multicard reader	1
	Ugreen multicard reader	1
12v to USB charger	4 port for 12v round charging port	1
Compass	Brunton hiker compass	1
	Davis Hand bearing compass	1
Binoculars	Nikon Travelite V	1
	Zhumell Xport Optics with compass	1
Spare Watch	Casio G-Shock Illuminator Model DW5600E-1V	1
Batteries	AAA Duracells, pack of 8	1
	AA Duracells, pack of 8	1
	9 volt Duracells, pack of 4	1
Batteries	CR2 3 volt	4
	D Duracells, pack of 8	1
Desk supplies	Weems and Plath 15" parallel ruler	1
	Triangle, pens and pencils, dividers, scissors, Swiss army knife, spare keys	1
Sextant	Dad's Tamaya sextant	1
Headlamp	Fenix HM70R rechargeable headlamp	1
	Black Diamond Spot 350 Submersible IPX8	2

ELECTRONICS | 305

Group	Description/Type	Quantity
Flashlights	Maglite 2D LED flashlights, with D cells	2
	Maglite mounting brackets, set	2
Cameras	Akaso V50X with accessories	1
	Akaso case (extra)	1
	Canon G7X with accessories	1
	GoPro Hero 7 camera with accessories	1
Communications	Iridium GO with install kit	1
	Iridium 9555 satphone	1
	Sony ICF-SW 12 shortwave receiver	1
	Yaesu FT-60 2m/440 MHz radio with charger	1
	Standard Horizon HX890 HF Marine radio with GPS and DSC.	1
	Charger for FTA-250L in ditch bag	1
	Charger for Standard Horizon HX890	1
	Garmin inReach SE+	1
	SMA to BNC adapter kit, 4 adapters	3
	BNC to UHF(PL259/SO259) adapter kit, 4 adapters	1
Computers	HP Elitebook 820 with Windows 7 and accessories	1
	Acer Travelmate B115 with Window 7 and accessories	1
Drones	Holystone HS720S	1
	DJI Mavic Air 2 with Smart Controller with 2 128GB Sandisk microSD cards V30	1
	Sandisk microSD cards, spare, 128GB V30	2
	Zeiss Fog Defender, lens anti-fog	2
	Zeiss Anti-fog wipes, box of 30	2
EPIRB	ACR 2830 GlobalFix V4 Cat 1, Model RLB-41. 2DCCAAD4FEFFBFF	1
PLB	ACR ResqLink View PLB-425 2DCEA4CEECFFBFF	1
	Ocean Signal PLB1	1
SSB (Ham) Radio Gear	ICOM IC-7300 HF transceiver	1

Group	Description/Type	Quantity
	ICOM AT-140 auto antenna tuner	1
	ICOM OPC-1465 shielded control cable for tuner	1
	18 feet RG8X coax cable with connectors	1
	75 feet GTO-15 high voltage wire	1
	MFJ-818 SWR meter	1
	MFJ-260C 300 watt dummy load	1
	10 feet RG8X coax cable with connectors	1
	Ancor Marine Grade RG8X 15 feet, one connector	1
	3 feet RG8X coax cable with connectors	1
	Ferrite RF chokes	10
	1/2" tinned braided copper strap for RF ground, 25 ft	1
	1" ID braided vinyl tubing to contain ground strap, 25 ft	1
Emergency Ditch Bag	Yaesu FTA-250L aviation band handheld transceiver with spare battery	1
	Standard Horizon HX890 Marine VHF with GPS and DSC, spare battery.	1
	Skyblazer II flares	4
	Signal mirror	1
	Whistle	1
	LED flashlight	1
	Packaged storm and survival kit	1

Appendix F – Medical Supplies

Condition	Description/Type	Quantity, (Source)
Books	Advanced First Aid Afloat, 5th edition	1 (OTC)
	Your Offshore Doctor, revised edition	1 (OTC)
Medical Kit	Adventure Marine 1500 Medical Kit	1 (OTC)
Supplemental Supplies:		
Antiseptic skin cleaner	Hibiclens, 32 oz bottle	2 (OTC)
Seasickness	Bonine, 16 ct pack	2 (OTC)
	Meclizine, 25 mg tablet, 100 ct bottle, Rugby	3 (OTC)
Burns	Silvadene, 1% cream, 400 gram container of salve.	1 (Pre)
	GlacierGel, pack of 6 sterile adhesive dressings	1 (OTC)
Antibiotics	Doxycycline, 100 mg tablet dose, 60 ct	1 (Pre)
	Azithromycin 500 mg tablet Travelers diarrhea. 12 ct.	1 (Pre)
Bleeding, Cuts	Bacitracin zinc cream 1 oz tube	3 (OTC)
	Neosoporin ointment, 1 oz tube	3 (OTC)
	Mupirocin, 2%, tube	1 (Pre)
	Skin stapler, sterile, disposal, with staple remover	1 (OTC)
	3" x yards self-adhesive bandage	3 (OTC)
	QuikClot, 3" x 24"	3 (OTC)
Coughs, Throat	Robitussin, liquid-gel capsule, 20 cap pack	2 (OTC)
Coughs, Throat	Ricola cherry flavor, 24 tablet bag	1 (OTC)
Diarrhea	Imodium, 24 ct pack	3 (OTC)
Ear treatment	Ciprofloxin 0.4%-Dexameth OTIC. 7.5 ml bottle	1 (Pre)
Eye	Erythoromycin, 0.5% , 3.5 oz tube	1 (Pre)
	Refresh, 0.5 fl oz bottle	2 (OTC)
Pain	Aspirin, 325 mg tablets, 100 ct bottle	1 (OTC)
	Advil, 200 mg tablets, 100 ct bottle	1 (OTC)

Condition	Description/Type	Quantity, (Source)
	Extra Strength Tylenol, 500 mg 100 ct	1 (OTC)
	Acetaminophen-COD #2, 30 ct. (Tylenol #2)	1 (Pre)
Stomach, Digestion	Tagamet, 200 mg tablets, 70 ct pack	1 (OTC)
	Tums 1000 ultra strength, 160 ct bottle	2 (OTC)
	Pepto-Bismol Liquidcaps, 48 ct pack	1 (OTC)
	Dulcolax tablets, box of 25	1 (OTC)
Skin Treatments	Tinactin cream, antifungal, 1 oz tube	2 (OTC)
	Benadryl cream, 1 oz tube	3 (OTC)
	Cortizone 10 cream, 2 oz tube	3 (OTC)
Salt deficiency	Thermotabs, 100 ct bottle	2 (OTC)
Antihistamine	Allegra, 100 mg tablet, 70 ct pack	1 (OTC)
Decongestant	Dayquil, 24 ct package	1 (OTC)
	Safeway Nighttime Cold and Flu Relief, 24 ct package	1 (OTC)
Sleep Aid	Zzzquil, LiquiCaps, 24 ct pack	2 (OTC)
Toothache	Clove Oil, 4 oz bottle	1 (OTC)
Nose	saline nasal spray, 3 oz bottle	2 (OTC)
Routine Meds, Vitamins	Atorvastatin, 80 mg tablet, 90 ct bottle, 1 year supply	4 (Pre)
	Centrum Silver Men, Multivitamin, 200 ct bottle	3 (OTC)
	Glucosamine/Chondroitin 1500 mg tablets, 120 ct bottle	4 (OTC)
	PreserVision AREDS 2, 120 ct bottle, 2/day	4 (OTC)
	Vitamin D3, 125 mcg softgels, 240 ct bottle, 1/day	2 (OTC)
	Baby aspirin, 81 mg. 1/day, Bayer 300 ct	2 (OTC)
	OTC = Over the Counter (Retail)	
	Pre = By prescription (in the U.S.)	

Appendix G – Charts, Books, and Flags

Item	Description/Type/Title	Author or Source
Navionics navdata cards	Europe, Central & West	Navionics
	U.S. East	Navionics
	Mexico, Caribbean to Brazil	Navionics
	Chile, Argentina & Easter Island	Navionics
	Africa Northwest	Navionics
	Australia Northeast	Navionics
	Pacific Islands	Navionics
	Africa, East	Navionics
	Indian Ocean and South China	Navionics
Antarctica Charts	Admiralty Chart #3560	Todd Navigation
	Admiralty Chart #1776	Todd Navigation
	Admiralty Chart #3463	Todd Navigation
	Admiralty Chart #3206	Todd Navigation
	Admiralty Chart #446	Todd Navigation
	Admiralty Chart #3207	Todd Navigation
	Admiralty Chart #226	Todd Navigation
Books	Atlantic Islands, 7th Edition.	Anne Hammick, Hilary Keatinge, Linda Lane Thornton
	Arctic and Northern Waters, 2nd Edition	Andrew Wilkes
	Cape Horn and Antarctic Waters	Paul Heinrey
	World Cruising Routes, 8th Edition	Jimmy Cornell
	World Voyage Planner, 2nd Edition	Jimmy and Ivan Cornell
	Cornells' Ocean Atlas	Jimmy and Ivan Cornell
	Sailing Directions, Antarctic Pilot, 9th Edition	UK Hydrographic Office
	Argentina, RCC Pilotage Foundation	Andy O'Grady and Peter Hill

Item	Description/Type/Title	Author or Source
	The Pacific Crossing Guide, 3rd Edition	Kitty Van Hagen
	Indian Ocean Cruising Guide, 2nd Edition	Rod Heikell
	Chile Cruising Guide, RCC Pilotage Foundation, 4th Edition	Andrew O'Grady
	Patagonia & Tierra del Fuego Nautical Guide, 3rd Edition	Marilina Rolfo & Giorgio Ardrizzi
	Embassy Cruising Guide Chesapeake Bay to Florida and ICW, 2021	Maptech
	U.S. Chart No. 1, 12th Edition	NOAA
	Antarctica Cruising Guide (tourist cruises), 4th Edition	Peter Carey and Craig Franklin
	Marine Diesel Engines, 3rd Edition	Nigel Calder
	Troubleshooting Marine Diesels	Peter Compton
	Boatowner's Mechanical and Electrical Manual, 4th Edition	Nigel Calder
	Singlehanded Sailing	Andrew Evans
	Storm Tactics Handbook, 3rd Edition	Lin & Larry Pardey
	High Latitude Sailing, 2020 edition	Jon Amtrup & Bob Shepton
	French for Cruisers	Kathy Parsons
	Spanish for Cruisers, 2nd Edition	Kathy Parsons
	Flying 7 Continents Solo	Harry Anderson
Courtesy flags	3 packages of courtesy flags: Europe Atlantic Coast Set, Circumnavigation Set, West Coasts of Americas Set	Yachtflags.com
	: Argentina, Ascension Island, Brazil, Easter Island, Falkland Islands, Greenland, India, Malaysia, Mayotte, Namibia, Pitcairn, Saint Helena, Sri Lanka, Thailand, Uruguay	Jimmy Green Marine
	Two Yellow Q flags, Taylor	Amazon

Appendix H – Antarctica Documents

The continent of Antarctica is inside an area regulated by the Antarctica Treaty System (ATS), an international treaty covering all the area south of 60 degrees south latitude. The treaty area is not controlled by any country. Some countries have made territorial claims to Antarctica, like Chile, but those claims are not recognized by other countries. More than 60 nations have signed the Antarctica Treaty agreeing to abide by its terms and conditions to protect the continent from commercial exploitation and environmental damage.

Traveling by boat or plane to Antarctica represents an "expedition" from your home country to the continent; in my case, an expedition of one since I was solo. The expedition must get permission from its home country to make the trip. This involves preparing and submitting several documents to the government to make sure the planned expedition complies with the Antarctica Treaty requirements. These documents are reviewed in detail by the appropriate authorities in your country and may require one or more revisions until they are acceptable. For the United States, the following documents are required:

1. Antarctica Advanced Notification Form DS-4131 submitted to the U.S. State Department
2. Initial Environmental Evaluation (IEE) submitted to the U.S. Environmental Protection Agency
3. Waste Permit Application submitted to the U.S. National Science Foundation which runs the U.S. Antarctica Program

The documents I created and submitted that successfully satisfied the requirements for a US expedition of one to Antarctica can be found on the following pages.

U.S. Department of State
ADVANCE NOTIFICATION FORM
TOURIST AND OTHER NON-GOVERNMENTAL ACTIVITIES IN THE ANTARCTIC TREATY AREA

OMB APPROVAL NO. 1405-0181
EXPIRES: 05/31/2021
ESTIMATED BURDEN: 10.5 HOURS

This information is requested in furtherance of U.S. obligations under Article VII(5)(a) of the Antarctic Treaty of 1959, and consistent with Antarctic Treaty Consultative Meeting Recommendation XVIII-1 and Resolution XIX-3. Information below should be submitted no later than three months prior to intended travel to the Antarctic Treaty Area. Responses will facilitate a determination of U.S. jurisdiction over the activity and permit timely dissemination to Parties to the Treaty of expedition details. Certain expedition information may be posted on the National Science Foundation's and the Antarctic Treaty Secretariat's Web sites in order to facilitate notification of and access by all Parties to the Treaty. All U.S. nationals organizing expeditions to Antarctica in the United States, or proceeding to Antarctica from the United States, should submit this form to the U.S. Department of State as indicated below . In addition to disclosure to other Parties to the Treaty, the information provided may be shared with the U.S. Environmental Protection Agency to ensure compliance with 40 CFR *(Code of Federal Regulations)* Part 8, Environmental Impact Assessment *(EIA)* of Nongovernmental Activities in Antarctica, as well as with other relevant U.S. agencies. The information also may be shared with appropriate domestic or foreign entities for law enforcement, search and rescue, or administrative purposes.

Include attachments for responses that require more space than the form provides. If an organizer is planning more than one expedition, details specific to each individual expedition should be provided as attachments to this form. Each organizer should prepare only one Advance Notification form.

The completed form should be submitted to the Antarctic Advisor, Office of Ocean and Polar Affairs, Bureau of Oceans, Environment and Science, U.S. Department of State, 2201 C Street NW, Washington DC 20520.

NOTE: For the purposes of this form, "expeditions to Antarctica" include activities south of Sixty degrees South Latitude, excluding commercial fishing voyages. Crew includes an expedition's captain and officers, helicopter pilots, and deck, engine, and hotel/catering staff. Expedition staff include guides, lecturers, and small boat drivers who are not otherwise counted as crew. Passengers include other persons accompanying the expedition, but exclude national representatives or observers.

A. Expedition Organizer

1. Name of Expedition Organizer *(Company, entity, or person(s) as appropriate)* Harry R. Anderson	2. Expedition Organizer's Contact Person Harry R. Anderson
3. Mailing Address *(Please also provide physical address if using a post office box)* xxx xxxxx xxxxx xx, Bainbridge Island, WA 98110	4. Nationality of Expedition Organizer USA
5. Principal Place of Business *(Home office)* xxx xxxxx xxxxx xx, Bainbridge Island, WA 98110	6. Total Number of Expedition Staff per Excursion 1
7. International Phone +1 XXX- XXX-XXX	8. International Fax N/A

9. Explain activities undertaken by the organizer, including, for example, acquiring the use of vessels or aircraft, hiring expedition staff, or planning itineraries.

The expedition will be the voyage of a single 41 foot aluminum hull yacht from Puerto Williams to the Antarctica Peninsula, and back, for the purpose of tourism. No other equipment, personnel, or resources will be required.

10. Explain if the organizer maintains substantial ties to a country or countries other than the United States; for example, a U.S. national who habitually resides in another country, or a company which is the subsidiary of an entity incorporated in or with other substantial ties to another country.

None.

11. Explain whether any organizing activities will be or are being performed by a party or parties other than the named expedition organizer; e.g., a sub-charter. Identify the nationality of individuals or commercial entities to whom the expedition organizer has delegated specified organizational responsibilities.

None.

12. Describe where the organizing activities conducted prior to the expedition will be or are being performed.

In the United States.

13. Specify the place(s) from which the expedition(s) will depart immediately prior to entering the Treaty Area.

From Puerto Williams, Chile

DS-4131

B. Details of Transport and Equipment to be Used for the Tour/Expedition

Complete these panels only once if all Tours/Expeditions planned do not vary in their use of transport or equipment; where these vary, complete the panel for every Tour or Expedition.

B1. Vessel/Aircraft Used for Transport To/From Antarctica

14. Vessel/Aircraft Registered Name		15. Vessel/Aircraft Type	
PHYWAVE		Allures 40.9 sailboat	

16. Country of Registration	17. Vessel/Aircraft Passenger Carrying Capacity	18. Vessel Ice Rating and Classification Society *(If applicable)*
USA	6	N/A

19. *(Check one)* ☐ Ship ☒ Yacht ☐ Aircraft ☐ Other _____	20. Vessel/Aircraft Fuel Capacity	21. Vessel/Aircraft Fuel Type
	900 liters	Diesel

22. Intended Use of Vessel/Aircraft

Transport crew from Chile to various anchorages along the Antarctica Peninsula.

23. Vessel/Aircraft Call Sign	24. Radio Frequency(ies) Monitored	25. INMARSAT Number(s)/Fax(es)	26. E-mail Address(es)
WDM7325	Marine channel 16	Iridium 8816 XXXXXXXX	harry.anderson17@gmail.com

27. Captain's/Commander's Name(s)	28. Total Number of Crew
Harry R. Anderson	1

B2. Equipment to be Used Within Antarctica

29. Number and Types of Aircraft to be Used

Number	Type	Use

30. Number and Types of Other Vessels or Vehicles to be Used *(e.g., small boats, snowmobiles)*

Number	Type	Use
1	9.6 foot RIB dinghy	to tranport crew ashore for day shore visits.

C. Contingency Planning

31. Type and Amount of Insurance Coverage, including Name(s) of Insurer(s)

Vessel damage insurance in the amount of the boat's value, liability insurance in the amount of US$ 1million, search and rescue insurance in the amount of $10,000. The insurer's name is Novamar Insurance Group. The policy covers vessel operation in North America, South America and the Antarctica Peninsula. In addition, the expedition leader has health insurance (Regence Blue Cross) and personal umbrella liability coverage in the amount of US$ 4 million (Allstate Insurance).

32. Arrangements for self-sufficiency and contingency plans including for medical evacuations and search and rescue in the event of an emergency.

The expedition is the voyage of a single yacht into the Antarctic Treaty Area from Puerto Williams, Chile. The yacht is equipped with the latest electronic navigation equipment, electronic and paper charts, HF radio, and satellite links for receiving weather forecasts. The vessel is a sailboat but it will also carry 900 liters of fuel, sufficent to travel 1500 nm under power alone, if necessary. The boat will have 60 days of provisions, more than twice that necesary for the planned expedition. The vessel is equipment with a covered life raft, PLB and EPIRB beacons, flares, satphone, and other signalling equipment in the event of an emergency. Search and rescue insurance and the financial resources of the expedition leader will cover the cost of rescue or evacuation, if necessary.

D. Expedition Details

NOTE: If more than one expedition is planned, please provide the information below in an attachment referring to each individual expedition. If more than one vessel will be used in carrying multiple expeditions, please organize the submission of information on individual expeditions under the name of the specific vessel that will carry those expeditions.

33. Planned Port of Embarkation	34. Planned Date of Embarkation *(mm-dd-yyyy)*
Puerto Williams, Chile	January 4, 2023 (depending on weather)
35. Planned Port of Disembarkation	36. Planned Date of Disembarkation *(mm-dd-yyyy)*
Puerto Williams, Chile	January 29, 2023
37. Planned Cruise/Flight Number or Voyage Name	38. Estimated Number of Passengers to be Carried per Excursion
Anderson Voyage to Antarctica	1 crew, no passengers

39. Activities to be Undertaken and Purpose

Sailing into Antarctica waters and the waters along the Antarctica Pennisula. Anchoring at several locations along the Antarctica Peninsula, as noted in Section 40 below, for the purpose of tourism and photography. Going ashore in the dinghy from the yacht PHYWAVE for the purpose of tourism, photography, and to set shorelines to help hold the yacht's anchored position. An Unmanned Aerial Vehicle (UAV) will be launched at some dinghy landing locations for the purpose of photography. The visits ashore at each location will last only a few hours each.

40. Proposed itinerary with dates and places to be visited. Include a proposed itinerary for all expeditions that will proceed south of 60 degrees South Latitude, even if there is no intention for individuals to disembark onto land.

1. Anchor in Whaler's Bay or Stancomb Cove at Deception Island, January 9-12, 2023
2. Anchor at Two Hummock Island, January 12-14, 2023
3. Anchor at Portal Point, January 14-15, 2023
4. Tie to the wreck of the whaling ship Governoren, Enterprise Island, Jaunary 15-17, 2023
5. Anchor at Waterboat Point, January 17-19, 2023
6. Anchor in the Melchior Islands in the channel between Eta and Omega Islands, January 19-23, 2023.

The itinerary dates are approximate and will depended on prevailing weather condtions. At each location the vessel's dinghy will be used to go ashore to set shore lines, as needed, and for short day hikes and photography. There will be no camping or overnight stays onshore.

Certification

	01-18-2022
Signature of Tour/Expedition Organizer	Date *(mm-dd-yyyy)*

Public reporting burden for this collection of information is estimated to average 10.5 hours per response, including time required for searching existing data sources, gathering the necessary documentation, providing the information and/or documents required, and reviewing the final collection. You do not have to supply this information unless this collection displays a currently valid OMB control number. If you have comments on the accuracy of this burden estimate and/or recommendations for reducing it, please send them to Antarctic Advisor, Office of Ocean and Polar Affairs, Bureau of Oceans, Environment and Science, U.S. Department of State, 2201 C Street NW, Washington DC 20520.

s/v *PHYWAVE* 2023 Antarctica IEE

Initial Environmental Evaluation

Sailing Vessel PHYWAVE Voyage to the Antarctica Peninsula

Yacht owner/captain, expedition leader:
Harry R. Anderson, Ph.D.

Bainbridge Island, WA 98110
hra@phywave.com
svphywave@gmail.com
website: www.phywave.com
home:
mobile:
satphone:

US contact:
Harry R. Anderson, Ph.D.

Bainbridge Island, WA 98110
hra@phywave.com
svphywave@gmail.com
website: www.phywave.com
home:
mobile:
satphone:

Summary

This IEE covers a proposed trip to the Antarctic Peninsula aboard the sailboat *PHYWAVE* scheduled for January 4 through January 29, 2023, for the purpose of tourism, a privilege acknowledged in Chapter VII of the Antarctic Treaty. One person will travel aboard a 41-foot aluminum hull Allures 40.9 sailboat. Brief landings by dinghy will be made at points on the peninsula for photography and day hiking.

Vessel operations and landing activities are expected to have no more than minor and transitory impacts on the Antarctic environment.

All activities on this voyage will be carried out in accordance with the Antarctic Treaty; the Environmental Protocol to the Antarctic Treaty on Environmental Protection and its Annexes; Antarctic Treaty Consultative Meeting (ATCM) Recommendation XVIII-1; the International Convention for the Prevention of Pollution from Ships (MARPOL); the International Agreement Concerning Safety of Life at Sea (SOLAS); and applicable domestic statutes and regulations, including the Marine Mammal Protection Act and the Endangered Species Act. These documents are listed in the References Section 11 of this IEE.

1. Description of Purpose & Activity

The primary purpose of this expedition is to sail solo to Antarctica and return to South America, and secondarily to enjoy the remoteness, solitude and scenery of Antarctica, and to take photographs and videos of the scenery. Explicitly, viewing wildlife is not a purpose of this expedition.

s/v *PHYWAVE* 2023 Antarctica IEE

2. Yacht Specifications

- *PHYWAVE* is an Allures 40.9 cutter
- Designer: Racoupeau Yacht Design
- Builder: Allures Yachting
- Year Built: 2021
- Cutter rig with genoa and staysail
- Aluminum hull with swing keel/centerboard
- LOA: 12.65 meters (41.50 feet)
- Beam: 4.15 meters (13.62 feet)
- Draft: keel/centerboard up: 1.06 meters (3.48 feet), down: 2.75 meters (9.0 feet)
- Displacement: 10.9 metric tons (24,000 lbs)
- Ballast: 4.2 metric tons (9260 lbs)
- Fresh water capacity: 330 liters (87 gallons) . *PHYWAVE* is also equipped with small desalination which turns sea water into fresh water so the fresh water supply is virtually unlimited.
- Fuel capacity: 500 liters (132 gallons) in internal tanks plus 400 liters auxiliary storage
- Holding tank capacity: 60 liters
- Engine: Volvo-Penta D2-50F with sail drive
- Equipped with solar panels, a wind generator, and a 6 kW diesel generator for battery charging
- CE Certification: Category A – Ocean
- USCG official number: 1322011
- FCC MMSI number: 368232960

s/v *PHYWAVE* 2023 Antarctica IEE

3. Crew

The captain and only crewmember is Dr. Harry R. Anderson. Dr. Anderson is an experienced yachtsman with more than 30 years of sailing experience including 12 years as owner and captain of *RAYTRACE*, a 37 foot Bavaria sloop he has sailed around the waters of the Pacific Northwest and Canada, as far north as Alaska. This experience includes more than 240 days as Master of the vessel, 95% of which were single-handed. Dr. Anderson also has American Sailing Association (ASA) Certifications 101, 103, 104, 105, and the International Proficiency Certificate. Before embarking on the voyage to Antarctica from Puerto Williams, Dr. Anderson will have sailed *PHYWAVE* from the east coast of the United States, across the Atlantic Ocean eastbound to Europe and Africa, across the Atlantic Ocean westbound to South America and south along its coast to Puerto Williams, more than 10,000 nautical miles at sea.

Dr. Anderson has been to Antarctica twice before.

In February, 2011, Dr. Anderson took a two week Quark Expeditions cruise to the Antarctica Peninsula (the "Crossing the Circle" cruise) aboard the ship Sergey Vavilov. During this cruise Dr. Anderson attended the requisite seminars on proper practices for protecting the flora and fauna of Antarctica, including maintaining appropriate distance while observing wildlife. The Quark cruise included several zodiac landings ashore where these procedures were followed.

In January, 2014, Dr. Anderson flew his single engine aircraft N788W from Punta Arenas, Chile, to King George Island. For that flight he submitted a complete IEE and a Waste Permit Application that were acceptable to the EPA and NSF, respectively. He also successfully obtained permission from the Chilean government and Chilean Air Force to land at King George Island.

From these previous experiences Dr. Anderson is very familiar with the standards and protocols for visiting Antarctica and protecting its environment.

Dr. Anderson is an experienced adventure pilot with more than 2250 hours of flight time in a variety of fixed-wing aircraft. More than 90% of those hours are solo, more than 97% as Pilot-in-Command. He holds a Commercial Pilot certificate for single-engine and multi-engine aircraft with an Instrument rating. He also holds a Private Pilot certificate for single-engine seaplanes. He has flown around the world twice, eastbound and westbound. He flew to Antarctica in 2014, as mentioned, and in 2018 he completed a transpolar flight over the North Pole from Resolute Bay, Canada, to Longyearbyen in the Svalbard Islands, Norway. From these wide-ranging international flights he has become highly experienced at worldwide navigation, interpreting weather forecasts, and expedition planning for Arctic and Antarctica regions. Many of his international flights are described in his 2015 book *Flying 7 Continents Solo*.

Dr. Anderson holds a BSEE degree from the University of California at Santa Barbara, a MSEE degree from Oregon State University, and a Ph.D. in Electrical Engineering from the University of Bristol in the United Kingdom. He is an expert in wireless communications network design, simulation and optimization. He has published numerous peer-reviewed technical papers and a graduate level reference text entitled *Fixed Broadband Wireless System Design* (2003, John Wiley: Chichester). He is a successful entrepreneur having founded, grown and sold high tech companies.

s/v *PHYWAVE* 2023 Antarctica IEE

Table 1 - Itinerary

Location	Arrival Date	Departure Date	Activity
Puerto Williams, Chile	12/13/2022	1/4/2023	wait for weather window to cross the Drake Passage southbound
Isla Lennox, Chile	1/4/2023	1/5/2023	interim stop before Drake Passage
Deception Island, Whaler's Bay	1/9/2023	1/12/2023	anchor, go ashore in dinghy
Two Hummock Island	1/12/2023	1/14/2023	anchor, shore ties, go ashore in dinghy
Portal Point	1/14/2023	1/15/2023	anchor, shore ties, go ashore in dinghy
Enterprise Island	1/15/2023	1/17/2023	tie to *Governoren* shipwreck, go ashore in dinghy
Waterboat Point	1/17/2023	1/19/2023	anchor, shore ties, go ashore in dinghy
Melchior Islands, anchor in small bight in the channel between Eta and Omega Islands	1/19/2023	1/24/2023	anchor, shore ties, go ashore in dinghy. Wait for weather window to cross Drake Passage northbound
Puerto Williams, Chile	1/29/2023		

In addition to his education and practical experience with Antarctic environmental protection methods aboard the Vavilov and his solo flight to King George Island, Dr. Anderson has read relevant sections of the documents listed in the References in Section 11 of this IEE which include several pertaining to minimizing environmental impact while visiting Antarctica.

4. Proposed Itinerary

Table 1 shows the proposed itinerary and activities for the *PHYWAVE* expedition to Antarctica. The locations represent anchorages which have been successfully used by yachts of similar size and configuration to *PHYWAVE*, that is, shallow enough (10-12 meters depth or less) with fair to good holding ground for successful anchoring and, in most cases, the ability to set shore ties.

4a. Itinerary Adjustments

The proposed itinerary, of course, is dependent on weather conditions. In particular, it is anticipated that *PHYWAVE* will wait at Puerto Williams for a suitable weather window to cross the Drake Passage southbound to Antarctica so the departure date may change, perhaps by several days. Similarly, the return voyage northbound across the Drake Passage will also require a suitable weather window. Some yachts have waited 10 days in the Melchior Islands for a suitable weather to return to Puerto Williams. While along the Antarctica Peninsula, depending on the prevailing wind and ice conditions, some of the listed anchorages may be undesirable or even unusable. Based on extensive study of previous yacht voyages to Antarctica, some as recent as the 2021-2022 season, and available publications, several other alternate anchorages have been identified where yachts have successfully anchored in the past. If conditions warrant, one or more of these anchorages may be added to, or substituted for, the locations listed in the itinerary.

ANTARCTICA DOCUMENTS | 319

s/v *PHYWAVE* 2023 Antarctica IEE

As stated in Section 1, the primary purpose of this expedition is simply to sail solo to Antarctica and return to South America. This means the expedition's activities can be extremely limited and still achieve this purpose. As a minimum, sailing to Antarctica, going ashore in one place like Deception Island, taking some photos, and sailing back to Puerto Williams would satisfy the primary purpose of this expedition. If conditions warrant, the proposed itinerary can be adjusted to accomplish that purpose only.

4b. Assessment of Alternatives

The identified need and activity is to exercise the tourism privilege acknowledged in Chapter VII of the Treaty. Voyaging to Antarctica is the only way to meet the identified need. Having noted that, the itinerary of this expedition to the Antarctic Peninsula will be altered as necessary to decrease its impact on the environment and on wildlife. Changing the itinerary in response to weather also serves to reduce risk of accidental release of pollutants due to shipwreck and of the impact caused by a search and rescue (SAR) incident.

The expedition consists of one person, a 41-foot sailboat, and a 9.5 foot dinghy. Stores of fuel and other potential pollutants are therefore limited. The activity will be led with an eye toward minimizing impact.

Cancelling a trip to Antarctica would remove its impact on the environment. Because this trip will have no more than minor or transitory impact, cancellation is not indicated.

5. Expedition Activities in Antarctic Waters

5a. Yacht Operations

Activities conducted from the yacht *PHYWAVE* include:

- Viewing scenery
- Sailing
- Motoring

Boats create an impact while underway by their visual presence and by the sound they emit. *PHYWAVE* is small enough and quiet enough that its movements will cause no more than a minor or transitory impact on wildlife, visitors, or the environment, especially compared to many large cruise ships that visit the Antarctic Peninsula during the austral summer.

While underway in Antarctica, a visual watch will be maintained both to reduce the risk of ice collision and to watch for other obstacles. Modern broadband radar will be in continuous use to detect icebergs or other hazards. The AIS receiver/transmitter will be used to detect and avoid other vessels.

The boat has is 51 hp engine that burns diesel fuel and creates some noise when it is running. There are no published specifications for how much noise it emits, either as a standalone engine or when installed in the boat. However, it should be noted the engine is installed in the center of the boat

s/v *PHYWAVE* 2023 Antarctica IEE

on the hull and surrounded by sound baffling material so as to minimize the engine noise so its impact on the people aboard the boat. Of course, this same sound baffling will reduce the amount of engine noise outside the boat. Such sound baffling is a standard design feature on modern yachts.

The IAATO publication *Cetacean Watching Guidelines* will be followed while underway.

5b. Dinghy Operations

The dinghy is a 9.5 foot AB dinghy with a rigid aluminum hull and inflatable tubes (RIB).

Activities conducted from the dinghy include:

- Landing ashore
- Dinghy cruises
- Shore viewing without landing
- Scenery viewing

Most of the dinghy operations are short trips to bring crew ashore to set shore ties, and for photography and day hikes.

The dinghy will also occasionally be used for cruising. During dinghy cruises the IAATO wildlife watching guidelines (References 6-9) will be followed.

The inflatable dinghy will be cleaned prior to departing South America. It will be free of foreign material that could be introduced to Antarctica during its use.

5c. Landings

The crew intends to make landings in Antarctica in the AB 9.5 RIB dinghy carried aboard *PHYWAVE*. For ocean passages the dinghy is normally strapped down, upside down, on the foredeck of *PHYWAVE*. In this position the aluminum bottom and inflatable side tubes will be thoroughly clean with a stiff brush in Puerto Williams before departure for Antarctica. The dinghy will also be flipped over on the foredeck so the interior can also be cleaned with a brush.

Crossing the Drake Passage the dinghy will remain strapped to the foredeck. On arriving at *PHYWAVE*'s first anchorage location at Deception Island, the dinghy will be lifted off the foredeck and placed in the water for use in landing ashore. After the landing is completed and the crew returns to *PHYWAVE*, the dinghy will be hoisted onto the arch on the stern of *PHYWAVE* and carried there during the short trips between the anchorages listed in Table 1. As described in Section 6e, the dinghy will be also cleaned between shore landings. Once *PHYWAVE* is ready to depart the Antarctica Peninsula, the dinghy will be returned to the foredeck and strapped down there for the passage north to Puerto Williams.

The landings will potentially take place at all the locations listed in Table 1, depending on weather and ice conditions. With only one person, the landings will have little impact. Landing durations will be a few hours during daytime, not overnight. While along the Antarctica Peninsula the boat will be anchored and stopped, never underway, when the crew member is sleeping.

s/v *PHYWAVE* 2023 Antarctica IEE

The yacht will be anchored as close to shore as practical and will be tied directly to shore when possible or necessary. Because of the swing keel, anchoring is possible in shallower water closer to shore than boats with standard fixed keels.

During landings no stoves, fuel, or food (other than survival rations) will be taken ashore. Planned activities include dinghy cruising, photography, and day hikes, but not camping. For safety, the dinghy will carry an emergency bag containing marine and aviation band VHF radios, GPS, a satphone, survival gear, packaged food like granola bars, drinking water, and the boat's flare gun. In case the dinghy's outboard motor fails, oars stowed on the dinghy will be used, and the dinghy will be landed within rowing range of the boat.

The crew will operate within the Code of Conduct for each site, including ASMAs as identified at www.ats.aq/e/protected.html. There will be no visits to ASPA's.

If there are cruise ships or yachts in an anchorage area where a landing is contemplated, an effort will be made to contact these other vessels on maritime VHF channel 16 to determine, if possible, their schedule for landings and coordinate with them so that *PHYWAVE* landings do not occur at the same time as the landings from other vessels. Since enjoying the solitude of Antarctica's natural environment is one goal of this expedition, avoiding going ashore when another crowd of people is already there is undesirable in any event.

Landings are planned using the IAATO's *Guidelines for Visitors to the Antarctic*, *Southern Ocean Cruising*, and *Status of Antarctic Specially Protected Area and Antarctic Specially Managed Area Management Plans*. The IAATO *Information for Yachts* will be followed.

UAV Operations

With suitable weather, an Unmanned Aerial Vehicle (UAV or "drone") will be launched to take photos and videos from an elevated perspective. Suitable weather means current and forecast surface wind speeds during the flight time of less than 12 knots with no current or forecast precipitation.

The UAV will only be launched from a shore location, typically adjacent to where the dinghy has been landed. Launching from a shore-based location is a superior approach compared to launching from a moving boat or a boat swinging at anchor, as some have proposed. Modern advanced UAV's are equipped with important Return-to-Home (RTH) safety features. When the UAV is first powered on it establishes a Home Position using its internal GPS. If the UAV should lose the signal from the controller, it will automatically return to the Home Position and land. This is an RTH safety feature. Similarly, if the UAV detects its internal battery power level is too low it with also execute the RTH procedure and land. In contrast, if the UAV is launched from a moving boat the Home Position established at launch may no longer be the location of the boat and the RTH safety features will send the UAV to a water landing.

As noted, the intended use of the UAV is to get photos and videos of Antarctica from a unique, elevated perspective. To get a suitable elevated perspective the UAV will be flown no higher than 75 meters above surrounding terrain and no farther than 400 meters from the launch point. The screen on the UAV controller continuously displays the UAV height above, and distance from, the Home Point so it easy to keep the UAV confined to this space. The operator will maintain visual line-of-sight with the UAV at all times. The UAV on board *PHYWAVE* has a maximum flight time of about 27 minutes. However, the planned flight times in Antarctica will be limited to about 10-15 minutes.

s/v *PHYWAVE* 2023 Antarctica IEE

The UAV flights are not intended for viewing wildlife as wildlife viewing is not a purpose of this expedition. Before launching the UAV, the operator will note the location of wildlife in the vicinity of the launch point and choose a flight route, and periodically modify that flight route and altitude as necessary, to avoid that wildlife, including airborne flocks of birds. If the presence of wildlife is too intense around the launch location, the UAV will not be launched.

Because of its many built in safety features such as automatic RTH, it is extremely unlikely, but not impossible, that the operator could lose control of the UAV and it will crash somewhere. If it crashes on land, it will be possible to hike to the location and recover the UAV. A "crash" would not necessarily be a violent event like an airplane crash. The UAV itself is a solidly-built device unlikely to break apart in such an event. The exception are the four plastic propellers (2 blades each) which may break off if the UAV crashes.

If the UAV crashes on water, the flotation devices attached to each of its four legs (as pictured here) will keep it afloat so it can be recovered with the dinghy.

It should be noted that as of January, 2021, there were more than 1.7 million UAV's registered with the FAA in United States, and countless other unregistered UAV's. Even with these large numbers the press essentially never reports a UAV crashing in some unintended place. It would be newsworthy if it were happening. While this is anecdotal evidence, it certainly reinforces the idea that it is extremely rare for operators to lose control of a UAV and have it crash.

The UAV carried aboard *PHYWAVE* is a DJI Mavic Air 2 model registered with the FAA in the United States, registration number FA3NT7A3ZH. In addition to being a licensed commercial pilot, Dr. Anderson is also a FAA-licensed Remote Pilot authorized to operate an Unmanned Aerial System (UAS). The drone will be operating in accordance with FAA Rules, Part 107, with particular attention to not disturbing wildlife as noted above.

The IAATO was contacted with regard to UAV operations (RPAS in their nomenclature). They do not permit recreational use of UAV's, only commercial use, which is understandable when considering the idea of a cruise ship full of passengers wanting to launch UAV's at the same time. A further request was made to IAATO for the technical and other guidelines they apply to the commercial use of UAV's by their member operators, when they authorize such use by operators. IAATO did not respond to that request. Consequently, at this point the guidelines they apply to commercial UAV operations by the IAATO operators are unknown so it is not possible to determine whether the *PHYWAVE* expedition's proposed UAV operations follow those guidelines.

The *PHYWAVE* expedition leader believes the proposed UAV operations as described above are modest and reasonable, with the goal of not disturbing wildlife or leaving any trace of the UAV operation at any location where the UAV may be launched.

s/v *PHYWAVE* 2023 Antarctica IEE

6. Expedition Impacts

6a. State of the Antarctica Environment

Geographical Description

The plan is to visit the islands west of the Antarctic Peninsula as far south as Waterboat Point (64° 49' South), ice conditions permitting. The landings at Portal Point and Waterboat Point will be the only landings on the Antarctica Peninsula itself.

Animal and Plant Life in the Region

In this region, the summer months of December to March are marked by a decrease in local ice cover, which makes travel by sea possible. The mainland is largely covered by permanent ice, but ice retreats sufficiently on the outer islands and some mainland regions to provide nesting sites for penguins, cormorants, terns, Dominican gulls, and skuas. Marine mammals, including whales and seals, migrate into the region to feed in the nutrition-rich cold Antarctic waters. At this time, various mosses and lichens grow on the rocks of the offshore islands and bare mainland areas, and algae bloom in the glaciers themselves. Underwater, sea life is abundant in this time of year, with krill blooms, and undersea plants and animals feeding and undergoing most of their annual growth and development.

Common species present during this time include:

- Penguins (Adelie, Chinstrap, Gentoo, and Emperor - occasional transients)
- Whales (Humpback, Southern right, and Minke)
- Flying birds (cormorants, dominican gulls, Antarctic terns, Antarctic skuas)
- Seals (Leopard, Weddel, Crabeater)
- Krill
- Mosses and lichens
- Undersea life

Aquatic Environment

Icebergs and floating pieces of ice (bergy bits, growlers, and brash) are prevalent at this time of year and contribute to the cold water temperature of the region (typically in the 1-2 degrees Celsius range), which is an important factor in the nutrient-holding capabilities of the water, since cold water is capable of holding more oxygen (from plankton photosynthesis and surface transmission) in suspension and thus supporting more life than warmer water.

In many regions, melt-water streams flow into the sea during the warmer summer months.

The Antarctic Polar Front, a shifting ocean zone which marks a usual sharp decrease in water temperature as one approaches Antarctica, serves to act as a barrier to warmer ocean currents and sea-borne pollution reaching the Antarctic Peninsula region.

s/v *PHYWAVE* 2023 Antarctica IEE

Terrestrial Environment

The mainland and many of the outlying islands of the Antarctic Peninsula are covered with permanent ice. Some melt-water runs off in the summer, and glacial retreat has been observed in many locations. Several regions covered by permanent ice as little as 20 years ago have now experienced significant retreat, including the former Renard Peninsula (which is now an island), the Jones Ice Shelf and the newly named Amsler Island. Most of the region's land is either exposed or snow-covered rock or permanent ice.

Human Environment

The Antarctic Peninsula is home to numerous national scientific programs which maintain bases, camps, and emergency depots. In addition to currently-occupied human habitation, there are also numerous historic sites, including huts, wrecked ships, whaleboats, barrels, and other artifacts from the exploration and whaling history of Antarctica. Whale skeletons can be found on the regions beaches and underwater, a result of Antarctic whaling.

Tourism

Numerous cruise ships and yachts make the voyage to Antarctica each austral summer season. Most of these ships and yachts will be making landings in the region, visiting bird nesting colonies, observing whales and seals while underway, and exploring historic sites and scientific bases in the region.

6b. Predicted Environmental State in the Absence of this Expedition

Given the numbers of cruise ships and yachts expected to visit the region during the 2022-2023 season, the estimated difference between the environmental state of the region in the absence of, or with, the expedition of a small yacht like *PHYWAVE* will be negligible.

6c. Potential Impact from Yacht Operations

Risk of a Yacht Fuel Spill

The most adverse impact of this expedition is that from a fire or shipwreck. The second most adverse impact is that from a fuel spill. *PHYWAVE* carries the following fuel:

1. 500 liters of diesel fuel to the boats main fuel tanks.
2. 200 liters of diesel fuel in 10 portable plastic cans.
3. 200 liters of diesel fuel in an ATL fuel bladder strapped down in the boat's cockpit.
4. 40 liters of gasoline in two 20 liter plastic cans for the dinghy's outboard motor.
5. 30 liters of propane in two fiberglass cylinders to run the gas stove onboard.

The following steps will be taken to reduce the risk of spill:

- Transferring fuel from portable fuel cans into the main fuel tank is done via a battery-powered electric transfer pump fitted to the spout of the fuel can, not by pouring from the cans. Similarly, transfer from the ATL fuel bladder will also be done via a portable battery-operated electric transfer pump. Transfers will only be done while at anchor.

s/v *PHYWAVE* 2023 Antarctica IEE

- Oil absorbent pads which soak up oil but not water are kept on board. They're used for spot cleaning of oil and fuel, and in the catch pan under the engine. The absorbent pads will be readily available to immediately address any minor fuel spill during a transfer.
- The bilge pumps will be operated manually. A visual check for oil in the bilge precedes each discharge of bilge water overboard. Although the Volvo-Penta engine is free of leaks, it is conceivable to see diesel or lube oil in the bilge. This is easily wicked up with a piece of oil absorbent pad.
- Bilges are kept clean. Visual inspection then allows the crew early warning of mechanical failures that put fluids into the bilge. This practice minimizes the risk of fuel discharge.
- The tank, fuel lines, and fittings meet ABYC and US federal standards.
- The dinghy motor and portable fuel can are returned to the yacht when not in use. The dinghy is never towed with either the motor attached or the fuel can aboard. The dinghy is normally stowed under the arch at the stern of the boat.

Response to a Yacht Fuel Spill

The response to a fuel spill is multi-step process including assessment, clean-up, disposal, and reporting(for Tier 3). All fuel spills will assessed as follows:

Tier 1: Small local spill that can be dealt with immediately by one person.

Tier 2: Medium spills that require the full resources of the vessel.

Tier 3: Large spills which exceed the resources of the vessel and thus require outside assistance.

Tier 1: Tier 1 spills are typically small spills confined to the vessel. For a Tier 1 spills the crew will soak up the fuel with absorbent pads designed for this purpose. 50 such pads are carried on board *PHYWAVE*. The contaminated pads use for this purposed will be stowed in a plastic container that is inert to hydrocarbon fuels. The pads will be properly disposed of when the yacht returns to Puerto Williams. For the cleanup process the crew will wear rubber gloves to avoid fuel inadvertently contacting the skin.

Tier 2: For Tier 2 spills the fuel may have spilled into water directly surrounding the yacht. In this case the crew will take immediate steps to contain the spill by using the dinghy to deploy the absorbent boom kept on board for this purpose. After containment, a hand siphon pump will be used to skim the fuel from the water's surface. Absorbent pads can also be used to soak up fuel from the water's surface. If any fuel has escaped containment, the dinghy can be used to agitate the water and accelerate the naturally occurring evaporation and dispersal of the fuel. The contaminated absorbent pads and boom components used for fuel spill clean-up will be stowed in a plastic container that is inert to hydrocarbon fuels. These pads and boom components will be properly disposed of when the yacht returns to Puerto Williams. For the cleanup process the crew will wear rubber gloves to avoid contact fuel contacting the skin.

Tier 3: Tier 3 spills require immediate notification via VHF and SATCOM to the base commander of the nearest installation, issuance of a CHILREP, and notification to the shore support officer. The reporting will include vessel name, callsign, MMSI, phone number, master's name, VHF channels monitored, vessel position, number of people on board and injuries(if any), names of *s/v PHYWAVE* 2023 Antarctica IEE

other vessels involved (collision, assistance, salvage), time and date of spill, vessel size (LOA, beam, draft, type), spill volume and type, condition of vessel, current weather, slick movement, assistance required, environmental impacts, current response actions, other mitigations, safe haven requirements, time of next report.

It should be noted that according to the NOAA Office of Response and Restoration, over 90% of the diesel in a small spill (less than 5,000 gallons) in the marine environment is either evaporated or naturally dispersed into the water column in time frames of a couple of hours to a couple of days. Diesel fuel is a light, refined petroleum product which is much lighter than water. It is not possible for diesel to sink and accumulate on the bottom as free oil would.

Emissions and Air Pollution from the Yacht

PHYWAVE carries five sources of combustion emissions:

- A Volvo-Penta D2-50F diesel engine
- A Webasto diesel cabin heater
- A 6 kW Northern Lights diesel generator
- A propane stove in the boat's galley
- A 6 hp Yamaha 4 stroke outboard motor for the dinghy (discussed below)

Careful maintenance means that these engines will work when they're needed. It also means that they run with fewer emissions. Spare parts and technical manuals for all of this equipment is kept on board.

The Northern Lights generator is only run when needed to supplement power generated from the engine alternator, solar panels, and wind generator. Diesel fuel for the generator comes directly from the main fuel tank. It emits some combustion byproduct when running. A large bank of AGM batteries provides efficient storage of power generated from solar and wind sources thus reducing the need to run the generator.

The cabin heater is a Webasto diesel system. It uses electricity to circulate heated air to fan units in several places in the cabin. The heating fuel is diesel, which comes directly from the engine's diesel tank without transfer. It emits some combustion byproduct.

The propane stove in the boat's galley will be used for cooking. Propane is a very low-carbon fuel so its combustion emissions are corresponding low. It is the best fuel to use for cooking on boat.

6d. Potential Impact from Dinghy Operations

General Operation

PHYWAVE's dinghy is a 9.5 foot AB RIB with a 6 hp Yamaha 4 stroke outboard motor. The dinghy is equipped with a bow locker where the fuel can is kept so there is no chance of it going overboard. The dinghy will be used to:

- Take lines ashore to secure the yacht while at anchor.
- Take the expedition member ashore to day hikes and photography.

s/v *PHYWAVE* 2023 Antarctica IEE

- Optionally to take sightseeing trips within a few miles of the yacht.

A dinghy may disrupt wildlife between the anchored yacht and shore, and wildlife onshore. The dinghy will be operated in a manner that minimizes that disruption. This will be done by first an assessing the location of wildlife before the dinghy is launched. A location on shore to land the dinghy will be chosen that is as far as practicable from the identified wildlife. If no such location is available; i.e. the entire available shore area for landing is populated with penguins, then the landing will be canceled. While en-route from the yacht to shore a route can be chosen, and the dinghy maneuvered, to stay well clear of wildlife, for example, a flock of birds floating on the water. Again, if such a route cannot be found, the landing will be cancelled or postponed. Observing the response of wildlife during dinghy operations is the only practical way to determine whether they are being disturbed. If there appears to be disturbance the dinghy operation will be cancelled and the crew will return to the yacht.

It should be emphasized that, unlike other yacht expeditions to Antarctica, viewing wildlife is not one of the purposes of *PHYWAVE*'s expedition as stated in Section 1 of this IEE. Having been to Antarctica twice before, Dr. Anderson has had the opportunity to view its wildlife and take many photos. Therefore, the *PHYWAVE* expedition has no motivation to get close to wildlife and will seek to avoid it.

Fueling

A single small 20 liter fuel can will be brought aboard the dinghy and used to run the outboard motor. The fuel can will be stored in the dinghy bow locker when in use, and secured inside a locker on the yacht when not in use. The outboard motor will be removed from the dinghy and secured on the yacht in a locker designed for this purpose when not in use. When not in use the dinghy is lifted out of the water and secured under the aft arch that's a fixed part of the yacht.

Since only one of two gasoline fuel cans will be used at any one time there will be no need to transfer fuel to prepare for operations in the dinghy. Eliminating the fuel transfer eliminates the possibility of a spill during transfer.

Risk of Dinghy Fuel Spill

There is a very small risk of gasoline spill inherent in dinghy operations. There is risk of accidents while underway. Fueling for the dinghy outboard motor will only be done on the yacht so it is very unlikely there will be a spill of dinghy fuel. As explained, the fuel can on the dinghy is kept in a closed and latched bow locker which eliminates the risk that fuel will leak from the can and exit the dinghy. The dinghy has an aluminum floor separate from the hull itself. The fuel hose from the tank in the bow locker is run under the floor and connected to the outboard motor so it out of the way and can't be disturbed by the crew boarding or leaving the dinghy. These features of the dinghy and how fuel is used reduces the risk of a fuel spill during dinghy operations.

Response to a Dinghy Fuel Spill

The details of *PHYWAVE*'s response to a fuel spill is described in detail in Section 6c. The particular case of a fuel spill from the dinghy would be classified as a Tier 1 (confined to the dinghy) or Tier 2 (some fuel may have spilled onto the water or shore where the dinghy has been landed). The most likely source of a fuel spill is a leaky hose connection which would be a Tier 1 spill. The response to a fuel spill during dinghy operations will use the same procedures described in Section 6c.

Version 3.0   September 20, 2022

s/v *PHYWAVE* 2023 Antarctica IEE

Dinghy Outboard Motor Emissions

Emissions will be minimal for two reasons. First, the motor is low power – only 6 hp. Second, there is only one person in the expedition so the amount of power needed from the motor to get somewhere is minimized. It is expected that less than 5 gallons of gasoline will be burned on the entire expedition.

Yacht and dinghy operations will conform to *"Appendix C, Guidelines for Small Boat Operations in the Vicinity of Ice,"* IAATO (2010).

Emergency Preparedness While Ashore

For safety, the dinghy will carry emergency grab bags containing both marine and aviation band VHF radios, GPS, a satphone, survival gear, packaged food like granola bars, drinking water, and the boat's flare gun. In case the dinghy's outboard fails, oars will be available, and the dinghy will be operated within rowing range of the boat, considering wind, waves, and ice.

6e. Potential Impact from Activities Ashore

Risks to Wildlife and Plant life

Local disruption: Humans moving around onshore in the proximity of wildlife have the potential to frighten or disturb wildlife, which can lead to disruption of behavior, avoidance of a location, cessation of feeding, or even abandonment of young.

Disease and Parasite Transmission: Humans are the only animal that visits multiple seal and bird colonies up and down the Antarctic Peninsula, so they present a risk of inter-colony contamination of diseases and parasites by transport on boots, clothing and equipment.

Introduction of Alien Species: Seeds, plants, parasites, or even mammals could be accidentally introduced. With the marked warming on the Antarctic Peninsula, it is conceivable that these accidental introductions could survive and come into competition with indigenous wildlife and plants.

Potential destruction of plant life: Lichens and mosses on the Antarctic Peninsula grow extremely slowly, and walking on them has the potential to injure or destroy plant life.

Site Briefings

Prior to each shore visit the guidelines for visitors to Antarctica will be reviewed as a reminder of the appropriate distance to stay away from wildlife and otherwise not disturb their normal activities. These guidelines include the crew staying a minimum of 5 meters away from wildlife such as penguins while ashore. The crew will stay on obvious trails, rocky areas, or snow fields to avoid stepping on lichens, mosses or disturbing other native plant life.

Decontamination and Shore Visits

The guidelines in IAATO publication *"Boot, Clothing and Equipment Decontamination Guidelines for Small Boat Operations"* will be followed for all shore visits.

Footwear ashore will be an open-pattern sole that allows easy cleaning, i.e., rubber barnyard boots. A Vikron S boot dip will be used to clean boots on the yacht when leaving for, or returning from,

s/v *PHYWAVE* 2023 Antarctica IEE

a shore excursion in the dinghy. Footwear, tripods, camera boxes, etc., will be decontaminated when brought aboard the yacht using a scrub brush and dish pan in the cockpit. Cameras will be transported in a container that's easily cleaned prior to stowing back aboard the yacht, i.e., a hard case rather than a fabric bag.

Clothing and Equipment

Outdoor clothing and footwear will be vacuumed, washed and inspected prior to departing Puerto Williams. Any equipment that will go ashore will be vacuumed to remove seeds and plant matter, including the dinghy and its equipment, between shore landings.

6f. Cumulative Potential Impact of the Expedition

Since this is a single, one-time only, expedition, there are no cumulative impacts to the Antarctica environment from this proposed expedition. With regard to cumulative impacts in light of other existing and known proposed activities, based on the minor and transitory nature of the impact from this proposed expedition, it is the conclusion of the expedition leader and vessel captain that there will be no cumulative impact on the Antarctica environment from this expedition.

7. Waste Management Plan

The *PHYWAVE* expedition will be guided by the general principal that the amount of wastes produced or disposed of in the Antarctic Treaty area shall be reduced as far as practicable so as to minimize impacts to the Antarctic environment and to minimize interference with the natural values of Antarctica. The specific details of the Waste Management Plan are given below. The Waste Management Plan complies with MARPOL 73/78 International Convention for the Prevention of Pollution from Ships and the relevant Antarctica Special Treaty Area Annexes, including Annex V, as set forth at Item 25 in the References Section 11.

7a. Garbage

There are two garbage disposal receptacles aboard *PHYWAVE*

- Galley: biodegradables in a covered garbage pail
- Galley: non-biodegradables in a waste basket, recyclables in a storage bag

Garbage from these areas will be dealt with as follows:

Inshore (within 12 miles of land or ice shelf)

- Biodegradables are stored in a covered garbage pail, which is emptied when necessary into a garbage bag kept onboard. Maximum particle size will be 1-inch diameter. Solids will be strained from grey water prior to discharge of grey water.

s/v *PHYWAVE* 2023 Antarctica IEE

- Non-biodegradables are stored in a waste basket, also in the galley. This is transferred as necessary to a separate garbage bag kept onboard.
- Recyclables are stored in its own garbage bag onboard. These will not be washed in an effort to prevent discharge of their contents as grey water. Recyclables will be disposed of appropriately upon *PHYWAVE*'s return to Puerto Williams.
- When inshore, grey water discharge will not include matter drained off cans (e.g., Tuna or chicken particles will be drained into the galley bin, rather than into the sink.)

Offshore: (Greater than 12 miles from land or ice shelf)

- Biodegradables will be reduced to 1" particle size prior to discharge overboard.
- Non-biodegradables are stored in a waste basket, also in the galley. This is transferred as necessary to a separate garbage bag kept onboard.
- Recyclables are stored in its own garbage bag onboard. These will not be washed in an effort to prevent discharge of their contents as grey water. Recyclables will be disposed of appropriately upon *PHYWAVE*'s return to Puerto Williams.
- Disposable batteries are separated for recycling both offshore and inshore.

Poultry Products

PHYWAVE will carry fresh eggs and chicken packaged for cooking into the Antarctica Treaty Area. Egg shells, chicken packaging and any poultry scraps will be separately stored in plastic bags on board for disposal when *PHYWAVE* returns to Puerto Williams. *PHYWAVE* does not have a freezer so it is not possible to freeze these waste products before disposable.

7b. Galley and Cleaning Wastes

Galley grey water is strained prior to disposal. Cooking oils and waste grease are poured into a sealed container. Biodegradable dishwashing detergent is used and cleaning agents are restricted in the Peninsula area.

The boat is cleaned primarily by sweeping while in the Peninsula region. Sweeping wastes are treated as non-biodegradable trash. Simply Green brand cleaner is occasionally used on countertops and other areas inside the boat and wiped with a paper towel.

7c. Sewage

MARPOL Annex IV applies to vessels of 400 gross tons or greater, and vessels of any size certified to carry more than 15 persons. 33 CFR 151.79 requires U.S. vessels certified to carry more than 10 persons to discharge beyond 12 miles when in Antarctic waters. Annex IV to the Protocol On Environmental Protection to the Antarctic Treaty, Article 6 Discharge Of Sewage applies to vessels certified to carry more than ten persons. *PHYWAVE* is 10.9 metric tons and is certified to carry 6 persons as an uninspected vessel. One person will be onboard while in Antarctic waters.

s/v PHYWAVE 2023 Antarctica IEE

7d. Discharge of Sewage

A holding tank will be used at all times. Discharge of the holding tank will done be at least three miles off shore and only while underway. A greater distance off shore is preferred so sewage will be discharged beyond twelve miles if conditions permit. Estimated sewage holding tank capacity with one person onboard is 25 days so it is not expected that any sewage discharge will occur while in the waters along the Antarctic Peninsula.

8. Emergency Contingency Plans and Insurance

All expeditions create some risk of requiring outside assistance. *PHYWAVE* is a new, modern, well-equipped vessel prepared for self-sufficiency to reduce the risk of needing outside assistance or search and rescue (SAR) resources as explained in the following sections. Since it was built in 2021, all of *PHYWAVE*'s equipment will be only about a year old when arriving in Antarctica and very unlikely to fail due to age or fatigue.

Dr. Anderson has long experience operating in remote areas where mechanics and parts are unavailable. The main precaution is preparation. The boat stocks extensive engine parts with technical manuals for the main diesel engine, the dinghy outboard motor, and the installed Northern Lights generator. The fact that the yacht is a sailboat gives it the ability to maintain headway with nearly all of its electromechanical devices inoperative. EPIRB and PLB units, a satphone, and a covered life raft, reduce the scope and difficulty of an SAR effort.

Redundancy and the capacity for repair are vital to self-sufficiency. Electronics are redundant, e.g., multiple GPS, chartplotters, autopilot, tablets, notebook computers, etc. The boat can be steered by wheel, mechanical autopilot, and emergency tiller. Electrical power can be generated four different ways – solar panels, wind generator, diesel generator, and main engine alternator. Systems that can't be backed up are planned for repair. Spares for pumps, rigging components, engines, heater, water maker and electrical systems are on the boat. While it was under construction, Dr. Anderson personally selected and customized the equipment on *PHYWAVE* for this Antarctic voyage.

8a. Vessel Preparation and Equipment

PHYWAVE Navigation and Boat Control Equipment

Vessel *PHYWAVE* is equipped with the latest in marine electronic navigation and boat control equipment, with primary and backup units in most cases.

- Two B&G 9" Zeus 3S chartplotters with GPS and Navionics electronic charts
- Five B&G Triton multi-function displays
- Redundant B&G autopilot drive units with redundant course calculators
- Two wireless remotes for the autopilot
- B&G Barograph
- B&G V3100 Class B+ AIS
- B&G Halo broadband radar
- Audible alarm for B&G electronics

s/v *PHYWAVE* 2023 Antarctica IEE

- Anchor windlass control and chain counter at the helm
- Wireless remote for the windlass
- Two Apple iPads with navigation apps and Navionics and iSailor charts, each independently connected to its own Dual XGS150A GPS receivers
- Optimized for single-handed operation with all halyards, sheets and reefing lines operated from the cockpit
- Electric halyard, reefing, and primary winches to easily manage the sails
- SOLAS aerial (parachute) and handheld flares and smoke markers
- Multiple fire extinguishers onboard
- Complete set of tools including cordless power tools and hand tools
- Complete leak repair kit

PHYWAVE Communications Equipment
- Iridium GO satellite link for text messages, email, and downloading weather forecasts
- ICOM IC-7300 HF band radio modified to transmit and receive on all HF frequencies. The radio is connected to an insulated backstay antenna through an ICOM AT-140 antenna tuner
- B&G VHF radio
- Standard Horizon HX890 handheld VHF radio with GPS and DSC
- Iridium 9555 satphone

PHYWAVE Emergency Grab Bag Contents:
- Standard Horizon HX890 marine band VHF band radio with GPS and spare battery
- Yaesu FTA-250L aviation band VHF radio with spare battery
- NOAA-registered Personal Locator Beacon (PLB), 406 MHz, with GPS
- Handheld USCG-approved flares
- Signaling mirror
- Survival knife
- Emergency rations
- Sleeping bag and tent
- Flashlight

Other emergency equipment on board *PHYWAVE*:

- NOAA-registered EPIRB (ACR model RLB-41, Category 1 - automatic)
- Winslow 4-person FA-AV (UL) covered life raft designed for arctic conditions
- Mustang cold water immersion (survival) suit
- Extensive medical kit

8b. Emergency Situations

Dealing with Inadequate Charts
The Antarctic waters are inadequately chartered. Whole islands and untold numbers of submerged rocks are absent from the charts.

s/v *PHYWAVE* 2023 Antarctica IEE

PHYWAVE carries NGA and UK Admiralty paper charts, Navionics electronic charts, iSailor electronic charts, the 2019 edition of the UK Admiralty *Antarctic Pilot* and *Sailing Directions,* and the RCC Pilotage Foundation's *Cape Horn and the Antarctic Waters.* In addition, *PHYWAVE* has copies of several hand-drawn sketches of anchorages and soundings done by other yachts over many years during visits to Antarctica. *PHYWAVE* has a swing keel which can safely rotate out of harm's way in some types of groundings. When retracted, the low draft allows the yacht to access more shallow and protected anchorages than does a boat with a fixed keel.

Dealing with Ice

Ice collision is always a risk in high latitude waters. Specific procedures will be used to minimize this risk with its potential to trigger a SAR incident.

- **While underway**: There will be continuous electronic (radar and AIS) monitoring and visual monitoring. Because a visual watch for ice is so important, the boat will only be underway during daylight hours when along the Antarctic Peninsula. A minimum distance of 200 meters will be maintained between the yacht and calving hazards.

- **While at anchor**: Anytime the boat is at anchor boat there will be continuous radar monitoring for ice. Anchoring will be in as shallow a depth as practical. This increases the odds that drifting ice will ground prior to reaching the anchored boat. AIS monitoring will also be used while at anchor to warn of any nearby approaching vessels.

PHYWAVE has a 10-12 mm thick aluminum hull which is very durable when contacting obstacles like ice. In the worst case the hull will deform rather than potentially crack and leak which is one of the main vulnerabilities of boats with fiberglass hulls operating in ice.

Recommendations in IAATO *Guidelines for Small Boat Operations in the Vicinity of Ice* will be followed. *PHYWAVE* will have a laser rangefinder onboard as recommended in these Guidelines to accurately assess the distance from ice hazards and calving glaciers.

Avoiding Fire

Aboard *PHYWAVE* the fire precautions include:

- The auxiliary engine and cabin heater run on diesel fuel which is much less volatile and explosive than is gasoline.
- Complying with USCG requirements for fire extinguishers
- No person on board smokes
- Buckets and a wash down pump augment the fire extinguishers

These precautions minimize the risk of a fire-related incident requiring a SAR response.

Dealing with Medical Emergencies

First aid training and on-board equipment are the first means of dealing with a medical incident. The boat stocks an extensive first aid kit with both over-the-counter and prescriptions medical supplies as advised by a medical consultant.

If the medical supplies and crew training and are not adequate to deal with the emergency, the response will need to be escalated to seeking professional medical help in Puerto Williams or

s/v *PHYWAVE* 2023 Antarctica IEE

Ushuaia. Depending on the medical incident, it may be possible for the crew to make these destinations aboard the boat.

Alternately, depending on the nature of the medical emergency, it is also possible to take the yacht to King George Island and anchor in Ardley Cove. From the airstrip on King George Island a medevac flight can transport a patient to Punta Arenas for advanced medical care.

Finally, depending on location, asking assistance from nearby yachts is also possible.

Note that medical emergencies do not necessarily require an SAR response because the vessel itself is not in peril and its location is known via the GPS position reported to MRCC as described in the next section.

8c. Search and Rescue (SAR) Plan

The entire expedition will be executed within the Chilean Maritime SAR area. *PHYWAVE* will adhere to the Chilean inland ship reporting system and CHILREP (Chile Ship Reporting System) system offshore. This will ensure that the Chilean MRCC (Maritime Rescue Coordination Center) remains informed of the vessel location and intentions. Self-rescue will always be considered the primary option and intent. Additionally, a contract is in place with GEOS Worldwide to support SAR coordination and to help cover SAR costs in addition to insurance.

Standard distress, urgency and safety messages will be broadcast using VHF CH16 and DSC in if it is not possible to execute a self-rescue. The 9555 satphone will be used to contact the MRCC and/or GEOS Worldwide.

Chile SAR Resource Contact Details:

MRCC Chile:
Email: mrccchile@directemar.cl , cbvradio@directemar.cl
Phone: +56 32 2208637 / +56 32 2208638 / +56 32 2208639
Iridium: +881622407584

MRSC (Maritime Rescue Sub-Center) Antarctica
Email: mrscantartica@directemar.cl , cpfides@directemar.cl
Phone: +56 32 2208556 / +56 32 2203381

MRSC Puerto Williams
Email: mrscpuertowilliams@directemar.cl
Phone: +56 61 2621090

Coastal Radio Stations in Antarctica:

Bahia Fidels, Chile MMSI 007250450 (VHF), Range 14 nm, 62 11S / 058 55W
Bahia Paraiso, Chile MMSI 007250470 (VHF), Range 14 nm, 64 49S / 062 51W

s/v *PHYWAVE* 2023 Antarctica IEE

Loss of Contact:
The Iridium GO, Iridium 9555 satphone and handheld VHF systems have internal battery power supplies and will continue to work in case of a loss of power on the vessel. Charged spare batteries for these devices are also kept on board. It is unlikely that all these devices would simultaneously fail so a total loss of contact is very unlikely. If a report in the 24-hour CHLREP reporting schedule is missed, and the vessel cannot be contacted by the Chilean MRCC, then the Chilean SAR system will be initiated.

The Response to Threats to Vessel Safety:
Prevention: The steps to prevent an SAR event have been taken and are ongoing, as discussed above.

Communication: As noted above, routine reports of position, with status, route and intentions, and weather observations, will be e-mailed at 1200 UTC to the MRCC.

Then, in this order:

1. Alert surrounding vessels with a PAN PAN on VHF DSC, and alert MRCC Chile and relevant MRSC via satphone, both to be cancelled if the situation can be rectified.
2. Deal with the threat using means and expertise already on the boat.
3. Request assistance from other yachts via VHF and possibly via satphone.
4. Request assistance from MRCC via satphone.
5. Broadcast a general call for assistance via VHF.
6. If unable to contact the MRCC or applicable MRSC directly, or other vessels to render assistance, GEOS Monitoring will be contacted via dedicated button on the Iridium GO terminal. If warranted, the EPIRB and/or PLB will be activated. Both beacons are registered with NOAA.

The boat carries a covered 4-person life raft. In the unlikely event the boat has to be abandoned, the life raft will be deployed, the survival immersion suit put on, and the emergency grab bag put aboard the life raft. The emergency grab bag contains the survival and signaling equipment listed above.

8d. Insurance

Vessel *PHYWAVE* carries hull insurance for the value of the boat and its equipment and liability insurance in the amount of $1,000,000. In addition, there is an insurance policy rider for $10,000 coverage for SAR. Dr. Anderson carries personal health insurance and a personal umbrella liability policy in the amount of $4,000,000.

9. Potential Impact on Climate Change

Contemporary climate change includes both global warming and its impacts on Earth's weather patterns. Unlike climate change that has occurred in the past, contemporary climate change is

s/v *PHYWAVE* 2023 Antarctica IEE

different in that the rate of change is much more rapid and is not due to natural causes. Instead, it is caused by the emission of greenhouse gases, mostly carbon dioxide and methane. Burning fossil fuels creates most of these emissions.

The proposed expedition has 3 pieces of equipment which burn fossil fuel and create emissions:

- a. The boat's 51 hp engine which burns diesel fuel
- b. The 6 hp motor on the dinghy which burns gasoline
- c. The boat's stove which burns propane gas

When compared to the enormous amount of greenhouse gas emissions the world produces from all sources that has led to climate change, the amount of emissions produced by emission sources used on the *PHYWAVE* expedition are infinitesimally small and negligible. The large commercial cruise ships that carry thousands of tourists to the Antarctica Peninsula each year produce vastly greater quantities of greenhouse gas emissions than will the proposed *PHYWAVE* expedition.

Consequently, it is reasonable to conclude the *PHYWAVE* expedition to will have no projected impact on climate change.

10. Conclusion

Based on careful consideration of the activities planned for this expedition to Antarctica, and the proposed minimization and mitigation measures that will be utilized, it is the conclusion of the expedition leader and vessel captain that this expedition will have no more than minor or transitory impact on the Antarctica environment.

Since this is a single, one-time only, expedition, there are no cumulative impacts to the Antarctica environment from this proposed expedition. With regard to cumulative impacts in light of other existing and known proposed activities, based on the minor and transitory nature of the impact from this proposed expedition, it is the conclusion of the expedition leader and vessel captain that there will be no cumulative impact on the Antarctica environment from this expedition.

September 20, 2022

s/v *PHYWAVE* 2023 Antarctica IEE

10. Reference Documents

1. *Admiralty Antarctic Pilot and Sailing Directions,* UK Hydrographic Office, 9th Edition, 2019.
2. *Cape Horn and Antarctic Waters,* Paul Heiney, Royal Cruising Club Pilotage Foundation, 1st Edition, 2017.
3. *ATCM Yachting Guidelines for Antarctica Cruises,* IAATO website.
4. *General Guidelines for Visitors to the Antarctic.* Recommendation 3, IAATO website.
5. *Checklist of Yacht Specific Items for Preparing Safe Antarctic Voyages.* ATCM XXXV Final Report. IAATO website.
6. IAATO. *Guidelines for Small Boat Operations in the Vicinity of Ice.* 2016.
7. IAATO. *General Information for Wildlife Watching*: IAATO website.
8. IAATO. *Cetacean Watching Guidelines*: IAATO Website.
9. IAATO. *Guidelines for Seal Watching*: IAATO Website.
10. IAATO. *Guidelines for Bird Watching*: IAATO Website.
11. IAATO. *Don't Pack a Pest.* Providence: IAATO website.
12. IAATO *Information for Yachts,* IAATO website.
13. IAATO. *Boot, Clothing and Equipment Decontamination Guidelines for Small Boat Operations.* IAATO website.
14. IAATO *Visitor Site Guidelines – 17. Whaler's Bay.* IAATO website.
15. IAATO *Visitor Site Guidelines – 42. Portal Point.* IAATO website.
16. IAATO *Visitor Site Guidelines – 20. Telefon Bay (East).* IAATO website.
17. Royal Cruising Club Pilotage Foundation. *Polar Yacht Guide.* v1.0, 2021.
18. Ardrizzi, Giogio, and Rolfo, Mariolina. *Patagonia and Tierra Del Fuego Nautical Guide.* Rome: Nutrimienti s.r.l., 2016.
19. Carey, Peter, and Franklin, Craig. *Antarctica Cruising Guide.* Wellington: Awa Press, 4th Edition, 2018.
20. Cornell, Jimmy. *World Cruising Routes.* London: Cornell Sailing Ltd., 8th Edition, 2019
21. Calder, Nigel, *Boatowner's Mechanical & Electrical Manual How to Maintain, Repair.* New York: International Marine/McGraw-Hill Education, 4th Edition, 2015,
22. Admiralty Nautical Charts 226, 445, 446, 1776, 3205, 3207, 3560, 3566, 4907, 225, 1740, 1774, 3206, 3210, 3213, 3463.
23. United States NGA charts 29002, 29102, 29105, 29106, 29121, 29122
24. ISM Code (International Management Code for the Safe Operation of Ships) Protocol on Environmental Protection to the Antarctic Treaty 1991

s/v *PHYWAVE* 2023 Antarctica IEE

   a. Annex I-Environmental Impact Assessment
   b. Annex II-Conservation of Antarctic Fauna and Flora
   c. Annex III-Waste Disposal and Waste
   d. Annex IV-Prevention of Marine Pollution
   e. Annex V-Area Protection and Management
25. MARPOL 73/78 International Convention for the Prevention of Pollution from Ships
   a. Annex I - Prevention of Pollution by Oil (Antarctic Treaty Special Area)
   b. Annex II - Prevention of Pollution by Noxious Liquid Substances Carried in Bulk (Antarctic Treaty Special Area)
   c. Annex III - Prevention of Pollution by Harmful Substances Carried in Packaged Form
   d. Annex IV - Prevention of Pollution by Sewage
   e. Annex V - Prevention of Pollution by Garbage (Antarctic Treaty Special Area)
   f. Annex VI - Prevention of Air Pollution Enforcement is via implementation by the country where the ship is registered (Flag State Control), backed up by inspections of countries at which the vessel calls (Port State Control)

s/v *PHYWAVE* 2023 Antarctica Waste Permit Application

Waste Permit Application

Sailing Vessel PHYWAVE Voyage to the Antarctica Peninsula

Yacht owner/captain, expedition leader:
Harry R. Anderson, Ph.D.

Bainbridge Island, WA 98110
hra@phywave.com
svphywave@gmail.com
website: www.phywave.com
home:
mobile:
satphone:

US contact:
Harry R. Anderson, Ph.D.

Bainbridge Island, WA 98110
hra@phywave.com
svphywave@gmail.com
website: www.phywave.com
home:
mobile:
satphone:

Summary

This Waste Permit Application is for a proposed trip to the Antarctic Peninsula aboard the sailboat *PHYWAVE* scheduled for January 4, 2023, through January 29, 2023. One person will travel aboard a 41-foot aluminum hull Allures 40.9 sailboat. Brief landings by dinghy will be made at points on the peninsula for photography and day hiking.

Vessel operations and landing activities are expected to have no more than minor and transitory impacts on the Antarctic environment.

All activities on this voyage will be carried out in accordance with the Antarctic Treaty; the Environmental Protocol to the Antarctic Treaty on Environmental Protection and its Annexes; Antarctic Treaty Consultative Meeting (ATCM) Recommendation XVIII-1; the International Convention for the Prevention of Pollution from Ships (MARPOL); the International Agreement Concerning Safety of Life at Sea (SOLAS); and applicable domestic statutes and regulations, including the Marine Mammal Protection Act and the Endangered Species Act.

1. Waste Permit Effective Dates

Since the exact dates for this voyage will be highly dependent on weather conditions which cannot be predicted this far in advance, it is requested that the Waste Permit be issued to be valid for the time period from January 1, 2023, to March 31, 2023.

s/v *PHYWAVE* 2023 Antarctica Waste Permit Application

2. Yacht Specifications

- *PHYWAVE* is an Allures 40.9 cutter
- Designer: Racoupeau Yacht Design
- Builder: Allures Yachting
- Year Built: 2021
- Cutter rig with genoa and staysail
- Aluminum hull with swing keel/centerboard
- LOA: 12.65 meters (41.50 feet)
- Beam: 4.15 meters (13.62 feet)
- Draft: keel/centerboard up: 1.06 meters (3.48 feet), down: 2.75 meters (9.0 feet)
- Displacement: 10.9 metric tons (24,000 lbs)
- Ballast: 4.2 metric tons (9260 lbs)
- Fresh water capacity: 330 liters (87 gallons). *PHYWAVE* is also equipped with small desalination which turns sea water into fresh water so the fresh water supply is virtually unlimited.
- Fuel capacity: 500 liters (132 gallons) in internal tanks plus 400 liters auxiliary storage
- Holding tank capacity: 60 liters
- Engine: Volvo-Penta D2-50F with sail drive
- Equipped with solar panels, a wind generator, and a 6 kW diesel generator for battery charging
- CE Certification: Category A – Ocean
- USCG official number: 1322011
- FCC MMSI number: 368232960

3. Crew

The captain and only crewmember is Dr. Harry R. Anderson. Dr. Anderson is an experienced yachtsman with more than 30 years of sailing experience including 12 years as owner and captain of *RAYTRACE*, a 37 foot Bavaria sloop he has sailed around the waters of the Pacific Northwest and Canada, as far north as Alaska. This experience includes more than 240 days as Master of the vessel, 95% of which were single-handed. Dr. Anderson also has American Sailing Association (ASA) Certifications 101, 103, 104, 105, and the International Proficiency Certificate. Before embarking on the voyage to Antarctica from Puerto Williams, Dr. Anderson will have sailed *PHYWAVE* from the east coast of the United States, across the Atlantic Ocean eastbound to Europe and Africa, across the Atlantic Ocean westbound to South America and south along its coast to Puerto Williams, more than 10,000 nautical miles at sea.

Dr. Anderson has been to Antarctica twice before.

In February, 2011, Dr. Anderson took a two week Quark Expeditions cruise to the Antarctica Peninsula (the "Crossing the Circle" cruise) aboard the ship Sergey Vavilov. During this cruise Dr. Anderson attended the requisite seminars on proper practices for protecting the flora and fauna of Antarctica, including maintaining appropriate distance while observing wildlife. The Quark cruise included several zodiac landings ashore where these procedures were followed.

s/v *PHYWAVE* 2023 Antarctica Waste Permit Application

In January, 2014, Dr. Anderson flew his single engine aircraft N788W from Punta Arenas, Chile, to King George Island. For that flight he submitted a complete IEE and a Waste Permit Application that were acceptable to the EPA and NSF, respectively. He also successfully obtained permission from the Chilean government and Chilean Air Force to land at King George Island.

From these previous experiences Dr. Anderson is very familiar with the standards and protocols for visiting Antarctica and protecting its environment.

Dr. Anderson is an experienced adventure pilot with more than 2250 hours of flight time in a variety of fixed-wing aircraft. More than 90% of those hours are solo, more than 97% as Pilot-in-Command. He holds a Commercial Pilot certificate for single-engine and multi-engine aircraft with an Instrument rating. He also holds a Private Pilot certificate for single-engine seaplanes. He has flown around the world twice, eastbound and westbound. He flew to Antarctica in 2014, as mentioned, and in 2018 he completed a transpolar flight over the North Pole from Resolute Bay, Canada, to Longyearbyen in the Svalbard Islands, Norway. From these wide-ranging international flights he has become highly experienced at worldwide navigation, interpreting weather forecasts, and expedition planning for Arctic and Antarctica regions. Many of his international flights are described in his 2015 book *Flying 7 Continents Solo*.

Dr. Anderson holds a BSEE degree from the University of California at Santa Barbara, a MSEE degree from Oregon State University, and a Ph.D. in Electrical Engineering from the University of Bristol in the United Kingdom. He is an expert in wireless communications network design, simulation and optimization. He has published numerous peer-reviewed technical papers and a graduate level reference text entitled *Fixed Broadband Wireless System Design* (2003, John Wiley: Chichester). He is a successful entrepreneur having founded, grown and sold high tech companies.

In addition to his education and practical experience with Antarctic environmental protection methods aboard the Vavilov and his solo flight to King George Island, Dr. Anderson has read relevant sections of the documents listed in the References in Section 6 of this Waste Permit Application which include several pertaining to minimizing environmental impact while visiting Antarctica.

4. Expedition Activities in Antarctic Waters

4a. Yacht Operations

Activities conducted from the yacht *PHYWAVE* include:

- Viewing scenery
- Sailing
- Motoring

Boats create an impact while underway by their visual presence and by the sound they emit. *PHYWAVE* is small enough and quiet enough that its movements will cause no more than a minor or transitory impact on wildlife, visitors, or the environment, especially compared to many large cruise ships that visit the Antarctic Peninsula during the austral summer.

s/v *PHYWAVE* 2023 Antarctica Waste Permit Application

While underway in Antarctica, a visual watch will be maintained both to reduce the risk of ice collision and to watch for other obstacles. Modern broadband radar will be in continuous use to detect icebergs or other hazards. The AIS receiver/transmitter will be used to detect and avoid other vessels.

The boat has is 51 hp engine that burns diesel fuel and creates some noise when it is running. There are no published specifications for how much noise it emits, either as a standalone engine or when installed in the boat. However, it should be noted the engine is installed in the center of the boat on the hull and surrounded by sound baffling material so as to minimize the engine noise so its impact on the people aboard the boat. Of course, this same sound baffling will reduce the amount of engine noise outside the boat. Such sound baffling is a standard design feature on modern yachts.

The IAATO publication *Cetacean Watching Guidelines* will be followed while underway.

4b. Dinghy Operations

The dinghy is a 9.5 foot AB dinghy with a rigid aluminum hull and inflatable tubes (RIB).

Activities conducted from the dinghy include:

- Landing ashore
- Dinghy cruises
- Shore viewing without landing
- Scenery viewing

Most of the dinghy operations are short trips to bring crew ashore to set shore ties, and for photography and day hikes.

The dinghy will also occasionally be used for cruising. During dinghy cruises the IAATO wildlife watching guidelines (References 6-9) will be followed.

The inflatable dinghy will be cleaned prior to departing South America. It will be free of foreign material that could be introduced to Antarctica during its use.

4c. Landings

The crew intends to make landings in Antarctica in the AB 9.5 RIB dinghy carried aboard *PHYWAVE*. For ocean passages the dinghy is normally strapped down, upside down, on the foredeck of *PHYWAVE*. In this position the aluminum bottom and inflatable side tubes will be thoroughly clean with a stiff brush in Puerto Williams before departure for Antarctica. The dinghy will also be flipped over on the foredeck so the interior can also be cleaned with a brush.

Crossing the Drake Passage the dinghy will remain strapped to the foredeck. On arriving at *PHYWAVE*'s first anchorage location at Deception Island, the dinghy will be lifted off the foredeck and placed in the water for use in landing ashore. After the landing is completed and the crew returns to *PHYWAVE*, the dinghy will be hoisted onto the arch on the stern of *PHYWAVE* and carried there during the short trips between the anchorages listed in Table 1. As described in Section 6e, the dinghy will be also cleaned between shore landings. Once *PHYWAVE* is ready to

s/v *PHYWAVE* 2023 Antarctica Waste Permit Application

depart the Antarctica Peninsula, the dinghy will be returned to the foredeck and strapped down there for the passage north to Puerto Williams.

The landings will potentially take place at all the locations listed in Table 1, depending on weather and ice conditions. With only one person, the landings will have little impact. Landing durations will be a few hours during daytime, not overnight. While along the Antarctica Peninsula the boat will be anchored and stopped, never underway, when the crew member is sleeping.

The yacht will be anchored as close to shore as practical and will be tied directly to shore when possible or necessary. Because of the swing keel, anchoring is possible in shallower water closer to shore than boats with standard fixed keels.

During landings no stoves, fuel, or food (other than survival rations) will be taken ashore. Planned activities include dinghy cruising, photography, and day hikes, but not camping. For safety, the dinghy will carry an emergency bag containing marine and aviation band VHF radios, GPS, a satphone, survival gear, packaged food like granola bars, drinking water, and the boat's flare gun. In case the dinghy's outboard motor fails, oars stowed on the dinghy will be used, and the dinghy will be landed within rowing range of the boat.

The crew will operate within the Code of Conduct for each site, including ASMAs as identified at www.ats.aq/e/protected.html. There will be no visits to ASPA's.

If there are cruise ships or yachts in an anchorage area where a landing is contemplated, an effort will be made to contact these other vessels on maritime VHF channel 16 to determine, if possible, their schedule for landings and coordinate with them so that *PHYWAVE* landings do not occur at the same time as the landings from other vessels. Since enjoying the solitude of Antarctica's natural environment is one goal of this expedition, avoiding going ashore when another crowd of people is already there is undesirable in any event.

Landings are planned using the IAATO's *Guidelines for Visitors to the Antarctic*, *Southern Ocean Cruising*, and *Status of Antarctic Specially Protected Area and Antarctic Specially Managed Area Management Plans*. The IAATO *Information for Yachts* will be followed.

UAV Operations

With suitable weather, an Unmanned Aerial Vehicle (UAV or "drone") will be launched to take photos and videos from an elevated perspective. Suitable weather means current and forecast surface wind speeds during the flight time of less than 12 knots with no current or forecast precipitation.

The UAV will only be launched from a shore location, typically adjacent to where the dinghy has been landed. Launching from a shore-based location is a superior approach compared to launching from a moving boat or a boat swinging at anchor, as some have proposed. Modern advanced UAV's are equipped with important Return-to-Home (RTH) safety features. When the UAV is first powered on it establishes a Home Position using its internal GPS. If the UAV should lose the signal from the controller, it will automatically return to the Home Position and land. This is an RTH safety feature. Similarly, if the UAV detects its internal battery power level is too low it with also execute the RTH procedure and land. In contrast, if the UAV is launched from a moving boat the Home Position established at launch may no longer be the location of the boat and the RTH safety features will send the UAV to a water landing.

s/v *PHYWAVE* 2023 Antarctica Waste Permit Application

As noted, the intended use of the UAV is to get photos and videos of Antarctica from a unique, elevated perspective. To get a suitable elevated perspective the UAV will be flown no higher than 75 meters above surrounding terrain and no farther than 400 meters from the launch point. The screen on the UAV controller continuously displays the UAV height above, and distance from, the Home Point so it easy to keep the UAV confined to this space. The operator will maintain visual line-of-sight with the UAV at all times. The UAV on board *PHYWAVE* has a maximum flight time of about 27 minutes. However, the planned flight times in Antarctica will be limited to about 10-15 minutes.

The UAV flights are not intended for viewing wildlife as wildlife viewing is not a purpose of this expedition. Before launching the UAV, the operator will note the location of wildlife in the vicinity of the launch point and choose a flight route, and periodically modify that flight route and altitude as necessary, to avoid that wildlife, including airborne flocks of birds. If the presence of wildlife is too intense around the launch location, the UAV will not be launched.

Because of its many built in safety features such as automatic RTH, it is extremely unlikely, but not impossible, that the operator could lose control of the UAV and it will crash somewhere. If it crashes on land, it will be possible to hike to the location and recover the UAV. A "crash" would not necessarily be a violent event like an airplane crash. The UAV itself is a solidly-built device unlikely to break apart in such an event. The exception are the four plastic propellers (2 blades each) which may break off if the UAV crashes.

If the UAV crashes on water, the flotation devices attached to each of its four legs (as pictured here) will keep it afloat so it can be recovered with the dinghy.

It should be noted that as of January, 2021, there were more than 1.7 million UAV's registered with the FAA in United States, and countless other unregistered UAV's. Even with these large numbers the press essentially never reports a UAV crashing in some unintended place. It would be newsworthy if it were happening. While this is anecdotal evidence, it certainly reinforces the idea that it is extremely rare for operators to lose control of a UAV and have it crash.

The UAV carried aboard *PHYWAVE* is a DJI Mavic Air 2 model registered with the FAA in the United States, registration number FA3NT7A3ZH. In addition to being a licensed commercial pilot, Dr. Anderson is also a FAA-licensed Remote Pilot authorized to operate an Unmanned Aerial System (UAS). The drone will be operating in accordance with FAA Rules, Part 107, with particular attention to not disturbing wildlife as noted above.

The IAATO was contacted with regard to UAV operations (RPAS in their nomenclature). They do not permit recreational use of UAV's, only commercial use, which is understandable when considering the idea of a cruise ship full of passengers wanting to launch UAV's at the same time. A further request was made to IAATO for the technical and other guidelines they apply to the commercial use of UAV's by their member operators, when they authorize such use by operators. IAATO did not respond to that request. Consequently, at this point the guidelines they apply to

s/v *PHYWAVE* 2023 Antarctica Waste Permit Application

commercial UAV operations by the IAATO operators are unknown so it is not possible to determine whether the *PHYWAVE* expedition's proposed UAV operations follow those guidelines.

The *PHYWAVE* expedition leader believes the proposed UAV operations as described above are modest and reasonable, with the goal of not disturbing wildlife or leaving any trace of the UAV operation at any location where the UAV may be launched.

5. Waste Management Plan

The *PHYWAVE* expedition will be guided by the general principal that the amount of wastes produced or disposed of in the Antarctic Treaty area shall be reduced as far as practicable so as to minimize impacts to the Antarctic environment and to minimize interference with the natural values of Antarctica. The specific details of the Waste Management Plan are given below. The Waste Management Plan complies with MARPOL 73/78 International Convention for the Prevention of Pollution from Ships and the relevant Antarctica Special Treaty Area Annexes, including Annex V, as set forth in the References Section.

5a. Garbage

There are two garbage disposal receptacles aboard *PHYWAVE*

- Galley: biodegradables in a covered garbage pail
- Galley: non-biodegradables in a waste basket, recyclables in a storage bag

Garbage from these areas will be dealt with as follows:

Inshore (within 12 miles of land or ice shelf)

- Biodegradables are stored in a covered garbage pail, which is emptied when necessary into a garbage bag kept onboard. Maximum particle size will be 1-inch diameter. Solids will be strained from grey water prior to discharge of grey water.
- Non-biodegradables are stored in a waste basket, also in the galley. This is transferred as necessary to a separate garbage bag kept onboard.
- Recyclables are stored in its own garbage bag onboard. These will not be washed in an effort to prevent discharge of their contents as grey water. Recyclables will be disposed of appropriately upon *PHYWAVE*'s return to Puerto Williams.
- When inshore, grey water discharge will not include matter drained off cans (e.g., Tuna or chicken particles will be drained into the galley bin, rather than into the sink.)

Offshore: (Greater than 12 miles from land or ice shelf)

- Biodegradables will be reduced to 1" particle size prior to discharge overboard.
- Non-biodegradables are stored in a waste basket, also in the galley. This is transferred as necessary to a separate garbage bag kept onboard.

s/v *PHYWAVE* 2023 Antarctica Waste Permit Application

- Recyclables are stored in its own garbage bag in a stern locker. These will not be washed in an effort to prevent discharge of their contents as grey water. Recyclables will be disposed of appropriately upon *PHYWAVE*'s return to Puerto Williams.
- Disposable batteries are separated for recycling both offshore and inshore.

Poultry Products

PHYWAVE will carry fresh eggs and chicken packaged for cooking into the Antarctica Treaty Area. Egg shells, chicken packaging and any poultry scraps will be separately stored in plastic bags on board for disposal when *PHYWAVE* returns to Puerto Williams. *PHYWAVE* does not have a freezer so it is not possible to freeze these waste products before disposable.

5b. Galley and Cleaning Wastes

Galley grey water is strained prior to disposal. Cooking oils and waste grease are poured into a sealed jar. Biodegradable dishwashing detergent is used and cleaning agents are restricted in the Peninsula area.

The boat is cleaned primarily by sweeping while in the Peninsula region. Sweeping wastes are treated as non-biodegradable trash. Simply Green brand cleaner is occasionally used on countertops and other areas inside the boat and wiped with a paper towel.

5c. Sewage

MARPOL Annex IV applies to vessels of 400 gross tons or greater, and vessels of any size certified to carry more than 15 persons. 33 CFR 151.79 requires U.S. vessels certified to carry more than 10 persons to discharge beyond 12 miles when in Antarctic waters. Annex IV to the Protocol On Environmental Protection to the Antarctic Treaty, Article 6 Discharge Of Sewage applies to vessels certified to carry more than ten persons. *PHYWAVE* is 10.9 metric tons and is certified to carry 6 persons as an uninspected vessel. One person will be onboard while in Antarctic waters.

5d. Discharge of Sewage

A holding tank will be used at all times. Discharge of the holding tank will done be at least three miles off shore and only while underway. A greater distance off shore is preferred so sewage will be discharged beyond twelve miles if conditions permit. Estimated sewage holding tank capacity with one person onboard is 25 days so it is not expected that any sewage discharge will occur while in the waters along the Antarctic Peninsula.

5e. Emissions and Air Pollution from the Yacht

PHYWAVE carries five sources of combustion emissions:

- A Volvo-Penta D2-50F diesel engine
- A Webasto diesel cabin heater

s/v *PHYWAVE* 2023 Antarctica Waste Permit Application

- An 6 kW Northern Lights diesel generator
- A propane stove in the boat's galley
- A 6 hp Yamaha 4 stroke outboard motor for the dinghy

Careful maintenance means that these engines will work when they're needed. It also means that they run with fewer emissions. Spare parts and technical manuals for all of this equipment are kept on board.

The Northern Lights generator is only run when needed to supplement power generated from the engine alternator, solar panels, and wind generator. Diesel fuel for the generator comes directly from the main fuel tank. It emits some combustion byproduct when running. A large bank of AGM batteries provides efficient storage of power generated from solar and wind sources thus reducing the need to run the generator.

The cabin heater is a Webasto diesel system. It uses electricity to circulate heated air to fan units in several places in the cabin. The heating fuel is diesel, which comes directly from the engine's diesel tank without transfer. It emits some combustion byproduct.

The propane stove in the boat's galley will be used intermittently for cooking. Propane is a very low-carbon fuel so its combustion emissions are corresponding low. It is the best fuel to use for cooking on a boat.

Combustion emissions from the outboard motor used on the dinghy will be minimal for two reasons. First, the motor is low power – only 6 hp. Second, there is only one person in the expedition so the amount of power needed from the motor to get somewhere is minimized. It is expected that less than 5 gallons of gasoline will be burned on the entire expedition.

The combustible emissions from the sources listed above are disposed of (dispersed by) the natural winds occurring along the Antarctica Peninsula. Because *PHYWAVE* is a small vessel compared to the much larger cruise ships that travel the waters of the Antarctica Peninsula during the austral summer, the emission contributions from this expedition will be minor, transitory and not cumulative.

6. Certification

I certify that, to the best of my knowledge and belief, and based upon due inquiry, the information submitted in the application for a waste permit is complete and accurate. Any knowing or intentional false statement will subject me to the criminal penalties of 18 U.S.C. 1001.

Date: September 20, 2022

Harry R. Anderson, Ph.D.
Expedition Leader

s/v *PHYWAVE* 2023 Antarctica Waste Permit Application

6. Reference Documents

1. *Admiralty Antarctic Pilot and Sailing Directions,* UK Hydrographic Office, 9th Edition, 2019.
2. *Cape Horn and Antarctic Waters,* Paul Heiney, Royal Cruising Club Pilotage Foundation, 1st Edition, 2017.
3. *ATCM Yachting Guidelines for Antarctica Cruises,* IAATO website.
4. *General Guidelines for Visitors to the Antarctic.* Recommendation 3, IAATO website.
5. *Checklist of Yacht Specific Items for Preparing Safe Antarctic Voyages.* ATCM XXXV Final Report. IAATO website.
6. IAATO. *Guidelines for Small Boat Operations in the Vicinity of Ice.* 2016.
7. IAATO. *General Information for Wildlife Watching*: IAATO website.
8. IAATO. *Cetacean Watching Guidelines*: IAATO Website.
9. IAATO. *Guidelines for Seal Watching*: IAATO Website.
10. IAATO. *Guidelines for Bird Watching*: IAATO Website.
11. IAATO. *Don't Pack a Pest.* Providence: IAATO website.
12. IAATO. *Boot, Clothing and Equipment Decontamination Guidelines for Small Boat Operations.* IAATO website.
13. IAATO *Visitor Site Guidelines – 17. Whaler's Bay.* IAATO website.
14. IAATO *Visitor Site Guidelines – 42. Portal Point.* IAATO website.
15. IAATO *Visitor Site Guidelines – 20. Telefon Bay (East).* IAATO website.
16. Royal Cruising Club Pilotage Foundation. *Polar Yacht Guide.* v1.0, 2021.
17. Ardrizzi, Giogio, and Rolfo, Mariolina. *Patagonia and Tierra Del Fuego Nautical Guide.* Rome: Nutrimienti s.r.l., 2016.
18. Carey, Peter, and Franklin, Craig. *Antarctica Cruising Guide.* Wellington: Awa Press, 4th Edition, 2018.
19. Cornell, Jimmy. *World Cruising Routes.* London: Cornell Sailing Ltd., 8th Edition, 2019
20. Calder, Nigel, *Boatowner's Mechanical & Electrical Manual How to Maintain, Repair.* New York: International Marine/McGraw-Hill Education, 4th Edition, 2015,
21. Admiralty Nautical Charts 226, 445, 446, 1776, 3205, 3207, 3560, 3566, 4907, 225, 1740, 1774, 3206, 3210, 3213, 3463.
22. United States NGA charts 29002, 29102, 29105, 29106, 29121, 29122

s/v *PHYWAVE* 2023 Antarctica Waste Permit Application

23. ISM Code (International Management Code for the Safe Operation of Ships) Protocol on Environmental Protection to the Antarctic Treaty 1991
    a. Annex I-Environmental Impact Assessment
    b. Annex II-Conservation of Antarctic Fauna and Flora
    c. Annex III-Waste Disposal and Waste
    d. Annex IV-Prevention of Marine Pollution
    e. Annex V-Area Protection and Management

24. MARPOL 73/78 International Convention for the Prevention of Pollution from Ships
    a. Annex I - Prevention of Pollution by Oil (Antarctic Treaty Special Area)
    b. Annex II - Prevention of Pollution by Noxious Liquid Substances Carried in Bulk (Antarctic Treaty Special Area)
    c. Annex III - Prevention of Pollution by Harmful Substances Carried in Packaged Form
    d. Annex IV - Prevention of Pollution by Sewage
    e. Annex V - Prevention of Pollution by Garbage (Antarctic Treaty Special Area)
    f. Annex VI - Prevention of Air Pollution Enforcement is via implementation by the country where the ship is registered (Flag State Control), backed up by inspections of countries at which the vessel calls (Port State Control)

www.ingramcontent.com/pod-product-compliance
Lightning Source LLC
Chambersburg PA
CBHW052010070526
44584CB00016B/1695